STOCHASTIC VOLATILITY IN FINANCIAL MARKETS

CROSSING THE BRIDGE TO CONTINUOUS TIME

Dynamic Modeling and Econometrics in Economics and Finance

VOLUME 3

Series Editors

Stefan Mittnik, *University of Kiel, Germany*
Willi Semmler, *University of Bielefeld, Germany* and
New School for Social Research, USA

STOCHASTIC VOLATILITY IN FINANCIAL MARKETS

CROSSING THE BRIDGE TO CONTINUOUS TIME

Fabio Fornari
Bank of Italy

and

Antonio Mele
Université du Littoral
and THEMA, Université de Paris X

KLUWER ACADEMIC PUBLISHERS
Boston / Dordrecht / London

Distributors for North, Central and South America:
Kluwer Academic Publishers
101 Philip Drive
Assinippi Park
Norwell, Massachusetts 02061 USA
Telephone (781) 871-6600
Fax (781) 871-6528
E-Mail <kluwer@wkap.com>

Distributors for all other countries:
Kluwer Academic Publishers Group
Distribution Centre
Post Office Box 322
3300 AH Dordrecht, THE NETHERLANDS
Telephone 31 78 6392 392
Fax 31 78 6546 474
E-Mail <services@wkap.nl>

 Electronic Services <http://www.wkap.nl>

Library of Congress Cataloging-in-Publication Data

Fornari, Fabio
    Stochastic volatility in financial markets : crossing the bridge to continuous time/
Fabio Fornari and Antonio Mele
        p. cm. -- (Dynamic modeling and econometrics in economics and finance;
    v. 3)
    Includes bibliographical references and index.
    ISBN 0-7923-7842-3 (alk. paper)
    1. Finance--Econometric models. 2. Capital market--Econometric models.
    3. Stochastic analysis. I. Mele, Antonio. II. Title. III. Series.

HG173 .F67 2000
332'.01'5195--dc21   00-028741

A Alessandra
F.F.

A Alessia e Florence
A.M.

CONTENTS

List of figures

List of tables

PREFACE

At an initial stage of the work this book was conceived as merely a collection of our previously published papers. We then came to the conclusion that owing to this structure its value-added for the reader could be very small, if any. The first attempt was then to try and link the various papers so as to bring continuity across the sections. Later on the papers have been completely re-drafted; many new sections and unpublished results have been added. The changes to the initial version result in a much shorter, more theoretical and, we hope, easy-to-read book. This book is not intended for beginners, though the interested, unexperienced, reader will find an up-to-date discussion as well as a deep analysis of the topic he or she will finally have to face after the initial warm-up process in the study of the subject. In our view the book is suitable for last year undergraduates willing to proceed to a higher degree in the field of finance, quantitative finance or financial economics; for PhD students taking finance exams or whose final dissertation is intended to deal with theoretical and empirical aspects of finance and financial markets econometrics. The book is also suitable for teaching in advanced courses dealing with time series topics including conditional heteroskedasticity, simulation-based econometric methods such as indirect inference, as well as continuous time finance. Useless to say, the book is suitable for researchers willing to deepen difficult theoretical issues as the convergence of difference equations to stochastic differential equations, filtering theory, market incompleteness or more applied topics as contingent claim pricing or the term structure of interest rates. Research departments of investment banks and research units dealing with risk-management could also fruitfully employ the ideas developed in this monograph. We show in deep detail how to setup models for the term structure with stochastic volatility or how to extract state prices from the prices of traded options, elements which are the key ingredients for any hedging strategies. The original idea of enriching the book with computer programs was successively dropped. The main reason for this was the low user-friendly nature of our programs, some of which developed in different versions of Gauss, Matlab, Rats and in Fortran 77, which were highly dependent on the nature of the specific problems at hand. We hope in the near future to be able to develop more general routines providing a systematic treatment of the issues contained and/or related to this book. In the meantime we would be willing to help readers with specific problems that may arise while going through the book. We may be reached at the following e-mail addresses: *f_fornari@hotmail.com* and *antonio_mele@hotmail.com*

F.F. — A.M.

INTRODUCTION

1.1 Background and aims of the monograph

Financial returns, albeit unpredictable according to the definition of Sims (1984), display both temporal dependency in their second order moments and heavy-peaked and tailed distributions. While such a phenomenon was known at least since the pioneer work of Mandelbrot (1963) and Fama (1965), it was only with the introduction of the autoregressive conditionally heteroscedastic (ARCH) model of Engle (1982) and Bollerslev (1986) that econometric models of changing volatility have been intensively fitted to data. ARCH models have had a prominent role in the analysis of many aspects of financial econometrics, such as the term structure of interest rates, the pricing of options, the presence of time varying risk premia in the foreign exchange market: see Bollerslev et al. (1992), Bera and Higgins (1993), Bollerslev et al. (1994) or Palm (1996) for surveys. The quintessence of the ARCH model is to make volatility dependent on the variability of past observations. An alternative formulation initiated by Taylor (1986) makes volatility be driven by unobserved components, and has come to be known as the stochastic volatility (SV) model. As for the ARCH models, SV models have also been intensively used in the last decade, especially after the progress accomplished in the corresponding estimation techniques, as illustrated in the excellent surveys of Ghysels et al. (1996) and Shephard (1996). Early contributions that aimed at relating changes in volatility of asset returns to economic intuition include Clark (1973) and Tauchen and Pitts (1983), who assumed that a stochastic process of information arrival generates a random number of intraday changes of the asset price.

Parallel to this strand of empirical research, option pricing theory has expanded into generalizations of the celebrated Black and Scholes (1973) and Merton (1973) evaluation formulae of European options. The Black-Scholes model, for instance, assumes that the price of the asset underlying the option contract follows a geometric Brownian motion, and one of the most successful extensions has been the *continuous time* SV model originally introduced by Hull and White (1987), Johnson and Shanno (1987), Scott (1987) and Wiggins (1987) (more recent related work includes Amin and Ng (1993), Duan (1995), Kallsen and Taqqu (1998) and Hobson and Rogers (1998)). In these models, volatility is not a constant, as in the original Black-Scholes model; rather, it is another random process typically driven by a Brownian motion that is imperfectly correlated with the Brownian motion driving the primitive asset price dynamics. Similar extensions have been introduced in the term structure literature.

In this monograph, we emphasize the use of ARCH models in formulating, estimating and testing the continuous time stochastic volatility models favored in the theoretical literature. The primary source of our research agenda came from work that Daniel B. Nelson published during the first half of nineties, and that is now collected in the second part of the book edited by Rossi (1996). In the first of his celebrated papers, Nelson (1990) was able to show that although ARCH processes are casted in terms of stochastic *difference* equations, they can be thought as reasonable approximations to the solutions of stochastic *differential* equations as the sampling frequency gets higher and higher. In technical terms, the volatility process generated within ARCH-type models converges in distribution towards a well defined solution of a stochastic differential equation as the sampling frequency increases. Since SV models are typically formulated in continuous time in the theoretical literature, Nelson's contribution appeared to many to be an important step towards 'bridging the gap' between the discrete time perspective followed by the applied econometrician and the continuous time perspective idealized by the theorist.

Yet, perhaps due to the great progress accomplished in the domain of the estimation of the parameters of stochastic differential equations through simulation-based methods expanding the early work of McFadden (1989), Pakes and Pollard (1989), Ingram and Lee (1991), Duffie and Singleton (1993), Smith (1990, 1993), Gouriéroux et al. (1993), Bansal et al. (1995) and Gallant and Tauchen (1996), Nelson's ideas were not pushed far enough in the subsequent empirical and statistical literatures; see Gouriéroux and Monfort (1996) for a systematic account of simulation-based econometric methods. One concomitant reason is that the continuous record asymptotics developed for ARCH models do *not* deliver a theory for the estimation of the relevant parameters; rather, such methods typically take the parameters as given, and study the limiting behavior of stochastic difference equations in correspondence of fixed, well-chosen (perhaps too well-chosen) sequences of parameters.

The methodology introduced by Nelson, however, revealed useful to show that appropriate sequences of ARCH models are able to estimate consistently the volatility of a given continuous time stochastic process as the sample frequency gets larger and larger, even in the presence of serious misspecifications: see Nelson (1992) and Nelson and Foster (1994) for the univariate cases, and Bollerslev and Rossi (1996) (p. xiii-xvii) for a very succinct primer on the filtering performances of ARCH models as applied to continuous time stochastic volatility models. As put by Bollerslev and Rossi (1996) (p. xiv), "one could regard the ARCH model as merely a device which can be used to perform filtering or smoothing estimation of unobserved volatilities".

We believe that this represents one of the most important aspects of Nelson's work. In addition to the point estimates of the parameters of stochastic differential equations systems, indeed, an essential ingredient for the practical implementation of any continuous time stochastic volatility model is obviously the knowledge of the volatility at some dates of interest. If one wishes to make use of an option pricing formula that takes stochastic volatility into account, for instance, one has to know not only the price of the asset underlying the contract, but also the instantaneous volatility of that price. However, volatility is obviously not observable—as it can instead be the case of a share price—, and obtaining estimates of it in continuous time is not an easy task; see, however, the recent work of Gallant and Tauchen (1998) that is based on reprojection techniques (previous work on the filtering techniques of stochastic volatility is succinctly reminded in section 1.2.1).[1]

Figure 1.1, taken from Fornari and Mele (1999a), visualizes one simulated path from which one can appreciate the 'typical' filtering of an ARCH model as applied to a restricted version of a theoretical short-term interest rate model presented in chapter 5:

$$\begin{aligned} dr(t) &= (\iota - \theta r(t))dt + r(t)^{1/2}\sigma(t)dW^{(1)}(t) \\ d\sigma(t) &= (\overline{\omega} - \varphi\sigma(t))dt + \psi\sigma(t)dW^{(2)}(t) \end{aligned} \qquad (1.1)$$

where $W^{(i)}, i = 1, 2$, are standard Brownian motions, and $\iota, \theta, \overline{\omega}, \varphi$ and ψ are real parameters whose values have been fixed at the corresponding estimates obtained with US data (see chapter 5 for some additional details, and Fornari and Mele (1999a) for a more technical presentation). The single trajectory reported in the figure represents a weekly sampled trajectory of $\sigma(t)$ obtained by simulating (1.1); the dotted line represents instead the trajectory of the (rescaled) volatility obtained when an ARCH model is fitted to the simulated weekly sampled trajectory of $r(t)$. The strength of such a visual, informal evidence has been formally tested in the Monte Carlo experiment conducted in

---

[1]We are not considering here the possibility of using a theoretical model to extract volatility and/or estimate parameters by means of cross sectional information (e.g., option and/or bond prices). If such a theoretical model had a closed-form solution, this could be an interesting device. Since continuous time stochastic volatility models typically have *not* closed form solutions, using cross sectional information for filtering volatility and estimating all the model's parameters is for the moment nearly unfeaseable, requiring an extremely fine numerical integration of partial differential equations in correspondence of each candidate of the parameter values. See, however, Fornari and Mele (1999a and 1999b) for related work on both term-structure and European option pricing issues. For cross sectional methods applied to option pricing objectives similar to our 1999b paper, see Chernov and Ghysels (1999).

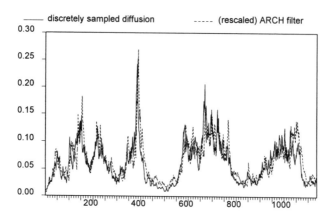

FIGURE 1.1. Typical filtering of the weekly sampled volatility diffusion $\sigma(t)$ in eqs. (1.1) by means of an ARCH model

Fornari and Mele (1999a), where a very low RMSE is shown to divide the two trajectories in thousands of simulations; notice that previous related work on Monte Carlo evidence concerning ARCH models as consistent volatility filters was already conducted as early as Schwartz et al. (1993).

Such results should reinforce the researcher's motivation on the use of ARCH models as approximations of diffusion processes. Yet, relatively little empirical work has been done in that direction. This point is also evidenced by Campbell et al. (1997) (p. 381), who notice that:

> "The empirical properties of [ARCH as approximators of continuous time stochastic volatility processes] have yet to be explored but will no doubt be the subject of future research."

The research presented in this monograph tries indeed to accomplish this task. We wish to outline two major steps in our research strategy. The first one consists in constructing continuous time economies displaying equilibrium dynamics to which ARCH models converge in distribution as the sample frequency gets infinite. This allows us to obtain a microeconomic foundation of the continuous time models that we take as the data generating mechanism. The utility of such an approach lies in the possibility of determining explicitly, within standard preference restrictions (e.g., CRRA utility functions), the risk-premia demanded by agents to be compensated for the fluctuations of the stochastic factors. Our primary field of application will be the theory of the term structure of interest rates with stochastic volatility, a field that is relatively less developed than the corresponding European option pricing domain where, instead, we take a more data-oriented approach (see section 1.3 for further introductory details).

Naturally, there are other continuous time candidates than the economies that we consider here. As shown in chapters 4 and 5, however, only a minor change in notation (and in the corresponding computer codes!) is required to bring our models in touch with these alternatives. In our theoretical model of the term structure of interest rates, indeed, stochastic volatility is generated by the variability of the economic fundamentals and, as is well-known since the seminal contribution of Harrison and Kreps (1979), any arbitrage-free specification of asset prices can be sustained by a competitive equilibrium. In chapter 10 of the Duffie's (1996) textbook, for instance, the reader can see such a phenomenon at work within the standard univariate representation of the Cox et al. (1985a) model; as concerns stochastic volatility, we show in chapter 4 that the choice of the primitive measure space and subsequent factor restrictions crucially determine the final predictions of our equilibrium model of the term structure. To resolve for such an indeterminacy, two natural alternatives are possible. The first one consists in specifying the primitives so as to obtain a computationally (or even analytically) tractable model, as in the case of the original single factor Cox et al. (1985a) model. Such an idea is fully exploited by Duffie and Kan (1996), who construct a class of 'exponential-affine' models "specifying simple relationships among yields" (p. 380); see also Brown and Schaefer (1995) for an earlier treatment of related issues. Another possibility fully exploits the idea that, given the imperfections of any model, it is an empirical issue as to which primitives will serve best at generating a model of the term structure of interest rates. In this case, one can look for economies that support dynamics that are more or less consistent with past data analysis or even with informal observation. Our reverse strategy is thus justified by this second possibility.

The second step of our research program is devoted to a more concrete econometric analysis of continuous time stochastic volatility models. Precisely, the concern lies in the estimation of the parameters of the stochastic differential equations characterizing our equilibrium economies. In the estimation strategy that we suggest, one first uses the moment conditions under which ARCH models converge in distribution towards the theoretical models, obtaining a *direct*, preliminary estimate of the model's parameters. Since such estimates are obtained by means of discrete time models that are typically not closed under temporal aggregation (Drost and Werker (1996)), one then tests and corrects possible *disaggregation* biases by using, this time, ARCH models as *auxiliary* devices in simulation-based schemes. Fornari and Mele (1999a, 1999b) have already applied such a strategy to option prices and US interest rate data, finding strong evidence that the correction made by indirect inference is not significant. In addition to being an appropriate tool to filter out stochastic volatility, such results also make a strong case for the use of ARCH models as approximating devices of the parameters of certain stochastic differential equations.

A related topic lies between the two above mentioned steps of our work: it consists of a better understanding of the functioning of ARCH models by resorting to the more easily tractable continuous time approach. This objective arises quite naturally, since ARCH models are intensively used (not only in mathematical finance as in this monograph), which would require a clear understanding of their theoretical characteristics. In this respect, too, the continuous time approach of Nelson (1990) offers an appropriate tool of analysis. Indeed, ARCH models are non linear stochastic difference equations, and some of their properties are quite cumbersome to establish. The task is easier when one examines their behavior as the sampling frequency tends to infinity. In this case, ARCH models are 'approximated' by stochastic differential equations, a relatively easier to study object: in other terms, one would use *diffusions as ARCH approximations* to get insights into the functioning of ARCH models. As an example, in his first contribution, Nelson (1990) showed that the GARCH(1,1) model of Bollerslev (1986) (see eq. (1.4) below) converges in distribution towards the following stochastic differential equation:

$$d\sigma(t)^2 = (\overline{\omega} - \varphi\sigma(t)^2)dt + \psi\sigma(t)^2 dW^\sigma(t), \qquad (1.2)$$

where W^σ is a standard scalar Brownian motion, and $\overline{\omega}$, φ, and ψ are real valued, non stochastic parameters. Now such a result implies that in continuous time, (1) σ^2 follows a stationary distribution that is an inverted Gamma; and (2) the error process from a given observation model is (approximately) unconditionally Student's t distributed, even if it is conditionally normal. Such results would not be obtained in a discrete time setting.

Our own contribution in this field consisted in deepening some of the previous findings. Precisely, we showed (Fornari and Mele (1997*a*)) that the limiting results obtained for the GARCH(1,1) hold as well for a fairly general model previously introduced by Ding et al. (1993) (see eq. (1.6) below), and for the model of Fornari and Mele (1997*b*). The first scheme admits a 'diffusion limit' that has the following form:

$$d\sigma(t)^\delta = (\overline{\omega} - \varphi\sigma(t)^\delta)dt + \psi\sigma(t)^\delta dW^\sigma(t), \ \delta \in \mathbb{R}_{++} \qquad (1.3)$$

and generalizes both the volatility equation in (1.1) and eq. (1.2). In addition to provide a flexible specification that can be useful in applied work related to mathematical finance—notably via the introduction of a sort of 'volatility concept' σ^δ—, eq. (1.3) enabled us to carry out a detailed analysis concerning the distribution of errors terms from the corresponding (discrete time) observation model: see section 1.2.4 for more details. On the other hand, the derivation of a diffusion limit in correspondence of our 1997*b* model was instructive to us, since despite the nonlinearities that it was designed to capture (see section 1.2.3

below for details), the kind of conditions required to obtain the convergence result were of the same essence as those of Nelson.

The remainder of this chapter has been designed to be a more systematic introduction to all these research themes to which we gave a contribution.

Next section provides a very selective overview of ARCH models. Given the many existing surveys on ARCH models, we only constrain ourselves to present those aspects of ARCH models that are connected with our own contribution: in section 1.2.1, we present the very basic ARCH models as well as their (discrete time) SV competitors; in section 1.2.2, we present the extensions of these models that are designed to capture some observed non linear dynamics of volatility, notably the fact that volatility tends to react asymmetrically to past shocks of different sign; in section 1.2.3 we deepen the previous issue, by arguing that volatility asymmetries are subject to reversals, i.e. positive shocks may sometimes induce more volatility than negative shocks; section 1.2.4 provides some details and motivation concerning our contribution to the approximation results for ARCH models. Section 1.3 covers some of the most important economic implications of continuous time stochastic volatility: section 1.3.1 presents the central issue of the problem in the option pricing domain, and insists on market incompleteness, the related impossibility to implement pure hedging strategies, and the existence of partial hedging strategies that could be optimal according to certain criteria; section 1.3.2 describes some of the existing models of the term structure of interest rates with stochastic volatility. Section 1.4 is an introduction to the statistical methodology that we use to conduct inference in our continuous time models. Finally, section 1.5 provides information about the plan of the remainder of the monograph.

1.2 Empirical models in discrete time

1.2.1 The basic models

The original ARCH model posits the existence of a relation between past squared innovations of an observation assets returns changes model and their current conditional variances. Let $\{\varepsilon_t\}_{t=1}^{\infty}$ be the error process of some observation model; then, the GARCH(1,1) model assumes that $\{\varepsilon_t\}_{t=1}^{\infty}$ is conditionally normal with variance changing through time in a fashion which resembles a restricted ARMA process, i.e.:

$$\varepsilon_t \;/\; I_{t-1} \sim N(0, \sigma_t^2)$$

$$\sigma_t^2 = \omega + \alpha \varepsilon_{t-1}^2 + \beta \sigma_{t-1}^2 \qquad (1.4)$$

where $\omega > 0$, $\alpha, \beta \geq 0$ are real, non-stochastic parameters and I_t is the information set dated t. In the original ARCH(p) model of Engle (1982), β was zero, and the volatility σ_t^2 was driven by a linear combination of p lagged squared error terms: $\sigma_t^2 = \omega + \sum_{i=1}^{p} \alpha_i \varepsilon_{t-i}^2$, $\alpha_i \geq 0$. The model can be estimated by standard maximum likelihood (ML) techniques. Very succinct presentations of the properties of such estimators are in the surveys cited at the beginning of the introductory section of this chapter.

A natural alternative to model (1.4) is given by the SV model, in which log-volatility typically follows an AR process. In the very first contributions, the corresponding estimation techniques relied typically on a simple method of moments (e.g., Scott (1987) and Wiggins (1987)) and the generalized method of moments of Hansen (1982) (e.g., Chesney and Scott (1989) and Melino and Turnbull (1990)). An alternative estimation technique is based on the Kalman filter (see Scott (1987) and Nelson (1988) for an early treatment of such issues): let r_t denote an asset return as of time t, and rewrite the observation equation

$$r_t = \sigma_t \cdot u_t, \ u_t \approx N(0,1)$$

as

$$\log r_t^2 = \log \sigma_t^2 + \xi_t, \ \xi_t \equiv \log u_t^2.$$

By postulating that the volatility propagation mechanism is

$$\log \sigma_t^2 = a + b \cdot \log \sigma_{t-1}^2 + \zeta_t, \ \zeta_t \approx N(0, \sigma_\zeta^2),$$

one sees that $\log r_t^2$ is written in a state space form; hence, the model can be estimated with the usual Kalman filtering techniques (see Harvey (1989) for a textbook on such techniques applied to economics). Due to non-normality of ξ, however, the likelihood function that results by the prediction error decomposition of the Kalman filter is not the exact one, but one can invoke the usual quasi-likelihood methods, as in Harvey et al. (1994). Jacquier et al. (1994) derive the exact filter, and extensions can be found in Jacquier et al. (1999). A comprehensive survey on related techniques can be found in Shephard (1996); notice that an important aspect of these methods consists in extracting volatility estimates, which is not the case for the method of moments. Furthermore, many of the preceding techniques were designed to estimate models that usually are naive discretization of the corresponding continuous time models favored in the theoretical literature; hence, they are likely to induce a discretization bias; see, for instance, Melino (1994) for one of the earliest discussion of this problem.

An alternative method to estimate a discrete time SV model can be based on the indirect inference methods that are succinctly described in section 1.4.

1.2.2 EXTENSIONS

A shortcoming of the GARCH model is that the sign of the forecast errors does not influence the conditional variance, which may contradict the observed dynamics of assets returns. Black (1976), for example, noted that volatility tends to grow in reaction to bad news (excess returns lower than expected), and to fall in response to good news (excess returns higher than expected). The economic explanation given by Black is that negative (positive) excess returns make the equity value decrease and the leverage ratio (defined as debt/equity) of a given firm increase (fall), thus raising (lowering) its riskiness and the future volatility of its assets. This phenomenon has consequently come to be referred to as *leverage effect* (Pagan and Schwert (1990), Nelson (1991), Campbell and Hentschel (1992)). It has to be said, however, that the negative correlation between asset returns and volatility seems to be too strong to be explained on the basis of the leverage effect only; see Christie (1982) and Schwert (1989a).

The basic attempts to include such features into a convenient econometric framework are the Exponential GARCH (EGARCH) model of Nelson (1991), the Glosten et al. (1993) (GJR) model, the asymmetric power ARCH model of Ding et al. (1993), the threshold ARCH model of Rabemananjara and Zakoïan (1993) and Zakoïan (1994), the Quadratic ARCH of Sentana (1991), or the SV model of Harvey and Shephard (1993a, 1993b) and Harvey et al. (1994). All such models include the sign of past forecast errors as conditioning information for the current values of the conditional variance.

In the EGARCH(1,1), for instance, the following equation generates σ_t:

$$\log \sigma_t^2 = \omega + \gamma_0 u_{t-1} + \gamma_1 (|u_{t-1}| - E|u_{t-1}|) + \beta \log \sigma_{t-1}^2,$$

where $u_t = (\frac{\varepsilon}{\sigma})_t$ and the asymmetric behavior of the log-variance with respect to changes in past errors is captured by the terms multiplying γ_0, γ_1. Notice further that such a formulation also allows one to relax positivity constraints on the other parameters ω, β.

In the GJR model, to cite another example, the following is the volatility generating process:

$$\sigma_t^2 = \omega + \alpha \varepsilon_{t-1}^2 + \beta \sigma_{t-1}^2 + \gamma s_{t-1} \varepsilon_{t-1}^2, \qquad (1.5)$$

with $\omega > 0$, $\alpha, \beta \geq 0$, and s_t is a dummy variable which equals one when ε_t is negative and is nil elsewhere. Here the asymmetry is captured by the term multiplying γ. When γ is negative, negative shocks ($\varepsilon < 0$) introduce more volatility than positive shocks of the same size in the subsequent period.

A fairly general model has been proposed by Ding et al. (1993). In this paper (see, also, Granger and Ding (1993, 1994)), the authors study US stock daily returns and show that the autocorrelation function (a.c.f.) of absolute returns raised to a positive power, say θ, is significantly different from zero and, further, is not the strongest one for $\theta = 2$ over a considerably wide range of lags.[2] Specifically, there are values of θ close to one which make such an a.c.f. the

---

[2]Granger and Ding (1993) attempted to link these findings to previous theoretical results of Luce (1980). Let x_t denote the series of returns on some speculative assets; let λ be a positive number. Then, Luce's results imply that the measure of risk per-

largest one for all the considered lags. Based on Monte Carlo evidence, Ding et al. (1993) also report that both the GARCH(1,1) of Bollerslev (1986) and the Taylor (1986) and Schwert's (1989b) model (TS henceforth) are able to reproduce the property that the a.c.f. of $|x_t|^\theta$ reaches its maximum in correspondence of $\theta \simeq 1$ for quite a high number of lags, despite the fact that the GARCH(1,1) makes the conditional variance a linear function of past squared innovations, and the TS model sets the conditional variance equal to the square of a linear function of past absolute innovations (see the third line in table 1). This motivated Ding et al. (1993) to propose the so-called Asymmetric Power ARCH (A-PARCH) model:

$$\sigma_t^\delta = \omega + \alpha(|\varepsilon_{t-1}| - \gamma\varepsilon_{t-1})^\delta + \beta\sigma_{t-1}^\delta, \ \gamma \in (-1,1), \ (\omega,\alpha,\beta,\delta) \in \mathbb{R}_+^4. \quad (1.6)$$

The main difference between (1.6) and standard ARCH equations is the power δ to which σ and $(|\varepsilon| - \gamma\varepsilon)$ are raised. In standard applications, δ is 2 or 1, while the A-PARCH imposes δ as a Box-Cox power transform on σ, which has to be estimated. Ding et al. (1993) show that model (1.6) encompasses at least seven classes of ARCH models already proposed; see table 1.1 for some of these models. Naturally, the leverage effect is also captured within this model (hence its definition as 'asymmetric'), notably throughout the term multiplying γ.

TABLE 1.1

GARCH(1,1)	eq. (1.4)
GJR	eq. (1.5)
Taylor-Schwert	$\sigma_t = \omega + \alpha\,|\varepsilon_{t-1}| + \beta\sigma_{t-1}$
Nonlinear ARCH	$\sigma_t^\delta = \omega + \alpha\,|\varepsilon_{t-1}|^\delta + \beta\sigma_{t-1}^\delta$

One disadvantage of all the previous formulations is that volatility asymmetries are nested into the ARCH scheme in an abrupt manner. In the GJR model (1.5), for instance, asymmetries in volatility are introduced by adding a term to the standard GARCH(1,1) that is the product of the squared residual times a step function of the residual: denote such a step function as $\underline{\alpha}(\varepsilon_t) \equiv \gamma \cdot s_t$. The dotted line in figure 1.2 represents $\underline{\alpha}$ when $\gamma < 0$. In a private conversation held with Timo Teräsvirta in January 1995, we suggested a natural generalization that replaces $\gamma \cdot s_t$ with a function that changes smoothly in the domain of definition of ε. The straight line in figure 1.2 depicts one possible $\underline{\alpha}$; generally, a creative use of standard techniques from the smooth transition

---

ceived by agents can be proportional to $E_t\,|x_{t+1}|^\lambda$ where E_t denotes the expectation operator conditional on the information set as of time t. Under market consensus on λ, and under the assumptions that (1) x_t distributes normally with zero mean and variance σ_t^2 and (2) $E_t\sigma_{t+1}^\lambda$ is the appropriate measure of volatility, then, standard volatility measures may fail to capture an adequate dynamic characterization of risk, since λ is not necessarily 2; rather, it can take any positive value.

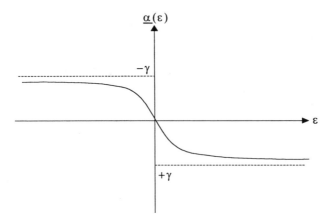

FIGURE 1.2. Smoothing volatility asymmetries ($\gamma < 0$)

modeling literature (see, e.g., Granger and Teräsvirta (1993)) can be employed to select an appropriate function $\underline{\alpha}$. To the best of our knowledge, Hagerud (1997) and Gonzalez-Rivera (1998) were the first papers that exploited such ideas by opening the route to the so-called 'smooth-transition' ARCH models.

1.2.3 VOLATILITY ASYMMETRIES: RAMIFICATIONS

According to empirical evidence originally reported in Rabemananjara and Zakoïan (1993), even the preceding asymmetric-type models might be unsuccessful in taking into account some nonlinearities of the volatility dynamics. In a study concerning disaggregated French returns, Rabemananjara and Zakoïan find that 'high' negative shocks increase future volatility more than high positive ones while at the same time 'small' positive shocks too often produce a stronger impact on future volatility than negative shocks of the same size. Thus, following the occurrence of a shock of a certain size, the asymmetric behavior of the volatility might become reversed; the modeling of such feature has also been the focus of two papers of ours (Fornari and Mele (1996, 1997b)).

Our first concern in Fornari and Mele (1997b) was to define the 'size' of the shock at which a volatility reversal may occur. The definition we adopted was based on the level of unexpected volatility generated by a shock at time $t-1$ (ε_{t-1}). Consider the information set dated $t-2$. The expected value of ε_{t-1}^2 is obviously σ_{t-1}^2; if, however, $\varepsilon_{t-1}^2 > \sigma_{t-1}^2$ ($\leq \sigma_{t-1}^2$), we said that ε_{t-1} generates (at time $t-1$) a level of volatility higher (lower) than expected (at time $t-2$). Consider now a very small negative shock at time $t-1$; if it produces a level of volatility at time $t-1$ lower than expected at time $t-2$, there should be no reason to believe that volatility at time t will increase as a consequence of the leverage effect. Roughly speaking, a small negative shock which generates lower volatility than expected may be regarded as good news; at the same time, positive shocks which generate lower volatility than expected may be regarded as relatively bad news. This might be a possible explanation of the mechanism according to which a reversal originates. Furthermore, it gives a natural explanation for what has to be regarded as a 'high' or a 'small' shock: a high shock ε is the one for which $\varepsilon^2 > \sigma^2$ and viceversa.

In Fornari and Mele (1997b), we also presented an informal economic argument justifying the occurrence of volatility reversals. In particular, we noticed that the Black's (1976) arguments based on changes in the leverage ratio could be deepened. The observation was that a change in the leverage ratio is likely to be followed by a change in the expected performance of the firm, the latter being a function of the differential between the expected average performance of the sector in which the firm operates and the overall cost of debt. Suppose that the economy has K productive sectors; one has that in the kth sector, $k = 1, ..., K$,

$$i_j = \rho_k + (\rho_k - r)\frac{D}{S_j}, \qquad (1.7)$$

where i_j and S_j are the expected profitability and the price of the stock, r the interest paid on debt, ρ_k the average performance of the kth sector, D the amount of debt, and $\frac{D}{S_j}$ represents the leverage ratio of the jth firm in the kth sector. Such a relation can be found in Modigliani and Miller (1958) (proposition II, p. 271). Consider now the case that $(\rho_k - r)$ is positive in eq. (1.7). Then, a negative shock on S_j may be regarded as more favorable than a positive shock; in fact it increases $\frac{D}{S_j}$ and the expected profitability of the firm: contrary to the celebrated Black's explanation, a positive shock may have a stronger impact on future volatility than a negative one of the same size. The Black's explanation, however, should be expected to be at work when the negative shock is very large. In this case, indeed, two things may be hypothesized to happen: first, economic agents may discount a recession of the kth sector, i.e. a fall of ρ_k; second, the cost of the debt might be thought to start rising sharply for the jth firm, which happens when r is positively related to $\frac{D}{S_j}$ (hence inversely related to S_j). Both events are likely to change the sign of $(\rho_k - r)$, hence causing volatility reversals.

Past empirical research had generally overlooked the impact of previous (unexpected or expected) volatility on its current expected level. Engle and Ng (1993), for example, propose to analyze the impact of news on the current conditional variance (i.e. on σ_t^2), keeping constant the information dated $t - 2$ and earlier, with all the lagged conditional variances evaluated at their unconditional value. An important point in our paper was to define a sort of *response function of the future expected volatility to past unexpected volatility*. Let, for example, $v \equiv \delta_0(\varepsilon^2 - \sigma^2)$, where δ_0 is a real constant. A simple model that takes into account the preceding remarks is:

$$\sigma_t^2 = w + \beta\sigma_{t-1}^2 + \alpha\varepsilon_{t-1}^2 + s_{t-1}v_{t-1}. \tag{1.8}$$

Let us suppose indeed that $\delta_0 < 0$. If $v_{t-1} < 0$ (i.e., 'high' shocks have occurred) then, *cæteris paribus*, negative shocks generate more volatility than positive ones. However, if $v_{t-1} > 0$ (i.e., 'small' shocks have occurred) positive shocks increase volatility more than negative ones. Thus, model (1.8) can take into account situations where the asymmetric behavior of the volatility is reversed.

Unfortunately, model (1.8) is too simple. Furthermore, it imposes a fixed probability of occurrence of reversals that is approximately 0.68. To clarify this point, let χ_1^2 denote a chi-squared random variable, and notice that when $\delta_0 < 0$,

$$\Pr\,(\text{reversal at } t) = \Pr(\varepsilon_{t-1}^2 < \sigma_{t-1}^2) = \Pr(\chi_1^2 < 1) \simeq 0.68,$$

whereas we would like to be endowed with a more flexible specification. Fornari and Mele (1997*b*) took

$$\sigma_t^2 = w + \beta\sigma_{t-1}^2 + \alpha\varepsilon_{t-1}^2 + s_{t-1}v_{t-1}, \tag{1.9}$$

where now

$$v_t \equiv \delta_0\varepsilon_t^2 - \delta_1\sigma_t^2 - \delta_2,$$

so that v_t is a constant plus a linear combination of the 'observed volatility' (ε_t^2) and its lagged expectation (σ_t^2), thus playing a role similar to that of an error correcting variable. Fornari and Mele (1997*b*) refer to model (1.9) as the Volatility-Switching (VS-) ARCH model.

Model (1.9) does not impose any a priori probability to the occurrence of reversals. Proceeding indeed with the same algebra as before, and assuming that $\delta_0 < 0$ (which was the case of our estimates),

$$\Pr(\text{reversal at } t) = \Pr(\varepsilon_{t-1}^2 < k_1\sigma_{t-1}^2 + k_2) = \Pr(\chi_1^2 < k_1 + k_2\sigma_t^{-2})$$

where $k_1 \equiv \frac{\delta_1}{\delta_0}$ and $k_2 \equiv \frac{\delta_2}{\delta_0}$. When $\delta_2 < 0$, the probability of reversals is an increasing function of the conditional precision process. This is in accordance with the explanation given above on the basis of relation (1.7): volatility reversals can occur when volatility is low. If, on the contrary, the estimates of (δ_1, δ_2) are such that $(-k_1, -k_2) \in \mathbb{R}_+^2$, the probability of reversal is nil; such a situation arises, for instance, once that $\delta_1 = \delta_2 = 0$, which is the restriction under which the VS-ARCH reduces to the GJR scheme. Thus, the VS-ARCH model allows a more detailed analysis of the asymmetric behavior of the volatility than the GJR model, enabling shifts in its direction, according to the size of past shocks. Furthermore, the existence of reversals can be

partly tested by ascertaining whether the VS-ARCH improves upon GJR.[3]
Fornari and Mele (1997*b*) were looking for international evidence by fitting the
VS-ARCH model to returns from seven stock exchanges. They found that on
average the VS-ARCH model outperformed the GJR, and provided evidence
of volatility reversals in almost all of the analyzed countries.[4]

Finally, it is worth noticing that a variant of VS-ARCH model has also been
estimated in Fornari and Mele (1996); it takes the following form:

$$\sigma_t^2 = \omega + \alpha \varepsilon_{t-1}^2 + \beta \sigma_{t-1}^2 + \gamma s_{t-1} \varepsilon_{t-1}^2 + \delta (\frac{\varepsilon_{t-1}^2}{\sigma_{t-1}^2} - k) s_{t-1}. \qquad (1.10)$$

The first three terms on the RHS are a standard GARCH(1,1) model. These,
together with the fourth term, define a GJR(1,1) model. The last term is
designed to capture the reversal of asymmetry that can be observed when
$(\frac{\varepsilon}{\sigma})^2$ reaches k, the threshold value. Estimation results from this model were
perfectly in line with those subsequently published in Fornari and Mele (1997*b*).

1.2.4 DIFFUSIONS AS ARCH APPROXIMATIONS

In addition to be useful devices in uncovering the filtering performances of
ARCH and, as it will be described in section 1.4, in enriching the estimation
techniques of continuous time stochastic volatility models, continuous time
methods can also be understood as a guidance to get interesting insights into
some properties of ARCH models in discrete time. In the introductory section
of this chapter, we mentioned that in his seminal paper Nelson (1990) showed
that the GARCH(1,1) error process follows (approximately) a Student's t, unconditionally. One of the tasks that we gave ourselves in our 1997*a* paper was
to obtain results in correspondence of the GARCH(1,1) error process when
the error process is not conditionally normal; also, we investigated what is the
form of such a distribution when innovations are conditionally normal and the
volatility propagation mechanism is eq. (1.6). More generally, we were looking
for the stationary distribution of the error process when the error process is
not conditionally normal and the volatility propagation process is eq. (1.6).
Similar issues were dealt with in our 1997*b* paper.

In chapter 2 we attempt to present a scheme that explores these issues;
we will draw heavily on the theoretical sections of our corresponding 1997
papers. In our scheme, the error process is taken to be conditionally *general
error distributed* (g.e.d.). Such a choice is useful on an analytical standpoint,

---

[3]It is worth signalling that Engle and Ng (1993) fitted different asymmetric models
(not the VS-ARCH) to stock returns from Japan and found the GJR to be the best
parametric scheme to model asymmetries.

[4]In our original paper, the models were estimated via a normal likelihood pro-
file. It is possible to show that our results are robust to a generalization of such a
distributional assumption.

while allowing at the same time for a fairly instructive first approximation treatment of non-normality issues. One reason to deal with non-normal errors came from well-known empirical findings of the mid eighties: the standardized residuals obtained by using the conditional standard deviation of an ARCH-type model is typically not normal, despite the use of conditionally normal likelihood profiles.[5]

Nelson (1991) was the first author to make use of the g.e.d. in the attempt to fit stock returns; as is well-known, the g.e.d. is characterized by a 'tail-thickness' parameter, denoted hereafter as v, that tunes the height of the tails; throughout this monograph, we will use the notation g.e.d.$_{(v)}$ to highlight the presence of such a parameter: see eqs. (2.1) for the corresponding analytical details. The g.e.d. encompasses a number of distributions such as the normal distribution or the Laplace distribution of the first kind; the Laplace distribution of the first kind was used by Granger and Ding (1993) to fit different ARCH models to stock returns data. It should be acknowledged, however, that Nelson (1991) reported that the g.e.d. did not fully account for all of the outliers using an EGARCH scheme for US stock market data. Alternatives to the g.e.d. are the Student's t used, for instance, in Engle and Bollerslev (1986), Bollerslev (1987), or Hsieh (1988) to model foreign exchange rates, or the generalized Student's t, used in Bollerslev et al. (1994) to model stock returns. The generalized Student's t distribution nests both the Student's t and the g.e.d., and is attractive since it has two shape parameters that take account of both the tails and the central part of the conditional distribution of the error process. Yet, Bollerslev et al. (1994) showed that even the likelihood function based on the generalized Student's t does not allow for a fully satisfactory treatment of tail events in US stock returns.

Our theoretical results can be summarized as follows. Under an appropriate discretization scheme, we first show that the solution of model (1.6) converges in distribution towards the solution of eq. (1.3). In a second step, we show that when the sampling frequency gets infinite, a conditionally g.e.d.$_{(v)}$ A-PARCH error process follows a stationary distribution that is a generalized Student's t distribution when $\delta = v$; the restriction $\delta = v$ was made for analytical convenience only, but the empirical section of Fornari and Mele (1997a) and Mele (1998) reported that it can hardly be rejected empirically. Obviously, the most interesting theoretical case is the general one in which $\delta \neq v$: while we do not have closed-form solutions in this case, numerical results suggest that *cæteris paribus*, low values of δ tend to: (1) raise the central part, and (2) increase the tails of the stationary distribution of the error process. Insofar as v is considered, we find that it shapes such a stationary distribution in the same

---

[5]The failure of conditional normality was documented by Bollerslev (1987) or Hsieh (1988) in exchange rate studies, and by Bollerslev et al. (1994) in stock returns enquiries.

manner as it does with the conditional one. Furthermore, chapter 2 also derives a closed-form solution for the instantaneous correlation between a continuous time asset price process and its instantaneous volatility, as approximated by the A-PARCH.[6] We find that the correlation is constant, and that its modulus never reaches unity for a reasonably wide set of parameters' values.[7] Finally, chapter 2 present analogous results for the VS-ARCH eq. (1.9), although we do not deal there with correlation issues, and we confine ourselves to the simplest situation where the error process is conditionally normally distributed.

1.3   Theoretical issues

1.3.1   EUROPEAN OPTION PRICING

Among the standard absence-of-frictions hypotheses underlying the celebrated Black and Scholes (1973) formula[8] for the price of European-type option contracts, an important assumption was the complete market structure that can be generated by assuming that the price of the asset underlying the option contract is a geometric Brownian motion:

$$dS(t) = \mu S(t)dt + \sigma S(t)dW(t), \qquad (1.11)$$

where μ and σ are two constants. Due to what Heston (1993a) (p. 933) figuratively terms "a surprising cancellation", the constant μ vanishes out from the final formula,[9] which is obviously not the case for the constant σ.

In addition to be inconsistent with time-series evidence, the constancy of σ also gives rises to empirical cross-sectional inconsistencies: when one compares the Black-Scholes formula with observed option prices and then inverts the formula to recover the σ in (1.11), one obtains that the resulting σ is in fact a U-shaped function of the strike of the option. Such a phenomenon has come to be known as the 'smile effect'.

To the best of our knowledge, Ball and Roma (1994) (p. 602) (see, also, Renault and Touzi (1996) for related work) were the first to point out that the smile effect emerges in a rather natural fashion when the data generating

---

[6]Such a result did not appear in the original 1997a paper, but in the 1999a one.

[7]In an independent work, Duan (1997) elegantly accomplishes similar tasks for models encompassing subclasses of the A-PARCH, but here we account for all the encompassed models, as well as more general distributional assumptions of the discrete model.

[8]See formula (3.16) in chapter 3.

[9]Heston (1993a) shows that the independence of the option pricing formula on the average appreciation rate of the underlying asset price is not a general property in correspondence of alternative asset price processes.

mechanism is a stochastic volatility one,

$$\begin{aligned} dS(t) &= \mu dt + \sigma(t)S(t)dW^{(1)}(t) \\ d\nu(t) &= \overline{\varphi}(t)dt + \overline{\psi}(t)dW^{\sigma}(t) \end{aligned} \qquad (1.12)$$

and yet one insists on inverting the Black-Scholes formula to recover a constant volatility. In system (1.12), ν is a monotone function of σ; the functions $\overline{\varphi}, \overline{\psi}$ are taken to be measurable with respect to the information set generated by the Brownian motions $W^{(1)}, W^{\sigma}$, and guarantee the existence of a solution to (1.12) (see chapter 3 for a more technical presentation on existence issues). The assumptions of the authors were essentially the ones underlying the Hull and White (1987) model; Renault (1997) presents a survey on the state-of-the-art on this issue, and Das and Sundaran (1999) develop further analytical results concerning the case in which W^{σ} can be written as $W^{\sigma} = \rho W^{(1)} + (1 - \rho^2)^{1/2}W^{(2)}$, where ρ is a constant in $(-1, 1)$, and $W^{(2)}$ is another Brownian motion, finding however that standard SV models are not entirely satisfactory.

The Black-Scholes setting was of course modified to take account of stochastic volatility, as in (1.12); Hull and White (1987), Scott (1987), or Wiggins (1987) were early attempts in that direction. Explicit solutions have proved hard to derive: if one excludes the approximate solution provided by Hull and White (1987) or the analytical solution provided by Heston (1993b),[10] one typically needs to derive the price of the call by implementing Monte Carlo methods (e.g., Johnson and Shanno (1987), Engle and Mustafa (1992) or Lamoureux and Lastrapes (1993)), or by numerically solving a certain partial differential equation, as in the seminal papers of Wiggins (1987):[11] see the following chapters.

It became rapidly clear, however, that the very problem associated with stochastic volatility was not the mere computational effort needed to generalize the Black-Scholes option pricing formula. Rather, a conceptual problem

---

[10]Such a solution was provided on the assumption that stochastic volatility was the solution of a linear mean-reverting "square-root" process; in a square root process, the instantaneous variance of the process is proportional to the level reached by that process: in model (1.12), for instance, $\overline{\psi}(t) = \psi\nu(t)^{1/2}$, where ψ is a constant. In fact, by delving into the computation details of Heston (1993b), one realizes that the role played by the "square-root hypothesis" in obtaining a closed-form solution resembles very much the role played by "variance-affinity" in the affine term-structure literature (see chapter 4 for details concerning the term structure of interest rates with stochastic volatility).

[11]Given the increase in the computational speed of modern computers, the numerical integration of a partial differential equation is not a real limitation; rather, it would suffice to slightly change a computer code to compare rather different stochastic volatility models: see chapter 5 for an illustration of this fact to our class of term-structure model with stochastic volatility that is developed in chapter 4. By contrast, the "human" computational time needed to find closed-form solutions in correspondence of realistic models can sometimes increase in an unreasonable way!

emerged, which is the fact that the presence of stochastic volatility generates market incompleteness. Heuristically, market incompleteness means that agents cannot hedge against future contingencies; one of the formal reasons here is that the number of assets is too low to span the entire space of contingencies. In an economy with diffusion state variables, for instance, incompleteness arises when the number of assets is less than the dimension of the Brownian motion driving the state variables: this is exactly the case of model (1.12), where trading strategies involving only one asset are not sufficient to duplicate the value of the option. In other terms, when the option price H is *rationally* formed at time t, it will be of the form $H(t) = H(t, S(t), \nu(t))$, where $\nu(t)$ is not adapted to the filtration generated by $W^{(1)}(t)$: therefore, trading with only the primitive asset does not allow for a perfect replication of H, which is the argument required to obtain one, and only one, arbitrage-free option price: see chapter 3 for a technical presentation.

To summarize, the presence of stochastic volatility introduces two inextricable consequences: (1) perfect hedging strategies are impossible; (2) there is an infinity of option prices that are admissible with the absence of arbitrage opportunities.

One way to treat the second issue would consist in making a representative agent 'select' the appropriate pricing function. This was the case of the Wiggins (1987) and Heston (1993b) models, for instance, who use the representative agent framework of Cox et al. (1985b). Furthermore, the use of a representative agent is justified on a solid microeconomic basis, since in these models the representative agent typically can trade with two assets (the primitive asset and the option contract), thus having access to a complete market structure.[12] The price to be paid to select a pricing function via preference restrictions of a representative agent, however, is that the resulting price is obviously not preference-free. In a sense, Hull and White (1987) also followed such a selection-by-preferences-restrictions strategy: in their framework, indeed, the authors supposed that agents are not compensated for the fluctuations of stochastic volatility i.e, the volatility risk premium is nil:[13] such an assumption is not confirmed empirically (see, e.g., Lamoureux and Lastrapes (1993)), and has been formally shown to be equivalent to an economy with a representative agent with logarithmic-type utility function (Pham and Touzi (1996)), a fact that was roughly known since Wiggins (1987). In Fornari and Mele (1999b), we take a data-oriented approach, by estimating what we termed a *volatility risk-premium surface*; see the end of section 1.3.2 for further introductory

---

[12]Bajeux and Rochet (1996) derived the conditions under which market completeness is ensured in a stochastic volatility framework. Romano and Touzi (1998) extended that framework by allowing, inter alia, for the existence of a correlation process between the primitive asset price and its instantaneous volatility.

[13]As a Hull and White pointed out (p. 283, footnote 1), a change in notation is sufficient to switch their model to a model with a constant volatility risk premium.

discussion, and chapter 3 for technical details.

A related utility-based approach has been developed by Davis (1997);[14] Davis' results were not designed directly for the stochastic volatility framework. Davis proposed to select a pricing function by a marginal rate of substitution argument: an agent has initial wealth equal to x, from which she generates final wealth equal to $V^{x,\pi}(T)$ by means of some portfolio process π; her problem is $\max_\pi E(u(V^{x,\pi}(T)))$. Now suppose that our agent diverts a small amount of her initial wealth x to buy an unhedgeable claim $\widetilde{X}$ that costs p; define $Q(d,p,x) = \sup_\pi E(u(V^{x-d,\pi}(T) + \frac{d}{p}\widetilde{X}))$. Davis defines a 'fair' price as the solution $\widehat{p}(x)$ of the following first order condition: $\frac{\partial}{\partial d}Q(d,\widehat{p},x)\big|_{d=0} = 0$.

An useful complement to utility-based approaches can be made by concentrating on hedging strategies: indeed, despite the fact that there are no *perfect* hedging strategies in incomplete markets, one can always look for some sort of 'imperfect', but *optimal* strategies. The notion of optimality is then generated by some loss function. As an example, if one considers strategies that simply make the volatility of the resulting strategy value the best approximation (in projection terms) of the volatility of an unhedgeable claim value, one gets that the following imperfect, pure hedging strategy:

$$\widetilde{\pi}(t) = (\frac{\partial H}{\partial S}S + \frac{\partial H}{\partial \nu} \cdot \overline{\psi} \cdot \rho \cdot \sigma^{-1})(t), \tag{1.13}$$

has the property in question within model (1.12); such a result generalizes a previous one obtained by Hofmann et al. (1992) to the case of a non-zero correlation. If one takes model (1.3) as the volatility generating mechanism, with $W^\sigma = \rho W^{(1)} + (1-\rho^2)^{1/2}W^{(2)}$, for instance, relation (1.13) then becomes:

$$\widetilde{\pi}(t) = (\frac{\partial H}{\partial S}S)(t) + \psi\rho \cdot (\frac{\partial H}{\partial \sigma^\delta})(t) \cdot \sigma(t)^{\delta-1},$$

and can be numerically evaluated by usual methods, such as those exploited in the last section of Hofmann et al. (1992). In an empirical study, Chernov and Ghysels (1999) have already made use of formula (1.13) within the Heston's framework. In addition to derive such a formula in a general diffusion context, chapter 3 also adds a few results connecting strategies like (1.13) to the Hull and White hypothesis that the volatility risk premium is nil.

Naturally, one may wish to consider criteria that are more general than the preceding one, but the price to be paid is a more complex analysis that has recently received a somewhat detailed treatment in mathematical finance: portfolio selection strategies belong to a very old research activity, but techniques in continuous time economies with incomplete markets have been introduced relatively recently; see the introduction to chapter 3 for a list of

---

[14]Such an approach is very close to that developed by Mankiw (1986) in a different context.

some of the most important initial contributions and surveys papers in this domain. Fundamentally, two approaches have been formulated. In the first one, one searches over strategies that minimize a loss function, and a more general formulation than the one considered above is, for instance, the continuous time incomplete market problem considered by Duffie and Richardson (1991): $\widehat{\pi}(p) = \arg\min_{\pi} E(V^{p,\pi}(T) - \widetilde{X})^2$. In a series of papers that are cited in the introduction of chapter 3, Schweizer subsequently defines an *approximation price*, equal to $\widehat{p} = \arg\min_{p} E(V^{p,\widehat{\pi}(p)}(T) - \widetilde{X})^2$. The second approach follows the revolutionary perspective introduced by Bensaid et al. (1992) in the transaction costs literature, and identifies the bounds of a continuum of arbitrage-free prices of the claim; such bounds correspond to the so-called 'dominating' strategies rather than the standard duplicating strategies of the complete markets case.[15] Such an approach can be extended to any well behaved situation in which markets are incomplete; see, for instance, Cvitanic et al. (1997) for an application to models with stochastic volatility. All such more general issues are not treated here.

1.3.2   THE TERM STRUCTURE OF INTEREST RATES

Despite the increased importance played by stochastic volatility in financial economics, only a few theoretical term structure models take into account such a phenomenon in the same fashion as one has observed for the European option pricing theory in the last decade.

A notable exception is the early equilibrium model of Longstaff and Schwartz (1992), in which the instantaneous interest rate is a linear combination of two factors, thus generating a two-factor model *à la* Cox et al. (1985a). Since volatility was driven there by the same Brownian motions driving the instantaneous interest rate, however, volatility acted in a way that is rather different from the one that is usually thought of in the traditional stochastic volatility literature, where volatility is typically *not* adapted to the filtration generated by the Brownian motion driving the observables. In fact, in one of the first empirical studies devoted to these issues, Andersen and Lund (1997a) convincingly propose to extend a model studied in Chan et al. (1992):

$$\mathrm{d}r(t) = (\iota - \theta r(t))\mathrm{d}t + \overline{\sigma}r(t)^{\eta}\mathrm{d}W(t), \tag{1.14}$$

where $\iota, \theta, \overline{\sigma}, \eta$ are real parameters, so as to incorporate a stochastic volatility factor in the following manner:

$$\begin{array}{rcl} \mathrm{d}r(t) & = & (\iota - \theta r(t))\mathrm{d}t + \sigma(t)r(t)^{\eta}\mathrm{d}W^{(1)}(t) \\ \mathrm{d}\log\sigma(t)^2 & = & \kappa(\alpha - \log\sigma(t)^2)\mathrm{d}t + \psi\mathrm{d}W^{(2)}(t) \end{array} \tag{1.15}$$

---

[15]One bound is the minimum cost that is needed to obtain at least the same payoffs as those promised by the claim. The other bound is obtained by using a symmetric argument.

where κ, α, ψ are real parameters that guarantee the existence of a solution to (1.15).

Model (1.14) is a univariate generalization of the square-root model of Cox et al. (1985a) model, which sets $\eta \equiv \frac{1}{2}$. In general, $\eta > 0$ makes interest rate volatility increase with the interest rate level. This is the so-called 'level-effect': as is clear, the parameter η measures the sensitivity of the instantaneous volatility to the level of the interest rate; in fact, Chan et al. (1992) suggest that $\eta > 1$ is empirically more plausible than $\eta < 1$. The drawback of model (1.14), however, is that it can not accommodate for the autocorrelation of volatilities in the fashion described in the preceding section. In contrast, this is not the case of a model like (1.1) or (1.15): as Andersen and Lund pointed out, a representation such as (1.15) is ad hoc, but it is also in accordance with "similar formulations for general financial time series", such as those presented in the preceding subsection.

On a theoretical standpoint, Fong and Vasicek (1991), Fornari and Mele (1994, 1995) or Chen (1996) have primitives with a more traditional stochastic volatility flavor than the model of Longstaff and Schwartz (1992), for they propose that the short term interest rate is the solution of:[16]

$$
\begin{aligned}
\mathrm{d}r(t) &= (\iota - \theta r(t))\mathrm{d}t + \sigma(t)r(t)^\eta \mathrm{d}W^{(1)}(t) \\
\mathrm{d}\sigma(t)^2 &= \kappa(\alpha - \sigma(t)^2)\mathrm{d}t + \psi\sigma(t)\mathrm{d}W^{(2)}(t)
\end{aligned}
\qquad (1.16)
$$

or:

$$
\begin{aligned}
\mathrm{d}r(t) &= (\iota - \theta r(t))\mathrm{d}t + \sigma(t)\mathrm{d}W^{(1)}(t) \\
\mathrm{d}\sigma(t)^2 &= \kappa(\alpha - \sigma(t)^2)\mathrm{d}t + \psi\sigma(t)^2\mathrm{d}W^{(2)}(t)
\end{aligned}
$$

The latter formulation appeared in our 1994 and 1995 papers, and was motivated by the fact that it represents the diffusion limit of an AR(1)-GARCH(1,1) process of the short term interest rate. Its main inextricable disavantages are that: (1) the short term interest rate can attain negative values; and (2) the model does not take account of the level effect.[17] Furthermore, that model was estimated via identification techniques *à la* Nelson, without controlling the adequacy of the approximating model via the consistency tests that will be succinctly presented in chapter 5. Our papers were written much before the date they were published and we did not have the same powerful techniques of today for estimating the parameters of a system of stochastic differential equations: such techniques are going to be discussed succinctly in the following section (see chapter 5 for a technical presentation).

The common theoretical drawback of the models of Fong-Vasicek, Fornari-Mele and Chen is that they do not arise from an equilibrium theory determining

---

[16]Parametric restrictions in these models were as follows: in Fong-Vasicek, $\gamma \equiv 0$, and in Chen, $\gamma \equiv \frac{1}{2}$. Actually the Chen's model is more general than (1.16) for it allows $\frac{\iota}{\theta}$ to follow a third diffusion model.

[17]Brenner et al. (1996) presented a discrete-time ARCH model that took care of the level effect.

the risk-premia demanded by agents to be compensated for the stochastic fluctuations of (r, σ^2).[18]

In chapter 4, we present an equilibrium model that attempts to overcome the preceding critiques. Its concern is to find economies in which generalized versions of systems like (1.1), (1.15) or (1.16) can be viewed as the *equilibrium* data generating process, and as a by-product of this we provide the partial differential equation that has to be followed by the equilibrium price of a default free bond. The approach that we follow is close to the framework of Cox et al. (1985b), with the exception that we replace linear activities with stocks.[19] As in Longstaff and Schwartz (1992), the primitives of the economy include two factors, but instead of generating equilibria in which the instantaneous interest rate is a linear combination of the factors, we specify the factor dynamics in a way that allows for the equilibrium short term rate to be linear in the first factor only. Stochastic volatility of the kind considered in this section then simply emerges because the first factor exhibits stochastic volatility—interpreted as the second factor—that is not adapted to the filtration generated by the Brownian motion driving the first factor. The model is derived under standard preference restrictions of a representative agent. Specifically, we assume logarithmic utility and find an equilibrium by using standard dynamic programming techniques. Such assumption and techniques are made for pedagogical purposes only. In Fornari and Mele (1999a), the model is solved by assuming a CRRA utility function and utilizing martingale techniques within a more pronounced general equilibrium framework.

To conclude, we would notice that the approach that is favored here might appear to be in contrast with the approach that we are following in our European option pricing empirical studies, where we do not assume any prior pertaining to the preferences of agents; see chapter 3. It has to be reminded, however, that apart from the work of Longstaff and Schwartz (1992), we do not know of any paper dealing with continuous time stochastic volatility models of the term structure in a fully articulated equilibrium framework: as explained above, it is instead a common practice to impose specific, *non-flexible* functional forms to otherwise unidentified risk-premia. However, imposing ad hoc risk-premia that rule out arbitrage opportunities would be an interesting

---

[18]In a subsequent paper, Andersen and Lund (1997b) try to examine the consequences of their model (1.15) on the term-structure of interest rates. As in the early contributions of Fong-Vasicek, Fornari-Mele and Chen, the authors's specification of the risk-premia is ad hoc. In addition to this, however, Andersen and Lund propose a three-factor model where the "long term" interest rate is another stochastic process—as in previous work of Chen—, and solve their model via Monte Carlo techniques.

[19]Such a modification essentially serves to jointly determine the dynamics of the stock price, which will be compared to the ones that are typically posited in the stochastic volatility pricing literature on European options.

agenda if the corresponding functional forms were general enough, especially when the final purpose of the researcher is to fit cross-sectional information. As noted, this is *not* the case of the above cited papers, but rather than undertaking such an objective, we preferred to pursue the more modest, yet logically preliminary task of developing more *theory* on the determinants of the risk premia within simple preference restrictions, which is for the moment more than an under-developed area. Naturally, one extension of our work would consist in applying a flexible, data-oriented approach to the determinants of the risk-premia, in the vein of our empirical work in the stochastic volatility option pricing area where, instead, it is now well-understood how risk-premia are affected by standard preference restrictions.

1.4 Statistical inference[20]

A recurrent difficulty arising in econometrics concerns the estimation of models giving rise to criterion functions that have no manageable analytical expressions. In modern finance theory, for instance, models are typically set in continuous time. Such a choice is justified by the fact that in continuous time, powerful mathematical techniques[21] exist, which have no counterparts in discrete time.[22] The resulting models are often diffusion processes, but jump diffusion processes are also part of a traditional research program. Furthermore, non-Markovian models have also been proposed, both in the term structure of interest rates (e.g., Heath et al. (1992), Comte and Renault (1996) (section 4.1)) and in the option pricing literatures (e.g., Comte and Renault (1998)). In this monograph, we constrain ourselves to Markovian models.

Apart from special cases such as the celebrated Black-Scholes or the Cox et al. (1985a) models, theoretical financial models typically give rise to transition and/or ergodic distributions for the observables that are not known explicitly, since these are solutions to parabolic partial differential equations that can only be solved numerically. Hence, the likelihood function implied by the measure induced by a discretely sampled diffusion can not be calculated explicitly.[23]

---

[20]This section is motivated by our applied research work on the estimation of the parameters of stochastic differential equations for the short term interest rates. Applications of the material discussed herein to stock returns, for instance, can be conceived in a straight forward manner. Furthermore, surveys that are more focussed on option pricing issues include Taylor (1994), Ghysels et al. (1996) and Shephard (1996).

[21]Essentially: stochastic calculus and elegant dynamic programming techniques and measure theory.

[22]See, however, Campbell et al. (1997) (chapter 11) for a survey of some interesting discrete time interpretations of continuous time models of the term-structure of interest rates.

[23]Following Lo (1988), ML estimation might also be feasible if the transition density

Accordingly, the proposed methods rely on nonparametric density estimation (e.g., Aït-Sahalia (1996*a*,*b*)) and/or closed-form approximations of the true (unknown) likelihood function of the discretely sampled diffusion (Aït-Sahalia (1998)), on generalized method of moments (e.g., Hansen and Scheinkman (1995), Conley et al. (1997)), or on the indirect inference principle.

Methods based on the indirect inference principle are particularly well suited to problems where the state is not fully observed, as it happens in the case of models with stochastic volatility. The quintessence of the methods relies on the simulation of the theoretical model. Its philosophy consists in comparing data simulated from the theoretical model with real data. If the model is a good description of reality (insofar as we are willing to accept the imperfections of *any* model!), then there should exist values of its parameters that make simulated data from that model 'resembling' to real data. On the statistical point of view, it is precisely the way how we think about comparing the two data sets that generates the so-called *auxiliary* criteria. In a classic contribution devoted to applied macroeconomics, for instance, Kydland and Prescott (1982) generated simulated moments from artificial economies corresponding to their models, from which they constructed reasonable 'confidence bands' that contained the sample-based moments corresponding to the US economy. The authors concluded that their model was a successful description of reality.

In a sense, the Kydland-Prescott procedure can be thought to be one of the latest antecedents of the modern simulation-based econometric techniques; Marcet (1994) has an excellent discussion concerning this point. The Kydland-Prescott techniques, however, did not insist on the formal statistical testing aspect of the story, which is of course a central issue of the modern methodology (see the debate of Kydland and Prescott (1996), Hansen and Heckman (1996) and Sims (1996)).

Back to finance, one of the first empirical study in which simulation-based methods were applied to estimating continuous time models of the short term interest rate was conducted by Broze et al. (1995*a*), who consider estimating a slightly more general version of the Chan et al. (1992) model (1.14): apart from methodology, one of the objectives of this study was to find empirically flexible functional forms of the diffusion of the short term interest rate, as opposed to the simple square root process of Cox et al. (1985*a*). It is instructive to remind that the issue of functional flexibility of the diffusion function of the short term interest rate has been pushed to the extreme by Aït-Sahalia (1996*a*), who estimated such a function nonparametrically. The basic idea can be explained

---

of the observables could be computed easily. When this is not the case, ML becomes computationally demanding. In the continuous time stochastic volatility case, for instance, ML would require to implement a numerical solution to a multi-dimensional partial differential equation at each iteration of the optimization algorithm. The likelihood would then be obtained by integrating out with respect to volatility.

as follows. Consider the following data generating process,

$$dr(t) = \mu(r(t); \theta)dt + \sigma(r(t))dW(t)$$

where, in the preceding notation, only the drift $\mu(r; \theta)$ has been parametrized with θ: the function σ has to be estimated non-parametrically. Now it is well known that if r has a stationary distribution, denoted as π, that has support in the extended positive line and boundary condition $\pi(0) = 0$, π is then the solution of the following ordinary differential equation:

$$\mu(r; \theta)\pi(r) = \frac{1}{2}\frac{\partial}{\partial r}(\sigma(r)^2\pi(r)), \ \pi(0) = 0.$$

The key observation now is that in lieu of solving for π for a given σ^2, one may also choice to integrate the preceding equation for a given π and obtain:

$$\sigma(r)^2 = \frac{2}{\pi(r)} \int_0^r \mu(x; \theta)\pi(x)dx.$$

After plugging in the preceding relation a non-parametric estimation of π obtained by standard methods (see, for instance, Härdle and Linton (1994)), one can obtain an estimate of σ^2 in a non-parametric way in correspondence of a given choice for μ. As concerns the drift function, Aït-Sahalia estimated a linear function in his original paper, but one can also add nonlinearities such as those considered in Aït-Sahalia (1996b) in a different context; see, also, Conley et al. (1997) or Stanton (1997) for related work. Issues pertaining to the nonlinearity of the drift function of the short term interest rate will be shortly presented in chapter 4.

As is clear, the preceding ideas are particularly interesting to apply to systems in which the state is completely observable: one of the main advantages of such an approach, indeed, is that it does not require any simulation of the system.[24] In contrast, this monograph deals with systems in which the state is partially observed due to the presence of stochastic volatility. This is one explanation for our choice of estimating continuous time stochastic volatility models via indirect inference.

A second explanation has been put forward in the introductory section of this chapter. Despite the great progress that has been made in the last decade in the estimation of the parameters of stochastic differential equations systems, one important aspect of our empirical research agenda is to understand to which extent ARCH models can be used as reliable approximators of continuous time stochastic volatility systems. Specifically, the quality of the filtering properties of ARCH models is now well-understood and, as stated in the introductory

---

[24]Hansen and Scheinkman (1995) and Aït-Sahalia (1998) also provide methods that are simulation-free. Again, such approaches are particularly well-suited to problems in which the state of the model is completely observable.

section, it has been further confirmed in a simulation study in Fornari and Mele (1999a) conducted in correspondence of a diffusion designed for the short-term interest rate dynamics (cf. eq. (1.1)). In contrast, there is no empirical work dealing with the quality of the approximation to the parameters of stochastic differential equations systems that is delivered by the moment conditions under which ARCH models converge to their continuous time counterparts. Now it turns out that one interesting way to address such an issue on a solid statistical-sounded basis just requires the simulation-based techniques that are associated with the indirect inference principle. Let us explain why.

As is clear, the preliminary step of any simulation-based method consists in an appropriate choice of the auxiliary criterion with which comparing real data with simulated data. In the context that is studied here, a natural auxiliary criterion can be based on the parameters' estimates of an ARCH model fitted to the available data.[25] In some cases, the estimation strategy would consist in finding parameters values of the continuous time model generating simulated data that, once sampled at the same frequency of the available data, can be fitted *with exactly the same ARCH model that fitted the real data*: this would be a just-identified problem. When, instead, the discrete time ARCH model has more parameters than the continuous time model, one obtains a classical over-identified problem, and the indirect inference estimator would now minimize an appropriate distance between the two sets of discrete time parameters (i.e., the parameters of the model applied to the observed data, and the parameters of the model applied on the simulated data).

The estimation strategy that we follow in our applied work focusses on the methodologically simple but empirically difficult just-identified case, in which the number of parameters of the discrete time model is equal to the number of parameters of the continuous time model. Naturally, our strategy does not spring out of nowhere and uses statistical techniques that were originally suggested in the seminal paper of Gouriéroux et al. (1993) (p. S108):

> "[Indirect inference] methods seem particularly promising when the criterion is based on approximations of the likelihood function, time discretization, range discretizations, linearizations, etc. In this case the method is simpler [...] and appears as an automatic correction for the asymptotic bias implied by the approximation."

It is clear how to identify the source of "the asymptotic bias implied by the

---

[25]Engle and Lee (1996) is the first paper we know in which ARCH models were exploited as direct and/or indirect devices for approximating stochastic differential equations. While the authors were concerned with stock returns data only, they also suggested (p. 352) to extend the Cox et al. (1985a) model to a setting with stochastic volatility of the kind described in the preceding section. As pointed out before, Andersen and Lund (1997a) is one of the first empirical studies that accomplished such a task.

approximation" in our context: as we reminded in the introductory section, most ARCH models are not closed under temporal aggregation, which suggests that using moment conditions ensuring the convergence towards a continuous time model should introduce an "asymptotic bias implied by the approximation" or, more correctly said, a *disaggregation* bias. Yet, ARCH models still have a natural interpretation in terms of the continuous time models that are supposed to approximate, since they are very close (in terms of the probability distributions generating them) to the continuous time models when the sampling frequency is high. Furthermore, it turns out that we are also endowed with a natural one-to-one interpretation of the sequence of the discrete time parameters of the auxiliary models in terms of the parameters of the continuous time model (see chapter 5 for technical details): as is clear, we exactly are in the position precognized by Gouriéroux et al. (1993), and we are only left with testing and correcting potential disaggregation biases.

The appropriate testing procedure has been designed within the logic of the indirect inference principle. It is based on testing procedures originally suggested by Gouriéroux et al. (1993) (section 4.2) that can be viewed as the natural substitutes of global specification tests in just-identified problems. Chapter 5 presents a technical description of the test, as well as the technical justification of it within our framework; it also succinctly describes the empirical results of Fornari and Mele (1999a), where it is shown that the disaggregation bias of fitting an ARCH model to weekly US interest rate data is not significant on the basis of that test. This is a particularly interesting empirical result. The simple reason is that Drost and Nijman (1993) constructively showed that ARCH models aggregate only when one weakens the concept of an ARCH model, which led the authors to introduce the so-called *weak-ARCH* process; more importantly, Drost and Werker (1996) generalized the Drost-Nijman setting and introduce the so-called GARCH diffusion which is, heuristically, the continuous time stochastic volatility process whose implied discrete differences form a weak-ARCH process. More precisely, a continuous time process $\{y(t)\}_{t \geq 0}$ is a GARCH diffusion if its implied differences process $\{(_h y_{h(k+1)} - {}_h y_{hk})\}_{k=1}^{\infty}$, $kk \leq t < h(k+1)$, is weak-GARCH for any $h > 0$, i.e., if there exist a sequence of parameters (w_h, α_h, β_h) and a covariance-stationary process,

$$_h \sigma_{hk}^2 = w_h + \alpha_h \cdot {}_h y_{h(k-1)}^2 + \beta_h \cdot {}_h \sigma_{h(k-1)}^2, \tag{1.17}$$

that is the best linear predictor of $(_h y_{hk} - {}_h y_{h(k-1)})^2$ in terms of 1, $_h \sigma_0^2$ and lagged values of $(_h y_{hk} - {}_h y_{h(k-1)})$ and $(_h y_{hk} - {}_h y_{h(k-1)})^2$. Take, for instance, the following diffusion,

$$\begin{aligned} dy(t) &= \sigma(t)dW^{(1)}(t) \\ d\sigma(t)^2 &= \theta(\omega - \sigma(t)^2)dt + \sqrt{2\lambda\theta}\sigma(t)^2 dW^{(2)}(t) \end{aligned} \tag{1.18}$$

where θ, ω, λ are parameters that satisfy $\theta > 0, \omega > 0$ and $\lambda \in (0, 1)$. Drost and Werker (1996) (prop. 3.1 p. 37) then show that there is a continuous mapping with an inverse from the parameters of the continuous time model (1.18) on to the parameters of the discrete time model (1.17).

We believe that the most natural interpretation of our empirical findings is that even though the ARCH models we use do not aggregate, they still remain, for a given frequency, an excellent approximation to the continuous time models towards which they converge in distribution, at least insofar as they are a natural proxy to the weak-ARCH models. Naturally, these are issues that deserve a deep theoretical investigation that we leave for further research.

A second way to implement the indirect inference principle has a rationale that is different from the one outlined above. Its main feature is to select, as an auxiliary device, an highly parametrized discrete time model that is used with the main purpose of calibration. Such an auxiliary model then generates a score (hence referred to as 'score generator'), and the objective becomes to search for the values of the parameters of interest that make such a score as close as possible to zero by using a long simulation of the theoretical model. Such a method has been introduced by Gallant and Tauchen (1996), and is referred to as efficient method of moments (EMM): heuristically said, the source of asymptotic efficiency comes here from the fact that if the true likelihood function is embedded in the density associated with the auxiliary model, then the EMM estimator achieves the same efficiency of the true ML estimator.[26] In practice, an embedding density can be built-up by providing additional parameters to the discrete time model with a semi-nonparametric (SNP) expansion of the distribution of the residuals by means of Hermite polynomials. In fact, as subsequently shown by Gallant and Long (1997), if the score generator is such an SNP, the efficiency of the EMM estimator can be made as close to the ML one as desired by taking the number of the auxiliary parameters large enough. One of the earliest applications of the EMM techniques to models of the stock prices with continuous time SV is in Gallant and Tauchen (1997), and the first application of EMM theory to continuous time SV models of the short term interest rate is in Andersen and Lund (1997a, b). Gallant and Tauchen (1997) also consider the application of EMM to interest rates models that have not stochastic volatility, while Gallant et al. (1997) apply the EMM technique to the discrete time SV models that have been succinctly presented in section 1.2.1. In all these applications, the score generator had a nonparametric density which also accommodated for an ARCH-type scale function.

---

[26]In this book, we are adopting the convention to include the EMM theory of Gallant and Tauchen (1996) as a part of the indirect inference principle.

1.5   Plan

Before giving the plan, it is useful to clarify what the following four chapters are and what are not: the rest of the monograph is intended as a succinct account of our past as well as ongoing research program in which we try to isolate our own contribution. Hence, the following chapters do *not* include extensive surveys on the state-of-the-art of the topics we treat. We only constrain ourselves to refer the reader to already published surveys or, when these are not available, provide a list of the papers that are related to our work, without however delving into the details.

Chapter 2 is devoted to a systematic presentation of our approximation results obtained in correspondence of some of the ARCH models presented in section 1.2. In addition to provide results that are useful when formulating and empirically implementing continuous time models with stochastic volatility, our objective also lies in finding results that can be useful up to a first order approximation treatment of the steady-state probabilistic properties of such models in discrete time.

Chapter 3 analyzes a few problems arising from the incomplete markets structure that is generated by the presence of continuous time stochastic volatility; our primary focus is on European-type options; we make use of a model with diffusion state variables. Although markets are incomplete insofar as one restricts attention to the primitive assets of the economy, the option itself can be taken to complete the markets; as a consequence of this, the risk premia demanded by agents to be compensated for the stochastic fluctuations of the state variables of the economy can be found via the preferences of a representative agent. As we mentioned in section 1.3.1, we then illustrate how we are currently attacking the problem: instead of imposing a functional form generated by a specific preference structure of a representative agent, as we do for the term structure model in chapter 4, we take the volatility risk-premium as a nonlinear function of the state variables of the model (i.e., a 'volatility risk-premium surface'), that can subsequently be estimated using cross-sectional information derived from option prices. One of the final objectives of the chapter is to provide a short description of hedging strategies that can be implemented within an economy with continuous time stochastic volatility. By delving into the simplest versions of the literature on risk-minimizing strategies—as opposed to the standard risk-neutralizing strategies *à la* Black-Scholes—we provide details concerning the construction of strategies for partial hedging in incomplete markets in the general version of the model, by focussing then on its stochastic volatility restrictions.

Chapter 4 presents a succinct overview of the theory of the term structure of interest rates within Markovian economies, and focusses essentially on the ramifications generated by 'injecting' stochastic volatility features into them. It then imposes restrictions to the model with diffusion state variables of chapter 3, and develops a class of equilibrium models in which the instantaneous interest rate exhibits stochastic volatility that is imperfectly correlated with the instantaneous interest rate level itself. As concerns the statistical inference, this chapter also provides a very first illustration of simulation-based econometric techniques that can be applied to estimate continuous time models of the short term interest rates. Furthermore, it explains the role played by the linearity of the diffusion functions of the state variables of the economy to assist in getting tractable models: our discussion will thus concern a very special case of the well-known literature on affine models of the term structure.

Chapter 5 presents in detail the econometric techniques that are required to make estimation and testing procedures applied to the parameters of our theoretical model of the term structure of interest rates. These techniques are based on a combined use of the approximation results of chapter 2 and the indirect inference principle. This chapter also presents methodology to obtain the solution of our theoretical model of the term structure of interest rates with stochastic volatility. We follow two approaches. In the first one, we use the Crank-Nicholson scheme to numerically integrate two-dimensional partial differential equations that typically accommodate for stochastic volatility; a Matlab code to implement the solution of our model is available upon request (our code takes approximately 1 minute to obtain the solution with Matlab 4.2 on a Pentium II 366 MHz with 64 Mbytes of memory). While the code has been specifically designed for solving our term structure model, only minor changes are required for that code to be used to solve related problems (e.g., models with different drift or diffusion functions and/or computation of transition measures in continuous time). Finally, we show how to implement a second, less traditional approach that is based on a method of iterated approximations.

CONTINUOUS TIME BEHAVIOR OF NON LINEAR ARCH MODELS

2.1 Introduction

This chapter presents convergence results for the A-PARCH model (1.6) that was originally proposed by Ding et al. (1993). We remind that in addition to be a particular convenient tool to model volatility asymmetries, such a model imposes a sort of Box-Cox power transformation to the conditional standard deviation. According to this model, the 'volatility concept' is thus not imposed a priori by the modeler, but it has to be estimated from data. By assuming that such a transformation is the same at every sampling frequency, we derive continuous time results for model (1.6). Such results are useful for three main reasons: (1) they help formulating continuous time models that are flexible with respect to the choice of the volatility concept (see chapter 5); (2) they provide a simple identification device through which estimating the correlation process between a continuous time asset price process and its instantaneous volatility; (3) they help understanding the role played by the volatility concept in determining the long run behavior of the error process of the model.

The chapter is organized in the following manner. The approximation results for model (1.6) are in the following section; section 2.3 contains comments concerning the moment conditions that are needed to guarantee the convergence of the discrete time model; section 2.4 provides a primer on the connection between the approximation results and option pricing; section 2.5 is devoted to the study of the stationary distribution of the A-PARCH models innovations; section 2.6 provides continuous time results for the VS-ARCH model (1.9), but the analysis there is not as deep as the analysis conducted for model (1.6). The appendices contain technical material.

2.2 Approximation results for a general class of non linear ARCH models

If h denotes the sampling interval, we partition time in (1.6) in a way that allows for the corresponding solution $\{_hY_{hk}\}_{k=1}^{\infty} \equiv \{_hS_{h(k-1)}, \, _h\sigma_{hk}^{\delta}\}_{k=1}^{\infty}$ to be a Markov process that converges weakly to an Itô process $\{Y(t)\}_{t\geq 0} = \{S(t), \sigma(t)^\delta\}_{t\geq 0}$ as $h \downarrow 0$:[1]

$$\log {}_hS_{hk} - \log {}_hS_{h(k-1)} = (\mu - \tfrac{{}_h\sigma_{hk}^2}{2})h + {}_h\varepsilon_{hk}$$

$${}_h\varepsilon_{hk} = {}_h\sigma_{hk} \cdot {}_hu_{hk}$$

$${}_h\sigma_{h(k+1)}^\delta - {}_h\sigma_{hk}^\delta = \omega_h + (\alpha_h |{}_hu_{hk}|^\delta (1 - \gamma_h s_k)^\delta h^{-\frac{\delta}{2}} + \beta_h - 1){}_h\sigma_{hk}^\delta$$

$$(2.1)$$

where S denotes an asset price (the price of a share, say), μ is a constant, and

$$_h\overline{u}_{hk} \approx \text{g.e.d.}_{(\upsilon)} = \frac{\upsilon \exp(-\tfrac{1}{2}\nabla_\upsilon^{-\upsilon} |{}_h\overline{u}_{hk}|^\upsilon)}{2^{1+\upsilon^{-1}}\nabla_\upsilon\Gamma(\upsilon^{-1})}, \quad \nabla_\upsilon \equiv \left(\frac{\Gamma(\upsilon^{-1})}{2^{2/\upsilon}\Gamma(3\upsilon^{-1})}\right)^{1/2}, \quad \upsilon \in \mathbb{R}_{++},$$

$_h\overline{u}_{hk} \equiv \frac{{}_hu_{hk}}{h^{1/2}}$, $s_k \equiv \text{sign}({}_hu_{hk})$, and $\Gamma(.)$ is the Gamma function. We require that:

$$(\{\omega_h\}, \{\alpha_h\}, \{\beta_h\}) \in \mathbb{R}_+^3, \quad \gamma_h \in (-1, +1)\ \forall h \in \mathbb{R}_+. \tag{2.2}$$

2.1 REMARK. Eqs. (2.1) do not encompass the case in which δ depends on h. Since different δ would correspond to different 'volatility concepts' (e.g., standard deviation dynamics, variance dynamics, etc.), we are therefore assuming that the volatility concept is invariant to time-scale changes.

The formal, probabilistic setup we shall employ to show the convergence of (2.1) to a diffusion is basically the same as that employed by Nelson (1990) to obtain the approximation results for the GARCH(1,1) model and the exponential ARCH. We only provide a short description of such a framework, which summarizes the setup of Stroock and Varadhan (1979). For each $h > 0$, let $(\Omega^{(h)}, \mathcal{F}^{(h)}, \mathcal{P}^{(h)})$ be a probability space, and $\mathcal{F}_{hk}$ a filtration of sub-σ-fields of $\mathcal{F}^{(h)}$ generated by $_hS_0, {}_hS_h, {}_hS_{2h}, ..., {}_hS_{h(k-1)}$ and $_h\sigma_0^\delta, {}_h\sigma_h^\delta, {}_h\sigma_{2h}^\delta, ..., {}_h\sigma_{hk}^\delta$. First, we want that the vector process $\{_hY_{hk}\}_{k=1,2,...}$ be constant between two adjacent intervals, that is: $_hY_t = {}_hY_{hk}$, $hk \leq t < h(k+1)$, for any integer k. Second, we define $\Pi^{(h)}(G\ /\ Y)$, $G \in \mathcal{B}(\mathbb{R}^2)$ (where $\mathcal{B}(\mathbb{R}^2)$ are the Borel sets on $\mathbb{R}^2$) as the transition probability in the following manner: $\Pi^{(h)}(.\ /\ Y)$ is a probability measure on $(\mathbb{R}^2, \mathcal{B}(\mathbb{R}^2))$; $\Pi^{(h)}(B\ /\ .)$ is Borel-measurable; $\forall y \in G, x \in \mathbb{R}^2, \mathcal{P}^{(h)}(_hY_{h(k+1)} \in G\ /\ {}_hY_{hk}) = \Pi^{(h)}(y\ /\ x)$. Third, we denote $\mathcal{P}^{(h)}(_hY_1 \in G) = \pi^{(h)}(G)$ as the distribution of the starting point. Finally, the distribution of the process is meant to be constituted by both the initial distribution and the transition probabilities.

---

[1] Let $\{_hX_{hk}\}_{k=0}^\infty$ be a discrete time Markov process and $\{X_t\}_{t\geq 0}$ an Itô process. When the probability laws generating the entire sample paths of $\{_hX_{hk}\}_{k=0}^\infty$ converge to the probability law generating $\{X_t\}_{t\geq 0}$, we say that $\{_hX_{hk}\}_{k=0}^\infty$ converges weakly to $\{X_t\}_{t\geq 0}$ and write this as $\{_hX_{hk}\}_{k=0}^\infty \Rightarrow \{X_t\}_{t\geq 0}$. In this chapter, the standard symbol $\xrightarrow{d}$ will be used to mean convergence in distribution of random variables.

Now we aim at creating a continuous time process by considering progressively smaller values of h. We shall make use of the following:

2.2 ASSUMPTION. *Assumptions 2 to 5 of Nelson (1990).*[2]

Consider the solution $\{S(t), \sigma(t)^\delta\}_{t \geq 0}$ of the stochastic differential system:

$$
\begin{aligned}
\mathrm{d} \log S(t) &= (\mu - \frac{\sigma(t)^2}{2})\mathrm{d}t + \sigma(t)\mathrm{d}W^{(1)}(t) \\
\mathrm{d}\sigma(t)^\delta &= (\overline{\omega} - \varphi\sigma(t)^\delta)\mathrm{d}t + \psi\sigma(t)^\delta \mathrm{d}(\rho W^{(1)}(t) + (1 - \rho^2)^{1/2}W^{(2)}(t))
\end{aligned}
$$
$$(2.3)$$

where $\{W^{(i)}(t)\}_{t \geq 0}$, $i = 1, 2$ are two independent $\mathcal{F}(t)$-standard Brownian motions.

We have:

2.3 THEOREM. *Let* $m_{\delta,v} = \dfrac{2^{\frac{2\delta}{v}-1}\nabla_v^{2\delta}\Gamma(\frac{2\delta+1}{v})}{\Gamma(v^{-1})}$, $n_{\delta,v} = \dfrac{2^{\frac{\delta}{v}-1}\nabla_v^\delta\Gamma(\frac{\delta+1}{v})}{\Gamma(v^{-1})}$,

$$
\rho = \frac{2^{\frac{\delta-v+1}{v}}\nabla_v^{\delta+1}\Gamma(\frac{\delta+2}{v})((1 - \gamma)^\delta - (1 + \gamma)^\delta)}{\Gamma(v^{-1})((m_{\delta,v} - n_{\delta,v}^2)((1 - \gamma)^{2\delta} + (1 + \gamma)^{2\delta}) - 2n_{\delta,v}^2(1 - \gamma)^\delta(1 + \gamma)^\delta)^{1/2}},
$$
$$(2.4)$$

and, for each h,

$$
Z_h = (m_{\delta,v} - n_{\delta,v}^2)((1 - \gamma_h)^{2\delta} + (1 + \gamma_h)^{2\delta}) - 2n_{\delta,v}^2(1 - \gamma_h)^\delta(1 + \gamma_h)^\delta.
$$

Suppose that the following conditions hold:

$$
0 < \overline{\omega} = \lim_{h \downarrow 0} h^{-1}\omega_h < \infty,
$$
$$(2.5)$$

$$
-\varphi = \lim_{h \downarrow 0} h^{-1}(n_{\delta,v}((1 - \gamma_h)^\delta + (1 + \gamma_h)^\delta)\alpha_h + \beta_h - 1) < \infty,
$$
$$(2.6)$$

$$
\psi^2 = \lim_{h \downarrow 0} h^{-1} \cdot Z_h \cdot \alpha_h^2 < \infty.
$$
$$(2.7)$$

Consider, finally, the condition:

$$
\gamma_h = \gamma, \ \forall h.
$$
$$(2.8)$$

Then,

$$
\{_h S_{h(k-1),h}\, \sigma_{hk}^\delta\}_{k=0,1,\ldots} \Rightarrow \{S(t), \sigma(t)^\delta\}_{t \geq 0} \ as \ h \downarrow 0.
$$

---

[2]The standard assumptions of Stroock and Varadhan (1979), which are essentially assumptions 1 through 4 of Nelson (1990), would suffice to guarantee that the sequence of a well behaved discrete time Markov process converges weakly to an Itô process. However, assumption 2.2 enables one to handle some technical situations in an easier way (see thm. 2.2 in Nelson (1990)).

PROOF. In appendix A. ∥

In his original paper, Nelson (1990) showed how to construct parameter sequences which satisfy moment conditions such as (2.5)-(2.7). This kind of analysis could easily be conducted here if $\gamma_h = 0, \forall h$, as in (2.8). In this case, in fact, an example of $(\{\omega_h\}, \{\alpha_h\}, \{\beta_h\})$ sequences matching (2.5)-(2.7) could be $\omega_h = \bar{\omega}h$, $\alpha_h = \alpha(h/2)^{1/2}$ and $\beta_h = 1 - \alpha n_{\delta,v}(2h)^{1/2} - \varphi h$. The proposed example shows that $(\{\omega_h\}, \{\alpha_h\}, \{\beta_h\}) \to (0, 0, 1)$ as $h \downarrow 0$. When $\gamma_h \neq 0$ the problem is more complicated. In fact, the search for converging parameters sequences results in a sort of arbitrage between the rate of convergence of α_h and γ_h towards their continuous time counterparts. It is easily checked, however, that the following candidate:

$$\omega_h = \bar{\omega}h, \qquad \alpha_h = \frac{\alpha}{2^{1/2}}h^p,$$
$$\beta_h = -\varphi h + 1 - n_{\delta,v}((1 - \gamma_h)^\delta + (1 + \gamma_h)^\delta)\alpha_h, \qquad (2.9)$$
$$1 - \gamma_h = \bar{\gamma}h^\ell, \quad \ell, p \geq 0 \text{ and bounded, and } 0 \leq \bar{\gamma} < 2,$$

actually converges when:

$$(\ell, p) = (0, \frac{1}{2}). \qquad (2.10)$$

In this case,

$$\psi^2 = \frac{1}{2}((m_{\delta,v} - n_{\delta,v}^2)(\bar{\gamma}^{2\delta} + \bar{\bar{\gamma}}^{2\delta}) - 2n_{\delta,v}^2\bar{\gamma}^\delta\bar{\bar{\gamma}}^\delta)\alpha^2, \qquad (2.11)$$

where $\bar{\bar{\gamma}} = 2 - \bar{\gamma}$.

Naturally, conditions (2.9)-(2.11) are not necessary to obtain the convergence. Specifically, condition (2.10) is equivalent to condition (2.8) and as is clear from the proof in appendix A, condition (2.8) is not necessary to ensure the convergence. Conditions (2.9)-(2.11) are just the simplest identifying assumptions that ensure the convergence.

As we mentioned in the previous chapter, Ding et al. (1993) showed that the discrete time model (1.6) encompasses at least seven classes of ARCH models; eq. (2.3) is therefore the diffusion limit of these models.[3] Notice that all such encompassed models exhibit a similar continuous time behavior: they are all mean reverting and possess second order moments (the volatility of volatility) proportional to the square of the volatility level. By Itô's lemma, however, the diffusion models which are not exploiting the same volatility concept (e.g., the GARCH and the TS) are *not* the same.

As argued in chapter 5 and in Fornari and Mele (1999b), theorem 2.3 could also help one to use ARCH models to get a preliminary estimate of the correlation process between an asset price process and its instantaneous volatility, and

---

[3]Nelson and Foster (1994) wrote down (eq. 6.8, p. 30) the structural form of (2.3) (with $\rho \equiv 0$) without providing the moment conditions (2.5)-(2.7).

avoids procedures such as those in Lamoureux and Lastrapes (1993), where the estimate of the correlation was simply the regression coefficient of continuous compounded daily returns on the series of volatility obtained after the estimation of a symmetric GARCH(1,1) model. Fornari and Mele (1999*b*) apply formula (2.4) to estimate the correlation of a continuous time model applied to future data, and find that the correction made by simulation-based methods is not very important.

As is clear from formula (2.4), a negative correlation may emerge in correspondence with the 'Black-Nelson effect'[4]—claiming that negative shocks introduce more volatility than positive ones of the same size (see section 1.2.2 in the previous chapter). One limitation of discrete time ARCH incorporating the Black-Nelson effect is that it is *future* volatility which is negatively related to current shocks. It has been shown here that considering progressively finer sample intervals shrinks the 'Black-Nelson lead' to zero. This kind of property was shown to hold, for the first time, by Nelson (1990), in correspondence with exponential ARCH of Nelson (1991)[5] (see section 1.2.1 in the previous chapter).

Figures 2.1 through 2.3 display the behavior of ρ considered as a function of γ, δ and υ. It has the opposite sign of γ, is nil when γ is nil, and its modulus is strictly less than one in correspondence with reasonable values of $(\gamma, \delta, \upsilon)$. This last property has important consequences: in continuous time and with Brownian information, markets *can* be complete when the correlation process between the primitive asset and its volatility is identically one; in that case, indeed, volatility behaves essentially as its underlying (traded) asset price process, and delta-hedging strategies can be fully implemented (see next chapter): that case is ruled out when one considers model (2.1) as data generating process for small values of h.

Furthermore, please notice that convergence results similar to theorem 2.3 can be obtained in correspondence with diffusion processes designed to represent the instantaneous interest rate dynamics: see, for instance, Fornari and Mele (1999*a*). Empirical evidence in Fornari and Mele (1995) combined with theorem 2.3 then suggest that in this case *instantaneous interest rate* changes should be *positively* correlated with instantaneous volatility changes. This is consistent with further empirical findings of Fornari and Mele (1999*b*), who find a negative correlation between future discount bond *prices* and their instantaneous volatility.

---

[4]Black (1976) and Nelson (1991).
[5]See also Duan (1997) for related work.

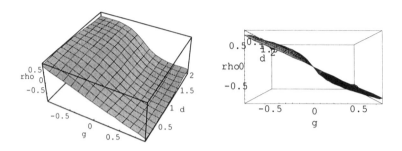

FIGURE 2.1. ρ as a function of γ and δ ($v = 2$)

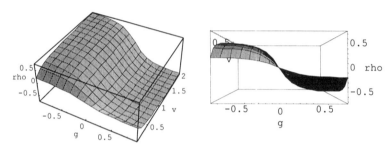

FIGURE 2.2. ρ as a function of γ and v ($\delta = 2$)

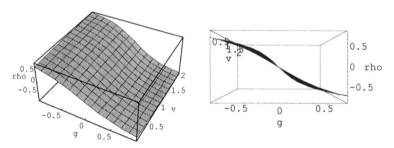

FIGURE 2.3. ρ as a function of γ and v ($\delta = 1$)

2.3   Interpretation of the moment conditions

In the previous section, (2.1) has been assumed to be the data generating process. The problem was to understand under which conditions (2.1) converges to a diffusion limit. We found that if eqs. (2.5)-(2.7) are satisfied, (2.1) converges to (2.3). In other terms, eqs. (2.5)-(2.7) describe the limiting behavior of the parameters in (2.1). It is important to realize that eqs. (2.5)-(2.7) have to hold simultaneously and this explains why, in the example (2.9), $p = \frac{1}{2}$, whereas

$\omega_h = h \cdot \overline{\omega}$. This determines an implicit relationship between the discrete time parameters in (2.1) as $h \downarrow 0$. Changing the distribution of error terms (by changing v), for example, does not imply a 'different value' of φ and ψ in the limiting diffusion. Here, φ and ψ are essentially fixed so that changing the distribution only determines a change of the sequences entering into the moment conditions (2.5)-(2.7).

In a recent paper, Corradi (1997) questions the realism of the moment conditions that Nelson (1990) originally imposed to show the weak convergence of the GARCH(1,1) towards a continuous time stochastic volatility model. Her reasoning can be generalized here as follows. In the third equation of (2.1), the term generating the diffusion terms of volatility is proportional to $(h^{-\frac{\delta}{2}}\alpha_h) \cdot |_h u_{hk}|^\delta$, which is of course $O_p(\sqrt{h})$ under the third moment condition in (2.7). In other terms, a condition for a diffusion to be obtained is to 'scale' the variance of $|_h u_{hk}|^\delta$ by a diverging sequence; another parametrization would be just $\alpha_h \approx O_p(h^q), q \in \mathbb{R}$. In this case, we would have three possibilities: (1) $q = \frac{1-\delta}{2}$, which is another way to express the condition under which (2.1) has a well-defined diffusion limit; (2) $q < \frac{1-\delta}{2}$, which implies that model (2.1) does not converge to any diffusion limit; and (3) $q > \frac{1-\delta}{2}$, which implies a 'degenerate' diffusion limit, i.e. with no diffusion terms. While recognizing that weak convergence results such as those contained in theorem 2.3 are obviously related to parametrization issues, our empirical studies (Fornari and Mele (1999a, b)) suggest that not only does the parametrization in (2.1) implies a reasonably good picture of the volatility dynamics, consistently with the theoretical results of Nelson and Foster (1994), but it is also not rejected by a test (designed within simulation-based techniques) that checks a posteriori the accuracy of the approximation.

2.4 Effectiveness of ARCH as diffusion approximations of theoretical models

In which way the ARCH models encompassed by (2.1) can effectively be used as diffusion approximations of continuous time models ? In order to answer this question and make this chapter as self-contained as possible, we now briefly review some foundational issues arising in the literature on stochastic volatility. The reader interested in more technical details is referred to the next chapters.

Let $[0, T]$ be a given time interval and $(\Omega, \mathcal{F}, P)$ a filtered probability space; here $\{\mathcal{F}(t)\}_{t \in [0,T]}$ is the P-augmentation of the filtration generated by a $(1 + d)$-dimensional Brownian motion $W(t) = (W^{(1)}(t), W^\sigma(t))$, where W^σ is d-dimensional. As evoked in chapter 1, the purpose of theoretical models with stochastic volatility is to provide a framework able to generalize the simple Black-Scholes scheme in which the price of an asset is a geometric Brownian motion. This can be accomplished by assuming a price process with stochastic volatility:

$$\begin{aligned}
\text{dlog } S(t) &= (\mu - \tfrac{\sigma(t)^2}{2})\mathrm{d}t + \sigma(y(t))\mathrm{d}W^{(1)}(t) \\
\mathrm{d}y(t) &= \varphi(y(t))\mathrm{d}t + \psi(y(t))\mathrm{d}W^{\sigma}(t)
\end{aligned} \tag{2.12}$$

Here y has to be interpreted as a partially observed multidimensional process, and φ, ψ are such that there exists a unique strong Markov solution to (2.12). To keep things relatively simple, we may assume that y and W^{σ} are scalars and that σ is the identity map.

Note that the perspective has changed here. The data generating process is now a diffusion and our concern is to understand which discrete time ARCH model should be chosen as a diffusion approximation to the second equation of (2.12).

Let r be the constant free-risk interest rate (its constancy is assumed here for sake of simplicity); let C be the price of a contingent claim, a European call option, for example. It is well known (e.g., Harrison and Kreps (1979)) that the existence of a probability measure equivalent to P, say Q, under which both $\{e^{-rt}S(t)\}_{t\in[0,T]}$ and $\{e^{-rt}H(t)\}_{t\in[0,T]}$ are Q-martingales implies the absence of arbitrage opportunities; the probability measure Q is often referred to as risk neutral. This implies that H satisfies:

$$\mathcal{D}^*[H] - rC = 0 \text{ for } t \in [0,T), \text{ with: } C(T) = (S(T) - K)^+, \tag{2.13}$$

where K is the strike of the option, T its expiration date, and $\mathcal{D}^*[.]$ is the Dynkin operator applied to (2.12) under Q. It can be shown that the solution of (2.13) is obtained via the Feynman-Kac theorem (e.g., Karatzas and Shreve (1991)):

$$H(t) = e^{-r(T-t)}E_t^Q(S(T) - K)^+.$$

An important point, here, is that it is practically impossible to obtain an *analytical* solution. A common practice, instead, is to resort to Monte Carlo methods (e.g., Engle and Mustafa (1992)), which are accomplished by simulating the path of (2.12) with μ being fixed at r.[6] This enables one to calculate a fair price of the call by means of the following formula:

$$\widehat{H}(t) = e^{-r(T-t)}\frac{1}{n}\sum_{i=1}^n(S^i(T) - K)^+, \tag{2.14}$$

where $S^i(T)$ is the price at time T simulated at the ith Monte Carlo round. Lamoureux and Lastrapes (1993), for instance, accomplished this through 1)

---

[6]This is so since the Q-martingale property of $\{e^{-rt}S(t)\}_{t\in[0,T]}$, the Itô's lemma and the Girsanov theorem (e.g. Karatzas and Shreve (1991) (thm. 5.1 p. 191)) imply that $\{S(t)\}_{t\in[0,T]}$ solves: $\text{dlog } S(t) = (r - \tfrac{\sigma(t)^2}{2})\mathrm{d}t + \sigma(t)\mathrm{d}\widetilde{W}^{(1)}(t)$ under Q, where $\widetilde{W}^{(1)}$ is a Q-Brownian motion. We have to stress that the set of all risk neutral probability measures is not a singleton here: in the following chapter, this important problem is treated in greater detail.

the preliminary estimation of a conditionally normal GARCH(1,1) model and 2) the conversion of the estimated parameters into their continuous time counterparts throughout the first approximation results of Nelson (1990).

Inspection of (2.12)-(2.14) reveals that the important issue, here, is the choice of the functional forms $\varphi(.,.)$ and $\psi(.,.)$. Apart from some isolated papers such as that of Lamoureux and Lastrapes (1993), however, this topic has never been motivated by data analysis; rather, as Taylor (1994) (p. 187) puts it: "it has often been suggested by intuitive reasoning and analytical convenience".

Consider then the following competing models in table 2.1:

TABLE 2.1

model A:	$d\sigma(t) = (\overline{\omega} - \varphi\sigma(t))dt + \psi\sigma(t)dW^\sigma(t)$
model B:	$d\sigma(t)^2 = (\overline{\omega} - \varphi\sigma(t)^2)dt + \psi\sigma(t)^2 dW^\sigma(t)$
model C:	$d\sigma(t)^2 = (\overline{\omega} - \varphi\sigma(t)^2)dt + \psi\sigma(t)dW^\sigma(t)$

The first formulation specifies standard deviation dynamics and can be found, for example, in the option pricing application made by Hofmann et al. (1992) and the term structure work of Fornari and Mele (1999a): it can be considered as the diffusion limit of the TS model. The remaining models specify variance dynamics: the functional form of model B is the same as the diffusion limit of the GARCH(1,1), and was exploited by Fornari and Mele (1994, 1995) in a yield curve application; model C represents a square root process and was proposed by Heston (1993b) as the volatility equation in a European option pricing model.

Now consider the last model. Notice that none of the models listed in table 1.1 admits a continuous time counterpart in a form of a square root process. As a consequence, none of the models encompassed by (1.6) can really permit to approximate model C. This means that in practice one can not use (at least traditional) ARCH models as diffusion approximations of model C. This claim has been made rigorous in the optimal filtering result of Nelson and Foster (1994) (p. 22).[7] Clearly, we are not asserting that ARCH models are the ones which best approximate a given data generating process. Continuous time ARCH, in fact, are as arbitrary as model C. We point out, instead, that if one really wishes to use an ARCH model as a diffusion approximation of a theoretical model, then such a theoretical model should be designed to have the same structural form as those encompassed by (2.3).

The volatility concept is also important. Suppose that the data generating mechanism is eq. (2.3) when in fact the modeler is assuming model A or model B, say, in table 2.1. Then, by applying Itô's lemma to (2.3), standard deviation

---

[7]Notice that Longstaff and Schwartz (1992) have already made use of ARCH models to estimate the volatility generated by square root processes.

and the variance equations are:

$$d\sigma(t) = (\tfrac{\bar{\omega}}{\delta}\sigma(t)^{1-\delta} - \tfrac{2\varphi+(1-\delta^{-1})\psi^2}{2\delta}\sigma(t))dt + \tfrac{\psi}{\delta}\sigma(t)dW^\sigma(t),$$
$$d\sigma(t)^2 = (\tfrac{2\bar{\omega}}{\delta}\sigma(t)^{2-\delta} - \tfrac{2\varphi+(1-2\delta^{-1})\psi^2}{\delta}\sigma(t)^2)dt + \tfrac{2\psi}{\delta}\sigma(t)^2 dW^\sigma(t),$$

$$(2.15)$$

which are quite different from model A and model B. In fact, eqs. (2.15) collapse to model A (model B) only if $\delta = 1$ (resp. $\delta = 2$).

Omitting to take into account these facts may result in a bias when one calculates $\widehat{H}$ through (2.14). Suppose, for instance, that the modeler wishes to make use of the variance concept when in fact the data generating process is system (2.3). Inspection of (2.12)-(2.13) reveals that $\widehat{H}$ depends on the current expectation of $\log S(T)$ under Q. Let

$$E_t^Q(\log S(T) \,/\, \delta \neq 2) \text{ (resp. } E_t^Q(\log S(T) \,/\, \delta = 2))$$

denote such current expectations when these are conditioned on the second equation of (2.12), and when this corresponds to eq.(2.3) with $\delta \neq 2$ (resp. $\delta = 2$). Next, apply thm. 8.4.2 p. 136 ff. in Arnold (1992) to get the solution of (2.3):

$$\sigma(t)^\delta = \sigma(0)^\delta e^{-(\varphi+\psi^2/2)t+\psi W^\sigma(t)} + \bar{\omega}\int_0^t e^{-(\varphi+\psi^2/2)(t-s)+\psi(W^\sigma(t)-W^\sigma(s))}ds.$$

Finally, by integrating (2.12) and exploiting the above equation to get the solution of $\{\sigma(t)^2\}_{t\geq 0}$ (for $\delta \neq 2$), it is easily shown that in general one has:

$$E_t^Q(\log S(T) \,/\, \delta \neq 2) \neq E_t^Q(\log S(T) \,/\, \delta = 2)$$

(such expectations exist under the assumptions and results presented up to here). We deduce that H is a function of δ and write this as $H(\delta)$. Then, if the modeler wishes to use a variance concept when the data generating process has a volatility equation with $\delta \neq 2$, her calculation $\widehat{H}(2)$ will generally differ from $\widehat{H}(\delta)$.

2.5   Limiting behavior of the error process

This section examines the asymptotic behavior of the error process of model (2.1). Let $P(\sigma^\delta)$ denote the stationary distribution of the volatility process (see the appendix for technical definitions). Appendix B provides the proof of the following, preliminary result:

2.4 LEMMA. *If (2.5)-(2.7) hold, and $\frac{2\varphi}{\psi^2} > -1$, then:*

$$_h\sigma_{hk}^\delta \xrightarrow{d} P(\sigma^\delta) = K_0^{-1}\sigma^{-\delta a}e^{-\frac{b}{\sigma^\delta}} \quad \text{as } h \downarrow 0 \text{ and } hk \to \infty, \qquad (2.16)$$

where: $K_0 = b^{1-a}\Gamma(a-1)$, $a = \frac{2(\varphi+\psi^2)}{\psi^2}$, *and* $b = \frac{2\bar{\omega}}{\psi^2}$.

The function appearing in (2.16) is an inverted Gamma. Note that when $(\delta, \gamma_h) \equiv (2,0), \forall h$, the stationary density function of the conditional precision process $\{\sigma(t)^{-2}\}_{t\geq 0}$ is a Gamma distribution with $a - 1$ degrees of freedom and parameter b, consistently with Nelson (1990); in such a case, Nelson also showed that the stationary distribution of the error terms is approximately a Student's t.

The starting point of this section is an analytically convenient situation that allows us to derive a closed form solution of the stationary distribution of the innovations process. It is based on the assumption that the tail thickness parameter of the g.e.d. is equal to the Box-Cox power transform applied to the local dynamics of the conditional standard deviation:

2.5 ASSUMPTION. $\delta = v$.

While there are no apparent reasons to expect that such an assumption holds in practice, Fornari and Mele (1997a) and Mele (1998) have provided a great deal of evidence for it. Below we provide a succinct description of such results.

2.6 THEOREM. *Let* $\eta \equiv 2a - 3 + 2\delta^{-1}$, $_hR_{hk} \equiv {}_h\bar{u}_{hk} \cdot {}_h\sigma_{hk}(\eta/2b)^{1/\delta}\nabla_\delta^{-1}$, *and, for each* h, *let* $_h\bar{u}_{hk}$ *be* g.e.d.$_{(\delta)}$. *Finally, let* $P_R^\delta(R)$ *be the stationary distribution function of* $_hR_{hk}$. *If* $\eta > 0$, *and the conditions of lemma 2.4 and assumption 2.5 hold, then:*

$$_hR_{hk} \xrightarrow{d} P_R^\delta(R) = \frac{\delta(1+\eta^{-1}|R|^\delta)^{-\frac{\eta+1}{2}}}{2\eta^{1/\delta}B(\frac{1}{\delta}; \frac{\eta+1}{2} - \frac{1}{\delta})} \quad \text{as } h \downarrow 0 \text{ and } hk \to \infty,$$

where $B(.;.)$ *is the Euler Beta function of the second kind.*

PROOF. In the appendix. ‖

2.7 REMARK. $P_R^\delta(R)$ is the Generalized Student's t distribution.

Theorem 2.6 says that innovations processes which are conditionally g.e.d.$_{(\delta)}$ are unconditionally Generalized Student's t distributed when the tail thickness parameter is exactly δ. Such a distribution was adopted by Bollerslev et al. (1994) to build *conditional* likelihood profiles in the modeling of high frequency financial data. It encompasses both the Student's t distribution and the g.e.d.$_{(\delta)}$. Note, in fact, that $P_R^\delta(R)$ is indeed the Student's t when $\delta = 2$ (consistently with Nelson (1990)), and it approaches the g.e.d.$_{(\delta)}$ when η is sufficiently large. This last case can be of interest, since $\eta = 2a - 3 + 2\delta^{-1}$ tends to infinity when $\delta \downarrow 0$. In such a circumstance, small values of δ generate innovations which are approximately unconditionally g.e.d.$_{(\delta)}$ with very fat tails.

Now we generalize:

2.8 THEOREM. *Let* $\delta \neq \upsilon$ *and* $_h\bar{\varepsilon}_{hk} \equiv {}_h\sigma_{hk} \cdot {}_h\bar{u}_{hk}$ *and, for each* h, *let* $_h\bar{u}_{hk}$ *be g.e.d.*$_{(\upsilon)}$. *Finally, let* $P^{\delta,\upsilon}(\bar{\varepsilon})$ *be the stationary distribution function of* $_h\bar{\varepsilon}_{hk}$. *If the conditions of lemma 2.4 hold, then, as* $h \downarrow 0$ *and* $hk \to \infty$:

$$_h\bar{\varepsilon}_{hk} \xrightarrow{d} P(\bar{\varepsilon}) = \frac{\upsilon\delta \int_0^\infty \sigma^{\delta(1-a)-2} \exp-(\frac{1}{2}\nabla_\upsilon^{-\upsilon}|\bar{\varepsilon}|^\upsilon \sigma^{-\upsilon} + b\sigma^{-\delta})d\sigma}{2^{1+\upsilon^{-1}}K_0\nabla_\upsilon\Gamma(\upsilon^{-1})}. \qquad (2.17)$$

PROOF. In the appendix. ‖

The preceding result provides the stationary distribution of the innovations process (1.6) observed at short time intervals when it is conditionally g.e.d.$_{(\upsilon)}$. While we do not provide its exact analytical form, we can solve numerically the integral appearing in (2.17). The main features of the above densities can be summarized as follows: (1) for any υ, low values of δ give rise to innovations processes which follow a stationary distribution with thick tails and high central peaks; (2) υ shapes the unconditional distribution in exactly the same manner as it does with the conditional distribution.

Figure 2.4, taken from Fornari and Mele (1999a), shows the shape of the invariant measure that is implied by thm. 2.8 and the estimates obtained in correspondence of model (5.3) in chapter 5 (see table 5.1, second row). Such estimates were obtained with $(\delta, \upsilon) = (1, 2)$. Accordingly, relation (2.17) reduces here to:

$$P(\bar{\varepsilon}) = \frac{\left(\frac{2\bar{\omega}}{\psi^2}\right)^{\frac{2\varphi+\psi^2}{\psi^2}}}{\sqrt{2\pi} \cdot \Gamma\left(\frac{2\varphi+\psi^2}{\psi^2}\right)} \int_0^\infty x^{-\frac{2\varphi+3\psi^2}{\psi^2}} \exp\left(-\frac{1}{2}\bar{\varepsilon}^2 x^{-2} - \frac{2\bar{\omega}}{\psi^2}x^{-1}\right)\mathrm{d}x, \; \bar{\varepsilon} \equiv \frac{\varepsilon}{\sqrt{h}}.$$

Figure 2.4 compares such a density with a normal density with variance equal to $\left(\frac{\bar{\omega}}{\varphi}\right)^2$ where, $\bar{\omega}, \varphi$ and ψ have been fixed at the values of the estimates of model (5.1) (see chapter 5) obtained with US data. Even with a conditional normal density, model (1.6) should play an excellent role in mimicking the steady state properties of the distribution of the unpredictable part of financial series that we studied in Fornari and Mele (1999a).

How might we relate such results to past theoretical research ? To correctly address the question, recall the optimal filtering result of Nelson and Foster (1994) (pp. 26-29), who found that the TS model is a better filter than the GARCH in the presence of *conditional* thick tailed residuals. This is somewhat different in nature from our results, which imply that the innovations process of models like TS are *unconditionally* thicker tailed than the GARCH (this is so since $\delta = 1$ in the TS and $\delta = 2$ in the GARCH). Further, a new fact is uncovered here: low values of δ are associated with innovations processes which are not only thick-tailed, but also high-peaked. As a result, innovations processes of models like the TS are also *unconditionally* more peaked than the GARCH.

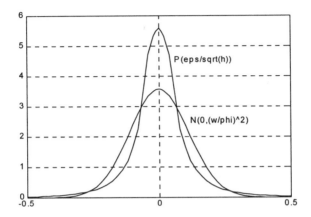

FIGURE 2.4. $P(\frac{\varepsilon}{\sqrt{h}})$ is the invariant distribution (2.17) obtained when $\delta = 1$ and $v = 2$. $N(0, (\frac{\omega}{\varphi})^2)$ is a normal density with standard deviation fixed at the steady state expectation of the volatility process in (2.3) as implied by the estimates of model (5.1) in chapter 5.

This holds, however, only when one considers fixed values of v. It can be the case that innovations processes with high values of δ are substantially as peaked as the innovations processes with low values of δ when the values of v which characterize the first ones are lower than the values of v which characterize the second ones. In fact, it is the combination of (δ, v) which determines the final shape of the stationary distribution of this model.

Are such results also related to empirical modeling issues ? The results of this section are about limiting probabilistic features of the innovations processes observed at short time intervals. Hence, they do not refer to modeling issues such as the maximum likelihood values of (δ, v). On a theoretical standpoint, it might be the case that the limiting behavior of the innovations processes uncovered in this section provides a satisfactory interpretative key of the (δ, v) maximum likelihood estimates behavior (since one observes ε_t rather than σ_t and u_t). Instead of proving this on the grounds of a mathematically sound theory, however, Fornari and Mele (1997a) addressed the issue on the basis of an empirical exploratory analysis that is succinctly presented below.

Our results can be summarized as follows. We made use of three stock market indices and four exchange rates. The estimates of both δ and v were concentrated around one (when $v = 1$, the g.e.d.$_{(v)}$ reduces to the Laplace distribution of the first kind). Insofar as we attempted to relate our theoretical results to the maximum likelihood behavior of δ and v, we proceeded to the following experiment. We gave definitions of outliers that were based on their relative distance from the mean of the estimated (unconditional) distribution; then we proceeded to subsequent estimation of the same model for all of our series while progressively dropping our selected outliers from the sample. What we observed is that the estimates of both v and δ increase as the number of outliers decreases. Finally, after performing Wald tests for the null $H_0 : \delta - v = 0$, we also concluded that the null could never be rejected.

2.6 Continuous time behavior of the volatility switching models

Following the research program developed in this chapter, we present analogous results for the VS-ARCH type models presented in the previous chapter, in which volatility is influenced not only by the sign of previous shocks, but also by the size of unexpected volatility induced by such shocks. Such results are presented in subsection 2.6.2. In subsection 2.6.1, we start first by deriving some basic properties of these models in discrete time. Only the case in which standardized errors are normally distributed is considered here. Furthermore, we do not develop results pertaining to the instantaneous correlation process between the asset price process and its instantaneous volatility process.

2.6.1 SOME PROPERTIES IN DISCRETE TIME

The unconditional moments of the model are important to understand why VS-ARCH type models should be able to capture a well-known characteristic of returns distributions, i.e. the fat tails. In the VS-ARCH model (1.9), for instance, the second moment of the innovations is (see appendix C):

$$E(\varepsilon^2) = \frac{w}{1 - \alpha - \beta}, \qquad (2.18)$$

and coincides with the corresponding moment of a GARCH(1,1): asymmetries do not affect the unconditional expectation of volatility; the fourth moment, however, is:

$$E(\varepsilon^4) = 3 \frac{(w^2 + \delta_2^2)(1 - \alpha - \beta) + 2w[(\alpha + \beta)w + \delta_2(\delta_1 - \delta_0)]}{(1 - \alpha - \beta)(1 - 3\alpha^2 - \beta^2 - 2\alpha\beta - 3\delta_0^2 - \delta_1^2 + 2\delta_0\delta_1)};$$

since δ_0, δ_1 and δ_2 measure the impact of v_{t-1} on σ_t^2, deeper asymmetries in volatility may result in more leptokurtic unconditional distributions for the innovations.

As in the previous model, the first unconditional moment of ε^2 in model

(1.10) is as in (2.18), but the fourth unconditional moment is given by:

$$E(\varepsilon^4) = 3E((\omega + \alpha\varepsilon^2 + \beta\sigma^2)^2 + \nu^2), \quad \nu \equiv \gamma\varepsilon^2 + \delta((\frac{\varepsilon}{\sigma})^2 - k).$$

Collecting the terms in $E(\varepsilon^4)$ yields

$$E(\varepsilon^4) = 3\frac{[\omega^2 + \delta^2(3 + k^2 - 2k)](1 - \alpha - \beta) + 2\omega(\omega(\alpha + \beta) + \gamma\delta(3 - k))}{(1 - \alpha - \beta)(1 - 3\alpha^2 - \beta^2 - 2\alpha\beta - 3\gamma^2)}.$$

Hence, the kurtosis of the model is given by

$$\frac{E(\varepsilon^4)}{[E(\varepsilon^2)]^2} = 3((\omega^2 + \delta^2(3 + k^2 - 2k))(1 - \alpha - \beta)$$

$$+2\omega(\omega(\alpha + \beta) + \gamma\delta(3 - k))) \times \frac{1 - \alpha - \beta}{\omega^2(1 - 3\alpha^2 - \beta^2 - 2\alpha\beta - 3\gamma^2)}.$$

The latter expression shows that both the fourth moment and the kurtosis are functions of δ, k and γ; there exist values of these parameters which generate coefficients of kurtosis higher than those implied by the simple GARCH(1,1) model. It is also worth noticing that, contrary to standard results (e.g., Bollerslev (1986)), such objects also depend on the intercept of the volatility equation.

2.6.2   CONVERGENCE ISSUES

At this point, it is important to investigate whether the diffusion limit (2.3) is able to generalize the diffusion of the VS-ARCH models; in this case, in fact, they would be indistinguishable from the A-PARCH in correspondence of high frequency sampling. It turns out that the answer is negative for both models. Partition time in (1.9) as

$$\begin{aligned}
{}_h\varepsilon_{hk} &= {}_hz_{hk} \cdot {}_h\sigma_{hk}, \; {}_hz_{hk} \sim N(0,h) \\
{}_h\sigma^2_{h(k+1)} - {}_h\sigma^2_{hk} &= w_h - \delta_{2,h}s_k \\
&\quad +(h^{-1}(\alpha_h + \delta_{0,h}s_k)\,{}_hz^2_{hk} + \beta_h - \delta_{1,h}s_k - 1)\,{}_h\sigma^2_{hk}.
\end{aligned}$$
(2.19)

It is shown informally in appendix A that if the standard conditions concerning the drift along with the following conditions

$$\begin{aligned}
\lim_{h\downarrow 0} h^{-1/2}\alpha_h &= \bar{\alpha} \\
\lim_{h\downarrow 0} h^{-1/2}\delta_{0,h} &= \bar{\delta}_0 \\
\lim_{h\downarrow 0} h^{-1/2}\delta_{1,h} &= \bar{\delta}_1 \\
\lim_{h\downarrow 0} h^{-1/2}\delta_{2,h} &= \bar{\delta}_2
\end{aligned}$$
(2.20)

are met, then $\{{}_h\sigma^2_{hk}\}_{k=0}^{\infty}$ converges in distribution to the solution of the following stochastic differential equation as $h \downarrow 0$:

$$d\sigma(t)^2 = (\bar{\omega} - \varphi\sigma(t)^2)dt + (\bar{\delta}_2^2 + \psi_1\sigma(t)^2 + \psi_2\sigma(t)^4)^{1/2}dW(t), \; \varphi \geq 0, \quad (2.21)$$

where
$$\begin{aligned}
\psi_1 &= -2\bar{\delta}_2(\bar{\delta}_0 - \bar{\delta}_1) \\
\psi_2 &= 2(\bar{\alpha}^2 + \bar{\delta}_0^2) + (\bar{\delta}_0 - \bar{\delta}_1)^2
\end{aligned}$$

This corrects formula (29) p. 56 in Fornari and Mele (1997b), where the $\psi_1 \sigma^2$ term in the diffusion function was omitted.

It is straight forward to check that such a diffusion limit is the same as in Nelson (1990) (eq. 2.40) when $\bar{\delta}_0 = \bar{\delta}_1 = \bar{\delta}_2 = 0$.

2.6.3 INVARIANT MEASURES

Let us start with the simple case in which $\bar{\delta}_0 = \bar{\delta}_1$. This corresponds to the diffusion limit (2.21) with $\psi_1 = 0$, which is the model actually studied in Fornari and Mele (1997b). Let $\psi \equiv \psi_2^{1/2}$; Fornari and Mele (1997b) then show that the stationary distribution of σ^2 is:

$$p(\sigma^2) \propto (r^2 + \sigma^4)^{-m} \exp(n \cdot \arctan(q \cdot \sigma^2)),$$

where $r^2 \equiv (\frac{\bar{\delta}_2}{\psi})^2, m \equiv \frac{\varphi}{\psi^2} + 1, n \equiv \frac{2\bar{\omega}}{\bar{\delta}_2 \psi}, q \equiv \frac{\psi}{\bar{\delta}_2}$. Note that in the case $\bar{\delta}_2 = 0$,

$$P(\sigma^2) \propto \sigma^{-4m} \exp(-\frac{b}{\sigma^2}),$$

where $b \equiv \frac{2\bar{\omega}}{\psi^2}$. The preceding distribution is an inverted Gamma, consistently with Nelson's (1990) results.

Note that when $\bar{\delta}_2 \neq 0$, there is a positive probability that the variance takes negative values, which is obviously also the case when $\bar{\delta}_0 \neq \bar{\delta}_1$. However, the results of this section have to be taken as *approximation* results that are produced to enhance our understanding of the functioning of the model in discrete time, as is the case in the analysis of the stationary distribution of the residuals to be presented succinctly below. In discrete time, for instance, we can always find conditions that ensure that the variance always remains positive, and such discrete time conditions often translate into continuous time conditions that makes the probability of negative variances rather negligible in practice.

To find the stationary distribution of the residuals, first find the stationary distribution of the standard deviation:

$$f(\sigma) \propto \sigma(r^2 + \sigma^4)^{-m} \exp(n \cdot \arctan(q \cdot \sigma^2)).$$

The VS-ARCH innovation process then approximately follows the following stationary density function:

$$p(x) = \int_0^\infty N(x \cdot \sigma^{-1}) f(\sigma) \sigma^{-1} d\sigma,$$

where $N'(.)$ is the standard normal density. Fornari and Mele (1997b) present some numerical results devoted to the understanding the shape of such a distribution.

In the general case in which $\bar{\delta}_0 \neq \bar{\delta}_1$, appendix B shows that the stationary distribution of the variance is:

$$
p(x) \quad \propto \quad (\delta_2^2 + \psi_1 x + \psi_2 x^2)^{-1-\frac{\varphi}{\psi_2}}
$$
$$
\times \exp(\frac{4\bar{\omega}\psi_2 + 2\varphi\psi_1}{\psi_2\sqrt{4\delta_2^2\psi_2 - \psi_1^2}} \cdot \arctan\frac{\psi_1 + 2\psi_2 \cdot x}{\sqrt{4\delta_2^2\psi_2 - \psi_1^2}}). \qquad (2.22)
$$

This density belongs to the family of Pearson's distributions. It is a Pearson type IV distribution. It is interesting to note that Föllmer and Schweizer (1993) (thm. 5.1) derive the same distribution for asset prices in a microeconomic foundation model of Brownian motion (there are errors in their derivation, however, that have been corrected in Föllmer (1995)). As the authors quoted from Johnson and Kotz (1970), "it seems that no common statistical distributions are of the type IV".

Appendix A: proofs on convergence issues

PROOF OF THEOREM 2.3. We start by considering the convergence of the volatility process. Consider the drift per unit of time of the volatility process in (2.1):

$$h^{-1}E((_h\sigma^\delta_{h(k+1)} -_h \sigma^\delta_{hk}) \,/\, \mathcal{F}_{hk})$$
$$= h^{-1}\omega_h + h^{-1}(n_{\delta,v}((1 - \gamma_h)^\delta + (1 + \gamma_h)^\delta)\alpha_h + \beta_h - 1)_h\sigma^\delta_{hk}. \qquad (2A.1)$$

To ensure that the drift per unit of time (2A.1) does not explode as h shrinks to zero, we impose the following Lipschitz conditions:

$$\lim_{h\downarrow 0} h^{-1}\omega_h = \overline{\omega} > 0,$$
$$\lim_{h\downarrow 0} h^{-1}(n_{\delta,v}((1 - \gamma_h)^\delta + (1 + \gamma_h)^\delta)\alpha_h + \beta_h - 1) = -\varphi.$$

The positiveness of $\overline{\omega}$ is required since $(\omega_h, \alpha_h, \beta_h)$ must be in the positive orthant for all h—by (2.2)—and therefore for $h \downarrow 0$, too; however, φ can be of either sign; assumption 2.2 is also satisfied by (2.5)-(2.7) (particularly, assumption 5 of Nelson (1990) is respected). Thus, as $h \downarrow 0$, the drift per unit of time of $_h\sigma^\delta_{h(k+1)} -_h \sigma^\delta_{hk}$ becomes:

$$\lim_{h\downarrow 0} h^{-1}E((_h\sigma^\delta_{h(k+1)} -_h \sigma^\delta_{hk}) \,/\, \mathcal{F}_{hk}) = \overline{\omega} - \varphi\sigma^\delta, \qquad (2A.2)$$

if and only if it is possible to show that the r.h.s. of (2A.2) and the limit $\lim_{h\downarrow 0} h^{-1}E((_h\sigma^\delta_{h(k+1)} - _h\sigma^\delta_{hk})^2 \,/\, \mathcal{F}_{hk})$ imply distributional uniqueness for $\{\sigma(t)^\delta\}_{t\geq 0}$. Now, the second order moment per unit of time of the volatility process in (2.1) is:

$$h^{-1}E((_h\sigma^\delta_{h(k+1)} -_h \sigma^\delta_{hk})^2 \,/\, \mathcal{F}_{hk})$$

$$= h^{-1}\omega_h^2 + h^{-1}(2\omega_h(n_{\delta,v}((1 - \gamma_h)^\delta + (1 + \gamma_h)^\delta)\alpha_h + \beta_h - 1))_h\sigma^\delta_{hk}$$
$$+ h^{-1}\alpha_h^2((m_{\delta,v} - n_{\delta,v}^2)((1 - \gamma_h)^{2\delta} + (1 + \gamma_h)^{2\delta}) - 2n_{\delta,v}^2(1 - \gamma_h)^\delta(1 + \gamma_h)^\delta)_h\sigma^{2\delta}_{hk}$$
$$+ h^{-1}(n_{\delta,v}((1 - \gamma_h)^\delta + (1 + \gamma_h)^\delta)\alpha_h + \beta_h - 1)^2 \cdot _h\sigma^{2\delta}_{hk}.$$

Substituting (2.5)-(2.7) into the preceding relation, and assuming the existence of the following limit:

$$\lim_{h\downarrow 0} h^{-1}((m_{\delta,v} - n_{\delta,v}^2)((1 - \gamma_h)^{2\delta} + (1 + \gamma_h)^{2\delta}) - 2n_{\delta,v}^2(1 - \gamma_h)^\delta(1 + \gamma_h)^\delta)\alpha_h^2 = \psi^2,$$

we conclude that the second order moment of the diffusion for $\{\sigma(t)^\delta\}_{t\geq 0}$ is:

$$\lim_{h\downarrow 0} h^{-1}E((_h\sigma^\delta_{h(k+1)} -_h \sigma^\delta_{hk})^2 \,/\, \mathcal{F}_{hk}) = \psi^2\sigma^{2\delta}, \qquad (2A.3)$$

if and only if the two r.h.s. of (2A.2) and (2A.3) imply distributional unique-ness for $\{\sigma(t)^\delta\}_{t\geq0}$. Suppose this to be the case; then, as regards the moment condition (2.7), it is easily checked that assumption 2.2 is satisfied with respect to assumptions 2 and 5 of Nelson (1990); thus, if $\{\sigma(t)^\delta\}_{t\geq0}$ were distribution-ally unique, then—by (2A.2) and (2A.3)—a diffusion limit for the volatility process in (2.1) could have the following structure:

$$d\sigma(t)^\delta = (\bar{\omega} - \varphi\sigma(t)^\delta)dt + \psi\sigma(t)^\delta dW^\sigma(t), \qquad (2A.4)$$

where $W^\sigma(t)$ is a standard Brownian motion. What is left now is just to show distributional uniqueness for the diffusion process (2A.4), i.e. completing the proof that (2A.4) satisfies the last requirement of assumption 2.2: the fulfill-ment of assumption 4 of Nelson (1990). But this follows from the continuous mapping theorem (e.g., Billingsley (1968)). Set, for example, $V(t) \equiv \log(\sigma(t)^2)$ and expand $V(t)$ via Itô's lemma:

$$dV(t) = -\frac{2\varphi + \psi^2 - 2\bar{\omega}\exp(-\frac{\delta}{2}V(t))}{\delta}dt + \frac{2\psi}{\delta}dW^\sigma(t).$$

Using now the same strategy as Nelson's (1990), it is a trivial exercise to verify that $\{V(t)\}_{t\geq0}$ satisfies condition B and the non-explosion condition given by Nelson (see Nelson (1990) (p. 17; p. 18, footnote 10; and appendix A, condition B and non-explosion condition, respectively)). Thus, $\{V(t)\}_{t\geq0}$ is distributional unique. Now, since $\{V(t)\}_{t\geq0}$ is distributional unique, $\{\sigma(t)^\delta\}_{t\geq0}$ is distributional unique as well by the continuous mapping theorem, and the proof that $\{\sigma(t)^\delta\}_{t\geq0}$ is the unique weak solution of (2A.4) is complete.

Until now, we were concerned with the convergence of the volatility process only. It is straight forward to see that the moment conditions (2.5)-(2.7) also guarantee the weak convergence of the asset price process to the first equation of system. Now we shall constructively show that $W^{(\sigma)}$ can be written as:

$$W^{(\sigma)}(t) = \rho W^{(1)}(t) + (1-\rho^2)^{1/2}W^{(2)}(t) \,, t \geq 0$$

with $W^{(2)}$ another $\mathcal{F}(t)$-Brownian motion. It is sufficient to show that the limit:

$$\lim_{h\downarrow0} h^{-1}E((\log {}_hS_{hk} - \log {}_hS_{h(k-1)})({}_h\sigma^\delta_{h(k+1)} - {}_h\sigma^\delta_{hk}) / \mathcal{F}_{hk})$$

is not ill-behaved. After that, an identification argument will do the work.

By (2.5)-(2.7), and the fact that $\frac{{}_hu_{hk}}{h^{1/2}}$ is g.e.d.$_{(v)}$ for each h,

$$\lim_{h\downarrow0} h^{-1}E((\log {}_hS_{hk} - \log {}_hS_{h(k-1)})({}_h\sigma^\delta_{h(k+1)} - {}_h\sigma^\delta_{hk}) / \mathcal{F}_{hk})$$

$$= \lim_{h\downarrow0} h^{-1}E(((\mu - {}_h\sigma^2_{hk}/2)h + {}_hu_{hk} \cdot {}_h\sigma_{hk})$$

$$\times (\omega_h + (\alpha_h |{}_hu_{hk}|^\delta (1 - \gamma_h s_k)^\delta h^{-\frac{\delta}{2}} + \beta_h - 1){}_h\sigma^\delta_{hk}) / \mathcal{F}_{hk})$$

$$= \lim_{h \downarrow 0} h^{-1} E({}_h u_{hk}(\alpha_h \,|{}_h u_{hk}|^{\delta} \,(1 - \gamma_h s_k)^{\delta} h^{-\frac{\delta}{2}} + \beta_h - 1) \cdot {}_h\sigma_{hk}^{\delta+1} \,/\, \mathcal{F}_{hk})$$

$$= \lim_{h \downarrow 0} h^{-1-\frac{\delta}{2}} \alpha_h \cdot E({}_h u_{hk} \,|{}_h u_{hk}|^{\delta} \,(1 - \gamma_h s_k)^{\delta} \cdot {}_h\sigma_{hk}^{\delta+1} \,/\, \mathcal{F}_{hk})$$

$$= \lim_{h \downarrow 0} \frac{\alpha_h}{h^{1/2}} (((1 - \gamma_h)^{\delta} - (1 + \gamma_h)^{\delta}) \int_{\mathbb{R}_+} x^{\delta+1} p(dx)) \cdot {}_h\sigma_{hk}^{\delta+1},$$

where $p(.)$ denotes the g.e.d.$_{(v)}$ density, or:

$$\lim_{h \downarrow 0} h^{-1} E((\log {}_h S_{hk} - \log {}_h S_{h(k-1)})({}_h\sigma_{h(k+1)}^{\delta} - {}_h\sigma_{hk}^{\delta}) \,/\, \mathcal{F}_{hk})$$

$$= \lim_{h \downarrow 0} \frac{\alpha_h}{h^{1/2}} ((1 - \gamma_h)^{\delta} - (1 + \gamma_h)^{\delta}) K \cdot {}_h\sigma_{hk}^{\delta+1}; \tag{2A.5}$$

here,

$$K = \frac{2^{\frac{\delta-v+1}{v}} \nabla_v^{\delta+1} \Gamma(\frac{\delta+2}{v})}{\Gamma(v^{-1})}.$$

We claim that the r.h.s. of (2A.5) is bounded and bounded away from zero. To see this, notice that by condition (2.7),

$$\psi^2 = \lim_{h \downarrow 0} (\frac{\alpha_h}{h^{1/2}})^2 \cdot Z_h < \infty,$$

and if $\gamma_h = \gamma$ for each h (condition (2.8)), then $Z_h = Z < \infty$ for each h, and:

$$\lim_{h \downarrow 0} (\frac{\alpha_h}{h^{1/2}})^2 = (\frac{\psi}{Z^{1/2}})^2,$$

which is bounded. By continuity, and (2A.5),

$$\lim_{h \downarrow 0} \frac{\alpha_h}{h^{1/2}} = \frac{\psi}{Z^{1/2}},$$

which shows that (2A.5) is bounded and bounded away from zero:

$$\lim_{h \downarrow 0} h^{-1} E((\log {}_h S_{hk} - \log {}_h S_{h(k-1)})({}_h\sigma_{h(k+1)}^{\delta} - {}_h\sigma_{hk}^{\delta}) \,/\, \mathcal{F}_{hk}) = \frac{\psi \overline{K}}{Z^{1/2}} \sigma^{\delta+1},$$

where:

$$\overline{K} = ((1 - \gamma)^{\delta} - (1 + \gamma)^{\delta}) K.$$

To identify ρ, we note that this has to solve the following equation: $\psi \rho = \frac{\psi}{Z^{1/2}} \overline{K}$, from which we find, finally:

$$\rho = \frac{\overline{K}}{Z^{1/2}}.$$

The proof is complete. ‖

CONTINUOUS TIME BEHAVIOR OF THE VOLATILITY SWITCHING MODEL. We are interested in analyzing rapidly the conditions under which the scheme in (2.19) converges weakly (i.e. in distribution) to an Itô process, as h drops to zero. To do this, we retain again Nelson's (1990) assumptions (1 to 5). We introduce notation for the filtration $\mathcal{F}_{hk}$, which is that generated by $\{_h z_{hi}\}_{i=0}^{k-1}$ and $\{_h\sigma_{hi}^2\}_{i=0}^k$.

We first evaluate the expected value per unit of time of $_h\sigma_{h(k+1)}^2 - _h\sigma_{hk}^2$ with $_h\sigma_{hk}^2$ generated by eq. (2.19). To avoid the explosion of the drift per unit of time as $h \downarrow 0$, we require the following Lipschitz conditions:

$$\lim_{h\downarrow 0} h^{-1} w_h = \overline{\omega} < \infty, \tag{2A.6}$$

$$\lim_{h\downarrow 0} h^{-1}(\alpha_h + \beta_h - 1) = -\varphi, \ \varphi \geq 0, \tag{2A.7}$$

obtaining

$$\lim_{h\downarrow 0} E(h^{-1}(_h\sigma_{h(k+1)}^2 - _h\sigma_{hk}^2) / \mathcal{F}_{hk})$$

$$= \lim_{h\downarrow 0}(h^{-1} w_h + h^{-1}(\alpha_h + \beta_h - 1) \ _h\sigma_{hk}^2)$$

$$= \overline{\omega} - \varphi\sigma^2.$$

The evaluation of $h^{-1}E((_h\sigma_{h(k+1)}^2 - _h\sigma_{hk}^2)^2 / \mathcal{F}_{hk})$ gives:

$$h^{-1}E((_h\sigma_{h(k+1)}^2 - _h\sigma_{hk}^2)^2 / \mathcal{F}_{hk})$$

$$= h^{-1}E(w_h^2 + \delta_{2,h}^2 s_k^2 + [h^{-2}(\alpha_h + \delta_{0,h}s_k)^2 \ _h z_{hk}^4 + (\beta_h - 1 - \delta_{1,h}s_k)^2$$
$$+2h^{-1}(\beta_h - 1 - \delta_{1,h}s_k)(\alpha_h + \delta_{0,h}s_k) \ _h z_{hk}^2] \ _h\sigma_{hk}^4$$
$$+2w_h[h^{-1}\alpha_h \cdot \ _h z_{hk}^2 + h^{-1}\delta_{0,h} \cdot s_k \cdot \ _h z_{hk}^2 + \beta_h - \delta_{1h} \cdot s_k - 1] \ _h\sigma_{hk}^2$$
$$-2\delta_{2,h}[h^{-1}\alpha_h \cdot s_k \cdot \ _h z_{hk}^2 + h^{-1}\delta_{0,h} \cdot s_k^2 \cdot \ _h z_{hk}^2 + \beta_h s_k$$
$$-\delta_{1h} \cdot s_k^2 - s_k] \ _h\sigma_{hk}^2 / \mathcal{F}_{hk})$$

$$= h^{-1}E(w_h^2 + \delta_{2,h}^2 + [3(\alpha_h^2 + \delta_{0,h}^2) + \beta_h^2 + \delta_{1,h}^2 + 1 - 2\beta_h$$
$$+2(\alpha_h\beta_h - \alpha_h - \delta_{0h}\delta_{1h})] \ _h\sigma_{hk}^4 + 2w_h(\alpha_h + \beta_h - 1) \ _h\sigma_{hk}^2$$
$$-2\delta_{2h}(\delta_{0h} - \delta_{1h}) \ _h\sigma_{hk}^2 / \mathcal{F}_{hk})$$

$$= h^{-1}E(w_h^2 + \delta_{2,h}^2 + [2(\alpha_h^2 + \delta_{0,h}^2) + (\alpha_h + \beta_h - 1)^2 + (\delta_{0,h} - \delta_{1h})^2] \ _h\sigma_{hk}^4$$
$$+[2w_h(\alpha_h + \beta_h - 1) - 2\delta_{2h}(\delta_{0h} - \delta_{1h})] \ _h\sigma_{hk}^2 / \mathcal{F}_{hk}),$$

whence

$$\lim_{h\downarrow 0} h^{-1}E((_h\sigma_{h(k+1)}^2 - _h\sigma_{hk}^2)^2 / \mathcal{F}_{hk})$$

$$= \lim_{h\downarrow 0}(h^{-1}w_h^2 + (\frac{\delta_{2,h}}{h^{1/2}})^2 + [2((\frac{\alpha_h}{h^{1/2}})^2 + (\frac{\delta_{0,h}}{h^{1/2}})^2) + h^{-1}(\alpha_h + \beta_h - 1)^2$$

$$+(\frac{\delta_{0,h}}{h^{1/2}} - \frac{\delta_{1h}}{h^{1/2}})^2] \, {}_h\sigma_{hk}^4 + [2h^{-1}w_h(\alpha_h + \beta_h - 1)$$

$$-2\frac{\delta_{2h}}{h^{1/2}}(\frac{\delta_{0h}}{h^{1/2}} - \frac{\delta_{1h}}{h^{1/2}})] \, {}_h\sigma_{hk}^2).$$

Using the Lipschitz conditions (2A.6)-(2A.7), we see that conditions (2.20) suffice to obtain the diffusion limit (2.21).

Appendix B: proofs on distributional issues

PROOF OF LEMMA 2.4. First, the Kushner conditions (1984) (chapter 6) required by Nelson (1990) (appendix B) to show thm. 2.3 in Nelson (1990) trivially hold here, and this enables us to simultaneously take $h \downarrow 0$ and $hk \rightarrow \infty$. Next, consider the Fokker-Planck equation associated with eq. (2.3):

$$\frac{\partial p(t, \sigma(t)^\delta / s, \sigma(s)^\delta)}{\partial t} = \frac{\frac{1}{2}\partial^2(\psi^2\sigma(t)^{2\delta} \cdot p(t, \sigma(t)^\delta / s, \sigma(s)^\delta))}{\partial(\sigma(t)^\delta)^2}$$
$$- \frac{\partial((\bar{\omega} - \varphi\sigma(t)^\delta) \cdot p(t, \sigma(t)^\delta / s, \sigma(s)^\delta))}{\partial\sigma(t)^\delta},$$

where p denotes the density function of $\sigma(t)^\delta$ conditional on the information set as of time $s < t$. Let:

$$P(\sigma^\delta) = \lim_{t\to\infty} p(t, \sigma(t)^\delta / s, \sigma(s)^\delta)$$

be the stationary distribution of σ_t^δ. It is a standard result that $P(\sigma^\delta)$ satisfies the following first order differential equation (e.g., Wong (1964)):

$$\frac{1}{2}\frac{\partial(\psi^2\sigma^{2\delta}P(\sigma^\delta))}{\partial\sigma^\delta} = (\bar{\omega} - \varphi\sigma^\delta)P(\sigma^\delta).$$

The reader can now check that (2.16) is indeed the solution of the last differential equation. ‖

PROOF OF THEOREM 2.6. First, notice that the invariance principle ensures that a suitable discrete time Markov process describing the asset price dynamics converges weakly to a standard Brownian motion regardless of the distribution of the error terms, say ${}_h\bar{u}_{hk}$, and provided the fact that ${}_h\bar{u}_{hk}$ has finite moments. However, this does not compromise the fact that ${}_h\bar{u}_{hk}$ preserves its distribution for each h, which is the reason why we required ${}_h\bar{u}_{hk}$ to be g.e.d.$_{(v)}$ for each h in the theorem.

Now consider the following lemma.

LEMMA 2B.1. *Let* $P^\delta_{(1/\sigma)}(\sigma^{-1})$ *be the stationary distribution function of* $_h\sigma^{-1}_{hk}$. *Then, under the conditions of lemma 2.4,*

$$_h\sigma^{-1}_{hk} \xrightarrow{d} P^\delta_{(1/\sigma)}(\sigma^{-1}) = \delta K_0^{-1}\sigma^{\delta(1-a)+1}\exp(-b\sigma^{-\delta}), \text{ as } h \downarrow 0 \text{ and } hk \to \infty.$$

PROOF. Nearly identical to lemma 2.4 and through the change of variables $\sigma^\delta \mapsto \sigma^{-1}$. ∥

Next, let $x_1 = {}_h\bar{u}_{hk}$ and $x_2 = \nabla_\delta(2b)^{1/\delta} \cdot {}_h\sigma^{-1}_{hk}$, where $_h\bar{u}_{hk}$ is g.e.d.$_{(v)}$. Consider assumption 2.5; then, it follows both by construction and lemma 2B.1 that the densities of x_1 and x_2 are:

$$f_1(x_1) = K_1^{-1}\exp(-\tfrac{1}{2}\left|\tfrac{x_1}{\nabla_\delta}\right|^\delta)$$

$$f_2(x_2) = \frac{\delta K_0^{-1}}{(2b\nabla_\delta^\delta)^{a-1}}x_2^{\delta(a-1)-1}\exp(-\tfrac{1}{2}\left|\tfrac{x_2}{\nabla_\delta}\right|^\delta)$$

where $K_1^{-1} = \dfrac{\delta}{\nabla_\delta 2^{1+\frac{1}{\delta}}\Gamma(\delta^{-1})}$. Define now two new variables:

$$y_1 = |x_1|^\delta + |x_2|^\delta$$
$$y_2 = x_1 x_2^{-1}$$

Given the strict positiveness of x_2, this system admits the following, unique transformation:

$$x_1 = y_2(\tfrac{y_1}{1+|y_2|^\delta})^{1/\delta}$$
$$x_2 = (\tfrac{y_1}{1+|y_2|^\delta})^{1/\delta}$$

with absolute Jacobian equating:

$$|J| = \left|\frac{D(x_1,x_2)}{D(y_1,y_2)}\right| = \frac{1}{\delta y_1}(\tfrac{y_1}{1+|y_2|^\delta})^{2/\delta}.$$

We conclude that the joint density of y_1 and y_2 is:

$$F(y_1,y_2) = f_1(x_1)f_2(x_2)|J|$$

$$= \frac{(K_0K_1)^{-1}}{(2b\nabla_\delta^\delta)^{a-1}}\exp(-\tfrac{1}{2}\nabla_\delta^{-\delta}(|x_1|^\delta + |x_2|^\delta))$$

$$\times x_2^{\delta(a-1)-1}y_1^{-1+2\delta^{-1}}(1+|y_2|^\delta)^{-2\delta^{-1}}$$

$$= \frac{(K_0K_1)^{-1}y_1^{a-2+\delta^{-1}}\exp(-\tfrac{1}{2}\nabla_\delta^{-\delta}y_1)(1+|y_2|^\delta)^{-(a-1+\delta^{-1})}}{(2b\nabla_\delta^\delta)^{a-1}}$$

$$= \frac{\delta y_1^{a-2+\delta^{-1}} \exp(-\frac{1}{2}\nabla_\delta^{-\delta} y_1)(1+|y_2|^\delta)^{-(a-1+\delta^{-1})}}{\Gamma(a-1)\Gamma(\delta^{-1})2^{a+\delta^{-1}}\nabla_\delta^{\delta(a-1)+1}}$$

$$= \frac{\delta y_1^{a-2+\delta^{-1}} \exp(-\frac{1}{2}\nabla_\delta^{-\delta} y_1)(1+|y_2|^\delta)^{-(a-1+\delta^{-1})}}{2B(\delta^{-1}; a-1)\Gamma(a-1+\delta^{-1})2^{a-1+\delta^{-1}}\nabla_\delta^{\delta(a-1)+1}}$$

$$= \frac{y_1^{a-2-\delta^{-1}} \exp(-\frac{1}{2}\nabla_\delta^{-\delta} y_1)}{2^{a-1+\frac{1}{\delta}}\nabla_\delta^{\delta(a-1)+1}\Gamma(a-1+\delta^{-1})} \times \frac{\delta(1+\eta^{-1}|y_3|^\delta)^{-\frac{\eta+1}{2}}}{2\eta^{\frac{1}{\delta}}B(\frac{1}{\delta}; \frac{\eta+1}{2}-\frac{1}{\delta})},$$

where $y_3 = \eta^{\frac{1}{\delta}} y_2$, η and $B(.;.)$ are defined in the theorem. The density of y_3 is thus:

$$f(y_3) = \frac{\delta(1+\eta^{-1}|y_3|^\delta)^{-\frac{\eta+1}{2}}}{2\eta^{\frac{1}{\delta}}B(\frac{1}{\delta}; \frac{\eta+1}{2}-\frac{1}{\delta})},$$

iff

$$\int_{-\infty}^{+\infty}(1+\eta^{-1}|y_3|^\delta)^{-\frac{\eta+1}{2}}dy_3 = 2\delta^{-1}\eta^{\frac{1}{\delta}}B(\frac{1}{\delta}; \frac{\eta+1}{2}-\frac{1}{\delta}).$$

To show the last relation, notice that:

$$\int_{-\infty}^{+\infty}(1+\eta^{-1}|y_3|^\delta)^{-\frac{\eta+1}{2}}dy_3 = 2\int_0^\infty(1+\eta^{-1}|y_3|^\delta)^{-\frac{\eta+1}{2}}dy_3$$

$$= 2\delta^{-1}\eta^{\frac{1}{\delta}}\int_0^\infty(1+x)^{-\frac{\eta+1}{2}}x^{\frac{1}{\delta}-1}dx,$$

where $\chi = \eta^{-1}|y_3|^\delta$, which is $2\delta^{-1}\eta^{\frac{1}{\delta}}$ times an Euler's Beta of the second kind, with parameters δ^{-1} and $\frac{1}{2}(\eta+1)-\delta^{-1}$. $\|$

PROOF OF THEOREM 2.8. We start by the following lemma:

LEMMA 2B.2. *Let* $P_{(\sigma)}^\delta(\sigma)$ *be the stationary distribution function of* $_h\sigma_{hk}$. *Then, under the conditions of lemma 2.4:*

$$_h\sigma_{hk} \xrightarrow{d} P_{(\sigma)}^\delta(\sigma) = \delta K_0^{-1}\sigma^{\delta(1-a)-1}\exp(-b\sigma^{-\delta}), \text{ as } h \downarrow 0 \text{ and } hk \to \infty.$$

PROOF. Nearly identical to lemma 2B.1. $\|$

Next, let $GED(x)$ denote the g.e.d.$_{(v)}$ density having x as argument. By integrating:

$$P(\bar{\varepsilon}) = \int_0^\infty GED(\bar{\varepsilon}(\sigma))P_{(\sigma)}^\delta(\sigma)\sigma^{-1}d\sigma = \int_0^\infty GED(\bar{\varepsilon}/\sigma)P_{(\sigma)}^\delta(\sigma)\sigma^{-1}d\sigma,$$

where $P_{(\sigma)}^\delta(\sigma)$ is given by lemma 2B.2. $\|$

THE STATIONARY DISTRIBUTION OF σ^2 IN THE VOLATILITY SWITCHING MODEL. Let $p(\sigma(t)^2 / \sigma(s)^2)$ be the probability density function of $\sigma(t)^2$, given the information set as of time s, $0 < s < t < \infty$. The Fokker-Planck equation associated with eq. (2.21) is:

$$\frac{\partial p(x \, / \, x^-)}{\partial t} = \frac{1}{2} \frac{\partial^2 ((\delta_2^2 + \psi_1 x + \psi_2 x^2) \cdot p(x \, / \, x^-))}{\partial x^2} - \frac{\partial ((\bar{\omega} - \varphi x) p(x \, / \, x^-))}{\partial x}.$$

A stationary density function (given it exists) must satisfy:

$$\frac{1}{2} \frac{\partial ((\delta_2^2 + \psi_1 x + \psi_2 x^2) p(x))}{\partial x} = (\bar{\omega} - \varphi x) p(x)$$

where $p(\sigma^2) = \lim_{t \to \infty} p(\sigma(t)^2 \, / \, \sigma(s)^2)$. Developing explicitly the above equation yields:

$$\frac{p'(x)}{p(x)} = \frac{2\bar{\omega} - \psi_1 - 2(\varphi + \psi_2)x}{\delta_2^2 + \psi_1 x + \psi_2 x^2}$$

Integrating and exponentiating gives the density in (2.22) of the text. $\|$

Appendix C

UNCONDITIONAL MOMENTS OF ε IN THE VOLATILITY SWITCHING MODEL. Let ε_t be zero mean conditionally normally distributed, with conditional variance σ_t^2. We have:

$$E(\varepsilon_t^{2m} \, / \, I_{t-1}) = (w + \beta\sigma_{t-1}^2 + \alpha\varepsilon_{t-1}^2 + s_{t-1}v_{t-1})^m \cdot \prod_{j=1}^{m}(2j - 1), \quad (2\text{C}.1)$$

where I_t is as in section 1.2.1 chapter 1. Setting $m = 1$ gives:

$$E(\varepsilon_t^2 \mid I_{t-1}) = w + \beta\sigma_{t-1}^2 + \alpha\varepsilon_{t-1}^2 + s_{t-1}v_{t-1}.$$

Recursive substitution yields:

$$E(\varepsilon^2) = \frac{w}{1 - \alpha - \beta}.$$

Setting $m = 2$, and sending time to infinity in (2C.1), so that the dependence of current values on the past is negligible, gives:

$$
\begin{aligned}
E(\varepsilon^4) &= 3E(w^2 + \alpha^2\varepsilon^4 + \beta^2\sigma^4 + \delta_0^2\varepsilon^4 + \delta_1^2\sigma^4 + \delta_2^2 - 2\delta_0\delta_1\varepsilon^2\sigma^2 \\
&\quad - 2\delta_0\delta_2\varepsilon^2 + 2\delta_1\delta_2\sigma^2 + 2\alpha w\varepsilon^2 + 2\beta w\sigma^2 + 2\alpha\beta\varepsilon^2\sigma^2) \\[6pt]
&= 3(w^2 + \delta_2^2) + (\beta^2 + 3\alpha^2 + 3\delta_0^2 + \delta_1^2 - 2\delta_0\delta_1 + 2\alpha\beta)E(\varepsilon^4) \\
&\quad + 6[w(\alpha + \beta) + \delta_2(\delta_1 - \delta_0)]\frac{w}{1 - \alpha - \beta}.
\end{aligned}
$$

Rearranging terms gives the formula of the text. $\|$

CONTINUOUS TIME STOCHASTIC VOLATILITY OPTION PRICING: FOUNDATIONAL ISSUES

3.1 Introduction

The past decade has witnessed a growing research interest in option pricing under constrained market participation. This chapter fucuses on issues related to market incompleteness due to the presence of continuous time stochastic volatility. When markets are incomplete, the value of a contingent claim is generally not attainable with a truly self-financing trading strategy, and absence of arbitrage opportunities is not sufficient to recover a unique rational price function of the claim, as in the celebrated Black and Scholes (1973) case.

Apart from the possibility of completing the market with the presence of additional, non-productive assets (as, for instance, the options themselves!), which allows one to obtain equilibrium restrictions on the price of a contingent claim that are driven by the preferences of a representative agent, there has recently been a growing research interest on studying interesting situations in which (1) there is not just an isolated price that is arbitrage free; or (2) there is the possibility of conceiving strategies 'resembling' the Black-Scholes ones. Accordingly, we may identify two main research strategies that deal with these problems. The first one tries to identify the bounds of a continuum of arbitrage-free prices of the claim; the survey of Karatzas (1997) (chapter 4), for instance, emphasizes such an approach. The second one looks for partial hedging strategies minimizing the risk incurred when hedging the claim by trading only the existing primitive assets; the term 'risk' will be made more precise below.

Refinements belonging to the second line of investigation are contained in this chapter. We work in continuous time. The original formulation of the problem is due to Föllmer and Sondermann (1986) and Bouleau and Lamberton (1989) in the case in which the tradable asset is a martingale under the primitive measure space; Duffie and Richardson (1991) and Schweizer (1992) presented results for (non-martingale) diffusion processes, while Schweizer (1994, 1996) developed deepening and ramifications; see He and Pearson (1991) and

Karatzas et al. (1991) for early related work; the preceding list is far from being exhaustive.

Formally, the problem can be formulated following two perspectives. In the first one, one optimizes a mean-variance criterion *with* a self-financing strategy; in this case, one says that the risk that is inherent to market incompleteness lies in the imperfect replication of the claim value process. In the second one, emphasized for instance in Föllmer and Schweizer (1991) and Hofmann et al. (1992), one makes use of certain strategies that are *not* self-financing, but that exactly replicate the value process of the claim; such strategies generate a random cumulative hedging cost, and the risk that is inherent to market incompleteness now lies in the randomness of the hedging cost.

In this chapter, we provide some properties of the hedging cost, such as its connections with the risk-premia demanded by agents to be compensated for the fluctuations of the (undiversifiable) risks. The primitives used here are less general than the primitives in Föllmer and Schweizer (1991), and are also a useful specialization of the model presented by Hofmann et al. (1992): specifically, we present a model with diffusion state variables, and consider strategies that simply make the volatility of the resulting strategy value the best approximation (in projection terms) of the volatility of the contingent claim value. Given a primitive probability space $(\Omega, \mathcal{F}, P)$, we shall say that such strategies are Z-mean-self financing if the corresponding cumulative hedging cost is a Z-martingale; here Z is a probability measure that is equivalent to P on $(\Omega, \mathcal{F})$. Contrary to a previous conjecture of Hofmann et al. (1992), we show that such a cost is a martingale under the set of all pricing, or 'risk-neutral' (in the sense of Harrison and Kreps (1979)), measures and that if the true pricing measure were really the minimal martingale measure introduced by Föllmer and Schweizer (1991),[1] the cost process would be a martingale even under the primitive measure space.

This last result is intimately related to the so-called Föllmer-Schweizer decomposition of the contingent claim value: up to a constant, such a decomposition expresses the value of the claim as the sum of certain cumulative gains from trade plus a martingale that is orthogonal to those gains, and the martingale part can be naturally interpreted as the cumulative hedging cost. The existence of a Föllmer-Schweizer -type decomposition is thus directly related to the fact that agents effectively price assets using the minimal martingale measure. Such results are obtained via intermediate results presenting an interest on their own. One of these is a Föllmer-Schweizer -type decomposition that

---

[1]The minimal martingale measure minimizes the Kullback-Leibler distance, or relative entropy, of the objective measure P with respect to any risk-neutral measure. The economic interpretation of the minimal measure is harder to discern. In the stochastic volatility setting, its interpretation is that agents do not wish to be compensated for the risk associated with the fluctuations of stochastic volatility, which is the hypothesis of Hull and White (1987).

we express in terms of the state variables. Such a decomposition was already derived by Hofmann et al. (1992), but here we give more information; particularly, we show how the cumulative hedging cost process can be ultimately computed in terms of the primitives of the model.

The chapter is organized in the following manner. Next section provides the basic setup; we present a model with productive, or 'primitive', assets in which information is diffusion information, and prices are *rational* functions of the state variables. Since we will assume that there are more state variables than primitive assets, our primitive security market model is incomplete and there is no way to give a unique price to a contingent claim. As noted before, the simplest way to attack such a problem consists in making use of the representative agent object in a model completed by non-productive assets, and here we succinctly present such an approach for two main reasons: first, such a representation helps introducing our applied research on the determinants of risk-premia in the stochastic volatility models; second, we introduce standard optimality equations that will be exploited in the next chapter to construct an equilibrium model of the term structure with stochastic volatility. Section 3.2 then concludes with the description of the strategies of the kind described above, and derives a decomposition of the contingent claim value process that is expressed in terms of such strategies and the state variables of the model.

Section 3.3 then adapts the framework of section 3.2 to a standard stochastic volatility model.

Section 3.4 contains refinements of section 3.2 and an appendix provides the proof that the minimal martingale measure is the equivalent martingale measure that is the nearest to the objective measure in terms of relative entropy; this was first shown by Föllmer and Schweizer (1991) in a general, unidimensional context; the proof here is restricted to the Brownian information case, but the analysis is conducted in the multidimensional case.

3.2 The reference model

3.2.1 PRIMITIVES

The first primitive is a probability space $(\Omega, \mathcal{F}, P)$. Information is available without costs and symmetrically to a continuum of identical agents on $(0, 1)$, and is released by the paths of a Brownian motion in $\mathbb{R}^d$

$$W = \{W(t) = (W^{(1)}(t), ..., W^{(d)}(t))'\}_{t \in [0,T]}, \ T < \infty.$$

We let $\mathbb{F} = \{\mathcal{F}(t)\}_{t \in [0,T]}$ be the P-augmentation of the natural filtration $\mathcal{F}^W(t) = \sigma(W(s), s \leq t)$ generated by W (with $\mathcal{F} = \mathcal{F}(T)$), and then consider a diffusion state process

$$Y^{(h)}(t) = Y^{(h)}(0) + \int_0^t \hbar_h(u, Y(u)) \mathrm{d}u + \int_0^t \sum_{j=1}^d \ell_{hj}(u, Y(u)) \mathrm{d}W^{(j)}(u), \ (3.1)$$

where $\hbar_h(t,y)$, $h = 1, ..., k$, and $\ell_{hj}(t,y)$, $h = 1, ..., k$ and $j = 1, ..., d$, are progressively $\mathcal{F}(t)$-measurable functions s.t. $[0,T] \times \mathbb{R}^k \mapsto \mathbb{R}$, and satisfy the usual regularity conditions ensuring a strong solution (e.g., definition 2.1 p. 285 in Karatzas and Shreve (1991)) to the preceding system.

Like the discrete time model of Lucas (1978), and unlike the continuous time model of Cox et al. (1985b), there are m *primitive* assets entitling to rights on the fruits, or *dividends* (the *numéraire*), of m trees; there is also an *accumulation factor*, and all assets are exchanged without frictions.

Let:
$$S_+ = \{S^+(t) = (S^{(0)}(t), ..., S^{(m)}(t))'\}_{t \in [0,T]}$$

be the $\mathcal{F}(t)$-adapted stochastic process of the accumulation factor price and the primitive prices. We suppose that these prices are *rationally* formed, which means that they are well defined functions of the state variables with standard smooth properties:

3.1 ASSUMPTION. *The primitive asset price function* $S_+ : ([0,T] \times \mathbb{R}^k) \mapsto \mathbb{R}_{++}^{m+1}$ *belongs to* $\mathcal{C}^{1,2}$.

The primitive price asset function is thus $S^{(i)}(t,y)$: it is the value of the ith primitive asset as of time t when the vector of the state variables is y. Finally, we introduce notation for the *discounted gain* process

$$\overline{G}^{(i)} = \frac{S^{(i)}}{S^{(0)}} + \overline{z}^{(i)}, \ i = 1, ..., m,$$

where, $d\overline{z}^{(i)} = \frac{1}{S^{(0)}} dz^{(i)}$, $i = 1, ..., m$, and $z^{(i)}(t) = \int_0^t \zeta^{(i)}(s)ds$, with $\zeta^{(i)} = \{\zeta^{(i)}(t)\}_{t \in [0,T]}$, an $\mathcal{F}(t)$-adapted process, standing for the dividend process. We close the model by assuming that $\zeta^{(i)}(t) = \zeta^{(i)}(t,y)$, all i, and that the price of the accumulation factor satisfies $S^{(0)}(t) = \exp(\int_0^t r(s)ds)$, $t \in [0,T]$, with $\{r(t)\}_{t \in [0,T]}$ a $\mathcal{F}(t)$-adapted process satisfying $E(\int_0^T r(t)dt) < \infty$. We define:

$$J \equiv \begin{pmatrix} \ell_{11} & \cdots & \ell_{1d} \\ \vdots & \ddots & \vdots \\ \ell_{k1} & \cdots & \ell_{kd} \end{pmatrix}, \ \frac{\partial S^{(i)}}{\partial Y} \equiv \left(\frac{\partial S^{(i)}}{\partial y_1}, ..., \frac{\partial S^{(i)}}{\partial y_k} \right) \text{ and } \frac{\partial S/S}{\partial Y} \equiv \left(\frac{\partial S^{(1)}}{\partial Y} \frac{1}{S^{(1)}}, ..., \frac{\partial S^{(m)}}{\partial Y} \frac{1}{S^{(m)}} \right)'.$$

By Itô's lemma,

$$dS^{(i)}(t) = \overline{\mu}_i(t,y(t)) \cdot S^{(i)}(t) \cdot dt + \sigma_i(t,y(t)) \cdot S^{(i)}(t) \cdot dW(t), \ i = 1, ..., m, \ (3.2)$$

where $\overline{\mu}$ and σ_i are $\mathcal{F}(t)$-adapted; specifically, σ_i is d-dimensional, with component $\sigma_{ij}(t,y)S^{(i)} = \sum_{h=1}^k \frac{\partial S^{(i)}}{\partial y_h} \ell_{hj}(t,y)$, and $\overline{\mu}_i(t,y)S^{(i)} = \frac{\partial S^{(i)}}{\partial t} + \sum_{h=1}^k \frac{\partial S^{(i)}}{\partial y_h} \hbar_h(t,y) + \frac{1}{2} \sum_{h=1}^k \sum_{j=1}^k \frac{\partial^2 S^{(i)}}{\partial y_h \partial y_j} \text{cov}(y_h, y_j),^2$ and has the interpretation of the

---

[2] $\text{cov}(y_h, y_j) = dy_h dy_j$, in the Itô's sense.

average appreciation rate referring to the ith primitive asset. Accordingly, we define the total appreciation rate as $\mu_i(t,y) = \bar{\mu}_i(t,y) + \bar{\zeta}_i(t,y)$, where $\bar{\zeta}^{(i)}(t) = (\frac{\zeta}{S})^{(i)}(t)$. We let σ denote the $m \times d$ matrix whose (i,j) entry is $\sigma_{ij}(t,y)$; this is: $\sigma = \frac{\partial S/S}{\partial Y} J$. In this book, we take $(\mu_i - \bar{\mu}_i)$ to be at most a deterministic function of time.

We formulate the standard:

3.2 ASSUMPTION. $\mathrm{rank}(\sigma) = m \leq d$, $P \otimes dt$-a.s.

Fruits can be continuously consumed between 0 and T; the consumption process is thus $c = \{c(t)\}_{t \in [0,T]}$, a positive adapted process satisfying $\int_0^T c(s) ds < \infty$, P-a.s., and a *strategy* is a predictable process in $\mathbb{R}^{m+1}$, denoted as $\theta = \{\theta(t) = (\theta^{(0)}(t), ..., \theta^{(m)}(t))\}_{t \in [0,T]}$, with $E(\int_0^T \|\theta(t)\|^2 dt) < \infty$. The value V of a strategy is

$$V(t) = \theta(t) \cdot S_+(t),$$

and has to solve

$$dV(t) = (\pi(t)'(\mu(t) - \mathbf{1}_m r(t)) + V(t)r(t) - c(t))dt + \pi(t)'\sigma(t)dW(t), \quad (3.3)$$

for the resulting strategy to be *self-financing*; here $\pi \equiv (\pi^{(1)}, ..., \pi^{(m)})'$, with $\pi^{(i)} \equiv \theta^{(i)} S^{(i)}$ and $\mu \equiv (\mu^{(1)}, ..., \mu^{(m)})'$. We impose a positive lower bound on V.

Markets clear when:

$$\pi(t) = S(t) \text{ and } c(t) = \sum_{i=1}^m \zeta^{(i)}(t), \ P \otimes dt\text{-a.s.}, \quad (3.4)$$

where S is the vector containing the m last entries of S_+.

We let $\mathcal{Q}$ be the set of measures equivalent[3] to P on $(\Omega, \mathcal{F})$ for $\overline{G}^{(i)}$.

3.3 ASSUMPTION. $\mathcal{Q}$ *is not empty.*

It is well-known that under all conditions formulated until now, (1) the securities market model is *viable* (following the terminology of Harrison and Kreps (1979)) if and only if assumption 3.3 holds, and a fortiori (2) there are not arbitrage opportunities (as defined, e.g. in def. 0.2.3 p. 4 in Karatzas (1997)) if and only if assumption 3.3 holds (see, e.g., thm. 0.2.4 p. 4-7 in Karatzas (1997) for (2)).

Let $L_{0,T,l}^2(\Omega, \mathcal{F}, P)$ be the space of all $\mathcal{F}(t)$-adapted processes $x = \{x(t)\}_{t \in [0,T]}$ in $\mathbb{R}^l$ and satisfying

$$0 < \int_0^T du \|x(u)\|^2 < \infty \quad P\text{-a.s.}$$

---

[3]Two measures are said to be equivalent if their null sets coincide.

Let 0_a be the zero process in $\mathbb{R}^a$, and define, for each $\mathcal{F}(t)$-adapted matrix process $\mathcal{A} = \{\mathcal{A}(t)\}_{t\in[0,T]}$ in $\mathbb{R}^{a_1 \times a_2}$, the subspace of processes:

$$\langle\mathcal{A}\rangle^\perp = \{x \in L^2_{0,T,a_2}(\Omega, \mathcal{F}, P) \; / \; \mathcal{A}(t) \cdot x(t) = 0_{a_1}, \; P \otimes \mathrm{dt}\text{-a.s.}\}.$$

Let

$$\widetilde{\lambda}(t) = (\sigma'(\sigma\sigma')^{-1}(\mu - 1_{m\times 1}r))(t);$$

under a standard Novikov's condition (e.g., Karatzas and Shreve (1991) (corollary 5.13 p. 199)) ensuring existence, the preceding can be interpreted as a risk premium process. In fact, *all* processes belonging to the set:

$$\mathcal{P} = \left\{\lambda \; / \; \lambda(t) = \widetilde{\lambda}(t) + \eta(t), \; \eta \in \langle\sigma\rangle^\perp\right\} \tag{3.5}$$

are bounded and can be interpreted as risk premia processes. More precisely, by defining:

$$\widetilde{\xi}(T) \equiv \frac{\mathrm{d}\widetilde{Q}}{\mathrm{d}P} = \exp(-\int_0^T \widetilde{\lambda}(t)'\mathrm{d}W(t) - \tfrac{1}{2}\int_0^T \left\|\widetilde{\lambda}(t)\right\|^2 \mathrm{dt}),$$

(the Radon-Nikodym derivative of $\widetilde{Q}$ with respect to P on $\mathcal{F}(T)$) and the density process of any $Q \approx P$ on $(\Omega, \mathcal{F})$:

$$\xi(t) = \widetilde{\xi}(t) \cdot \exp(-\int_0^t \eta(u)'\mathrm{d}W(u) - \tfrac{1}{2}\int_0^t \|\eta(u)\|^2 \mathrm{du})$$

(a strictly positive martingale on P), one has:

3.4 LEMMA. *$Q \in \mathcal{Q}$ if and only if it is of the form:* $Q(A) = E(1_A\xi_T) \; \forall A \in \mathcal{F}(T)$.

PROOF. Standard: adapt, for instance, proposition 1 p. 271 in He and Pearson (1991), or lemma 3.4 p. 429 in Shreve (1991) to the primitive price system (3.2). ∥

We shall have occasion to refer to all $Q \in \mathcal{Q}$ as *pricing measures* in the remainder. Because $\dim(\langle\sigma\rangle^\perp) = d - m$, (3.5) and lemma 3.4 show immediately that $\mathcal{Q}$ is a singleton if and only if $m = d$. As it will be seen in section 3.2.2, the case $m = d$ corresponds to the situation in which the security market model (3.2) is *complete*, which means that a trading strategy involving only the assets introduced in this subsection generates any $\mathcal{F}(T)$-measurable random variable. See the following subsection for more technical details.

These facts were established in a general setting by Harrison and Pliska (1983).

The so called Föllmer-Schweizer measure, or minimal martingale measure (Föllmer and Schweizer (1991)), has sometimes been of interest in the literature:

3.5 DEFINITION. The *minimal equivalent martingale measure* is defined to be: $\widetilde{Q}(A) \equiv E(1_A \widetilde{\xi}_T) \, \forall A \in \mathcal{F}(T)$.

In the stochastic volatility setting, the economic interpretation of $\widetilde{Q}$ is that the risk associated to the fluctuations of stochastic volatility is not compensated, which is the hypothesis made in the seminal paper of Hull and White (1987). For the mathematical interpretation, the minimal martingale measure is the one that minimizes the Kullback-Leibler distance, or relative entropy, of the objective measure P with respect to any $Q \in \mathcal{Q}$ (see the appendix). This kind of results was shown to hold by Föllmer and Schweizer (1991), in the unidimensional case, but in a context more general than that of Brownian information.

3.2.2 INCOMPLETENESS ISSUES

We formalize the concept of 'spanning' in the setting of this section. Heuristically, a set of securities is said to span a given vector space if any point in that space can be generated by a linear combination of the security prices. Here, spanning means that trading with a set of securities allows one to generate any $\mathcal{F}(T)$-random variable. Such a random variable can have the simple interpretation of the payoff of a contingent claim, a European claim in zero net supply say, or net consumption in a two-dates economy with a continuum of intermediate financial transaction dates à la Harrison and Kreps (1979) or Duffie and Huang (1985). Heuristically, we say that we face a complete markets model if there exist strategies that duplicate any $\mathcal{F}(T)$-random variable. Formally, if $V^{x,\pi}(t)$ denotes the solution of eq. (3.3) in correspondence of an initial capital equal to x, portfolio π, and $c \equiv 0$, spanning refers to the possibility that $V^{x,\pi}(T) = X$ a.s., where X is a square-integrable $\mathcal{F}(T)$-measurable random variable mapping Ω on to the real line.

As it is well known, the necessary and sufficient condition for market completeness here is that $m = d$. Let us see the sufficiency part. The solution of eq.(3.3) is:

$$((S^{(0)})^{-1} V^{x,\pi})(t) = x + \int_0^t ((S^{(0)})^{-1} \pi' \sigma)(u) dW^*(u),$$

where W^* is a new standard Brownian motion defined on Q^*, an arbitrary measure that belongs to $\mathcal{Q}$. For any $\widetilde{X} \in L^2(\Omega, \mathcal{F}, P)$, consider the Q^*-martingale

$$M(t) = E^{Q^*}((S^{(0)})^{-1}(T) \cdot \widetilde{X} \, / \, \mathcal{F}(t)). \tag{3.6}$$

By virtue of the representation theorem of continuous local martingales as stochastic integrals with respect to Brownian motions (e.g., Karatzas and Shreve (1991) (thm. 4.2 p. 170)), there exists $\varphi \in L^2_{0,T,d}(\Omega, \mathcal{F}, P)$ such that M can be written as:

$$M(t) = M(0) + \int_0^t \varphi(u)' dW^*(u) \quad \text{a.s. in } t \in [0, T].$$

Now consider the portfolio $\hat{\pi}' = S^{(0)}\varphi'\sigma^{-1}$. In terms of $\hat{\pi}$, M is:

$$
\begin{aligned}
M(t) &= M(0) + \int_0^t (S^{(0)})^{-1}\hat{\pi}'\sigma)(u)dW^*(u) \\
&= ((S^{(0)})^{-1}V^{M_0,\widehat{\pi}})(t) \quad \text{a.s. in } t \in [0,T].
\end{aligned}
$$

In particular,

$$
M(T) = ((S^{(0)})^{-1}V^{M_0,\widehat{\pi}})(T) \quad \text{a.s.}
$$

Comparing this with (3.6),

$$
V^{M_0,\widehat{\pi}}(T) = \tilde{X} \quad \text{a.s.}
$$

This is completeness.

In the preceding proof, the spanning property of a set of securities prices was checked by working directly with a (in fact, the only) measure that belongs to $\mathcal{Q}$. Equivalently, we can now take as a target the construction of a $\mathcal{F}(t)$-P-semimartingale. The reason of such a switching is that working directly with P enables us to produce results concerning the dynamics of some uninsurable risks (see theorem 3.8 below). In our setting, the starting point is the following representation of a $\mathcal{F}(t)$-P semimartingale:

$$
dA(t) = dF(t) + \tilde{\gamma}(t)dW(t), \tag{3.7}
$$

where F is a VF (*variation finie*) process and $\tilde{\gamma} \in L^2_{0,T,d}(\Omega, \mathcal{F}, P)$. As before, the problem is to look for the existence of a strategy π satisfying

$$
\tilde{\gamma}(t) = (\pi'\sigma)(t) \quad P \otimes dt\text{-a.s.}, \tag{3.8}
$$

for this is a condition for a self-financing strategy to duplicate A. Note that when the preceding condition is satisfied, one can also equate the drift of V with dF and obtain

$$
\frac{dF(t)}{dt} = \pi(t)'(\mu(t)-\mathbf{1}_m r(t))-r(t)V(t) = \pi(t)'(\mu(t)-\mathbf{1}_m r(t))-r(t)F(t), \tag{3.9}
$$

where the second equality follows from the fact that if drifts and diffusions terms of F and V are to be identical, then $F(t) = V(t)$ $P\otimes dt$-a.s.

When $m < d$, there are generically no candidate solutions for π. Economically, this implies that $V^{x,\pi}(T) \in M \subset L^2(\Omega, \mathcal{F}, P)$ when $m < d$. It is also possible to show the converse, and this motivates the popular definition:

3.6 DEFINITION. *The security market model (3.2) is complete if and only if* $m = d$.

3.2.3   MODELS COMPLETED BY NON-PRODUCTIVE ASSETS

Even though the security market model (3.2) were to be incomplete, the market structure to which agents could actually have access might be *completed* by the presence of non-productive assets in zero-net supply. Examples of non-productive assets include European options or bonds. The analysis of this chapter focusses on European-type contingent claims but a simple change in interpretation suffices to let this model include bonds, which is what we actually do in the next chapter.

The exact condition under which non-productive assets complete the market is that the augmented volatility matrix $\hat{\sigma} = (\ \sigma \quad \sigma_\ell\ )'$ is square and has full-rank; here σ_ℓ denotes the volatility matrix of the European contingent claims, and is defined similarly to σ. Such a condition is simple to interpret: rewrite the augmented price system as

$$
\begin{pmatrix} dS^{(1)}/S^{(1)} \\ ... \\ dS^{(m)}/S^{(m)} \\ dH^{(1)}/H^{(1)} \\ ... \\ dH^{(n)}/H^{(n)} \end{pmatrix} = \begin{pmatrix} \bar{\mu}_1 \\ ... \\ \bar{\mu}_m \\ \bar{\mu}_1 \\ ... \\ \bar{\mu}_n \end{pmatrix} dt + \hat{\sigma} dW, \ m+n = d, \tag{3.10}
$$

where $H^{(\cdot)}$ is the price of the .-th European contingent claim, and $\bar{\mu}^\ell \equiv (\bar{\mu}_1, ..., \bar{\mu}_n)'$ is defined as $\bar{\mu}$. Then the condition $\text{rank}(\hat{\sigma}) = d$ means that observing prices is equivalent to observing the sources of uncertainty of the economy.

When agents have access to an economy with a complete market structure, there is always a representative agent economy that supports the prices of the initial economy (see e.g. Huang (1987) for the diffusion case). Thus, under the condition $\text{rank}(\hat{\sigma}) = d$, we can average out without any loss of generality and pursue the analysis in terms of a representative agent. Our concern lies in describing the equilibrium restrictions on system (3.10) that are implied by the intertemporal preferences of such a representative agent. Notice that we are going to provide only heuristic but standard results; more technical details can be obtained by adapting here the analysis of Cox et al. (1985b). Furthermore, such an analysis makes use of standard dynamic programming techniques; see Fornari and Mele (1999a) for a restricted version of this model that is treated by means of martingale techniques.

The representative agent maximizes $\mathcal{J}(t, V(t), y(t)) \equiv \int_t^T u(c(u))du, \ t \equiv 0,$ under a generalized version of eq. (3.3) that also includes trading with the non productive assets; under mild technical conditions (such as assumption A9 p. 369 in Cox et al. (1985b)), as well as the equilibrium conditions in (3.4), one has the following first order conditions: $0 = u_c - \mathcal{J}_V$, and

$$
\begin{cases} \mathbf{0}_m = (\mu - \mathbf{1}_m r)\mathcal{J}_V + (\sigma\sigma'\pi + \sigma\sigma'_\ell\pi_\ell)\mathcal{J}_{VV} + \sigma\mathcal{J}'\mathcal{J}_{VY} \\ \mathbf{0}_m = (\mu^\ell - \mathbf{1}_n r)\mathcal{J}_V + (\sigma_\ell\sigma'_\ell\pi_\ell + \sigma_\ell\sigma'\pi)\mathcal{J}_{VV} + \sigma_\ell\mathcal{J}'\mathcal{J}_{VY} \end{cases} \tag{3.11}
$$

where π_ℓ is a n-dimensional vector process that includes wealth invested in the European claims, and fulfils the same properties as π. While the economic formulation followed her is more in the spirit of the discrete time Lucas' (1978) tree model, conditions (3.11) are qualitatively similar to the ones of Cox et al. (1985b).

In equilibrium $\pi = S$ and $\pi_\ell = 0$, and system (3.11) reduces to:

$$\begin{pmatrix} \mu - \mathbf{1}_m r \\ \mu^\ell - \mathbf{1}_n r \end{pmatrix} = \widehat{\sigma} \cdot \lambda \tag{3.12}$$

where

$$\lambda \equiv -(\sigma' S \frac{\mathcal{J}_{VV}}{\mathcal{J}_V} + J' \frac{\mathcal{J}_{VY}}{\mathcal{J}_V}). \tag{3.13}$$

This shows that the optimizing behavior of the representative agents *induces* the existence of a measure belonging to $\mathcal{Q}$. In particular, notice that the second relation in (3.12) completely characterizes the price of non-productive assets, such as options, but such prices are obviously not preference-free.

3.2.4 PARTIAL HEDGING STRATEGIES IN INCOMPLETE MARKETS: A BASIC EXAMPLE

The perspective that is going to be followed in the present subsection differs from the one of the previous subsection, for it focusses on what can be hedged when the security market model (3.2) is incomplete, rather than on what should be the price of the completing assets in a representative agent economy. Accordingly, now we come back to eq. (3.7). Our first concern consists in providing concrete examples of what can be a $\mathcal{F}(T)$-P-semimartingale in the diffusion state model of this section. Consider, for instance, the price process of a European contingent claim, a European call option say, and let $H(t)$ denote its price at t. A rationally formed price process of the claim is one that takes the form $H(t) = H(t, y(t))$. Provided $H \in \mathcal{C}^{1,2}([0,T) \times \mathbb{R}^k)$ it satisfies by Itô's lemma,

$$dH(t) = (\overline{\mu}^H H)(t)dt + (\frac{\partial H}{\partial Y} J)(t)dW(t), \tag{3.14}$$

where $\overline{\mu}^H H = \frac{\partial H}{\partial t} + \sum_{l=1}^k \frac{\partial H}{\partial y_l} \hbar_l(t, y) + \frac{1}{2} \sum_{l=1}^k \sum_{j=1}^k \frac{\partial^2 H}{\partial y_l \partial y_j} \mathrm{cov}(y_l, y_j)$, $\frac{\partial H}{\partial Y}$ is defined similarly to $\frac{\partial S^{(i)}}{\partial Y}$, and

$$H(T, y) = \widetilde{X}.$$

Here $\overline{\mu}^H H$ and $\frac{\partial H}{\partial Y} J$ play the roles played by $\frac{dF}{dt}$ and $\widetilde{\gamma}$ of subsection 3.2.2, and the volatility identification

$$(\frac{\partial H}{\partial Y} J)(t) = (\pi' \sigma)(t) \quad P \otimes dt\text{-a.s.}, \tag{3.15}$$

would correspond to relation (3.8). As an example, if the price of a stock is the only state variable of the economy, with $\hbar(.) = \mu S$, $\text{cov}(.) = \sigma^2 S^2$ (μ, σ^2 constants) and $m = d = 1$, then $\frac{\partial H}{\partial Y} J = \frac{\partial H}{\partial S} \sigma S$, $\pi = \frac{\partial H}{\partial S} S$, and by eq. (3.9),

$$\frac{\partial H}{\partial t} + \frac{\partial H}{\partial S} \mu S + \frac{1}{2} \frac{\partial^2 H}{\partial S^2} \sigma^2 S^2 = \pi(\mu - r) - rH = \frac{\partial H}{\partial S} S(\mu - r) - rH.$$

This is the partial differential equation followed by the arbitrage free price of a derivative security. Imposing the boundary condition of a European call option $H(T, s) = (s - K)^+$ (where K is the strike), one obtains that the solution is the celebrated Black and Scholes (1973) formula:

$$
\begin{aligned}
H(t, S(t)) &= S(t)\phi(d_1) - Ke^{-r(T-t)}\phi(d_2), \\
d_1 &= \frac{\log(S(t)/K) + (r + \sigma^2/2)(T-t)}{\sigma(T-t)^{1/2}}, \quad d_2 = d_1 - \sigma(T-t)^{1/2}, \quad (3.16) \\
\phi(x) &= \frac{1}{(2\pi)^{1/2}} \int_{-\infty}^{x} e^{-u^2/2} du.
\end{aligned}
$$

As noted in subsection 3.2.2, relations such as (3.15) generically fail to hold in the incomplete markets case $m < d$. Yet, for each t, we might consider the best approximation (in projection terms) of $\frac{\partial H}{\partial Y} J$

$$\widetilde{\pi}(t) = \arg \min_{\pi \in L^2_{0,T,m}(\Omega, \mathcal{F}, P)} (J' \frac{\partial H'}{\partial Y} - \sigma'\pi)(t)' \cdot (J' \frac{\partial H'}{\partial Y} - \sigma'\pi)(t),$$

which also minimizes pointwise

$$\widetilde{\mathcal{H}}_0^T(\pi) \equiv E(\int_0^T \left\| (\frac{\partial H}{\partial Y} J)(t) - (\pi'\sigma)(t) \right\|^2 dt).$$

$\widetilde{\mathcal{H}}_0^T(\pi)$ can be considered as a sort of (non-monetary) loss due to the (generic) impossibility of a perfect hedge in an incomplete market setting. We shall denote the value of this problem as

$$\mathcal{H}_0^T \equiv \widetilde{\mathcal{H}}_0^T(\widetilde{\pi}).$$

The solution of the program is

$$\widetilde{\pi}(t)' = (\frac{\partial H}{\partial Y} J\sigma'(\sigma\sigma')^{-1})(t). \quad (3.17)$$

When (μ, σ) are also deterministic, which is obviously not the case here, we could follow Schweizer (1992) (p. 177) and notice that $\widetilde{\pi}$ can be interpreted as the pure hedging demand component of the feedback-form solution[4]

$$\pi^*(t) = \widetilde{\pi}(t) + ((\sigma\sigma')^{-1}(\mu - \mathbf{1}r))(t) \cdot \delta(t), \quad \delta(t) \equiv H(t) - V^*(t) \equiv H(t) - V^{\pi^*}(t)$$

---

[4] π^* has been obtained by exploiting the inner product associated with the normal equations for orthogonal projection, as originally suggested by Duffie and Richardson (1991), and by exploiting the FS-type decomposition given in thm. 3.8 below, as in Schweizer (1992).

of the general self-financing problem

$$\min_{\pi \in L^2_{0,T,m}(\Omega,\mathcal{F},P)} E(\widetilde{X} - V^{x,\pi}(T))^2. \tag{3.18}$$

We shall limit attention to (3.17), and slightly generalize Hofmann et al. (1992) (p. 158) by defining a strategy by relation (3.17) and

$$(\theta^{(0)}S^{(0)})(t) = H(t) - \widetilde{\pi}(t)'\mathbf{1}_m, \quad t \in [0,T]. \tag{3.19}$$

For each $t \in [0,T)$, the value of such a portfolio is $H(t)$, and $\widetilde{X}$ a.s. for $t = T$. Yet, the *cumulative hedging cost*, defined as

$$C(t) \equiv H(t) - \sum_{i=0}^{m} \int_0^t (\widetilde{\theta}^{(i)} dS^{(i)})(u), \ t \in [0,T],$$

is not a constant as in the case of complete markets: $\widetilde{\pi}$ is not self-financing.[5] Aim of section 3.4 is to provide results establishing under which conditions the strategy defined by (3.17) and (3.19)—simply referred to as $\widetilde{\pi}$ in the remainder— is 'mean'-self-financing strategy, i.e., 'self-financing in average': see section 3.4, definition 3.11, for a more technical definition. To anticipate the results, we show that under a natural assumption on H (see assumption 3.7 below), $\widetilde{\pi}$ is Z-mean-self-financing for all measures $Z \in \mathcal{Q}$, and P-mean-self-financing if and only if the 'true' pricing measure is the minimal martingale measure.[6]

In this section we shall focus on a decomposition of a European contingent claim process that is useful mainly for interpretative purposes. Such a decomposition is obtained by making use of $\widetilde{\pi}$ and a special assumption (assumption 3.7). Our results are inspired by and large by previous work of Hofmann et al. (1992). However, Hofmann et al. (1992) do not write π in any closed-form solution and in fact, by using $\widetilde{\pi}$, we are parametrizing (see, also, remark 3.9(2) below).[7] Furthermore, by using (3.17), we shall give more information about the dynamics of the contingent claim price than Hofmann et al. (1992). Specifically, (3.17) will help making the theory interpretable in terms of the first primitives of the model. The following section contains the main applications to the central theme of this book.

The special assumption of this section is that the discounted price process of the European contingent claim behaves like the primitive asset prices under all the equivalent martingale measures:

---

[5]Notice that the standard $(\theta^{(0)}S^{(0)})(t) = V(t) - \widetilde{\pi}(t)'\mathbf{1}_m$ would make the corresponding strategy self-financing, but the probability that the value of (3.18) is positive would be obviously strictly positive in this case.

[6]When markets are incomplete, absence of arbitrage opportunities can only provide a set of economically admissible prices. We are assuming that the "true", unknown price of the contingent claim is induced by an (unknown *but*) unique pricing measure belonging to $\mathcal{Q}$—possibly induced by the preferences of the agents—.

[7]An early parametric example resembling (3.17) was provided by Schweizer (1992) (p. 178 form. (4.4)), and see He and Pearson (1991) (thm. 7 p. 287-288) for related work.

3.7 ASSUMPTION. Q *is also the set of martingale measures that are equivalent to* P *on* $(\Omega, \mathcal{F})$ *for* $\overline{H} \equiv \frac{H}{S^{(0)}}$.

Under mild regularity conditions, $\overline{H} \equiv \frac{H}{S^{(0)}}$ is a $(Q \in \mathcal{Q})$-martingale when markets are complete, or may be completed thanks to a certain number of non-primitive assets, as seen in the previous subsection. When markets are incomplete, however, H can not be duplicated with a self-financing strategy and, in the terminology of Hofmann et al. (1992) (p. 164), the preceding assumption makes the claim a 'compatible asset'.

The following result is related to the Föllmer-Schweizer decomposition of H (see comments at the beginning of section 3.4), and represents the state-variables equivalent of Hofmann et al. (1992):

3.8 THEOREM. *Let assumption 3.7 hold. Then, for each* $t \in [0, T]$, *the following decomposition holds:*

$$H(t) = H(t, \widetilde{\pi}) + H^c(t, \widetilde{\pi}), \qquad (3.20)$$

where $H(\widetilde{\pi})$ *and* $H^c(\widetilde{\pi})$ *are solutions of the following stochastic differential equations:*

$$\begin{cases} \mathrm{d}H(t, \widetilde{\pi}) &= (\widetilde{\pi}(t)'(\mu(t) - \mathbf{1}_m r(t)) + H(t)r(t))\mathrm{d}t + (\widetilde{\pi}'\sigma)(t)\mathrm{d}W(t) \\ \mathrm{d}H^c(t, \widetilde{\pi}) &= (\frac{\partial H}{\partial Y} J \eta)(t)\mathrm{d}t + (\frac{\partial H}{\partial Y} J)(t) \cdot (\mathbf{I}_{d \times d} - (\sigma'(\sigma\sigma')^{-1}\sigma)(t))\mathrm{d}W(t) \end{cases} \qquad (3.21)$$

where $\eta \in \langle \sigma \rangle^{\perp}$.

PROOF. We start by writing $J' \frac{\partial H}{\partial Y}'$ as the sum of two components. The first one is

$$(\sigma'\widetilde{\pi})(t) = (\sigma'(\sigma\sigma')^{-1}\sigma)(t) \cdot (J' \frac{\partial H}{\partial Y}')(t),$$

and the second one is

$$w(t) = (\mathbf{I}_{d \times d} - (\sigma'(\sigma\sigma')^{-1}\sigma)(t)) \cdot (J' \frac{\partial H}{\partial Y}')(t).$$

By the Itô's lemma applied to $\frac{H}{S^{(0)}}$, and the preceding decomposition of $\frac{\partial H}{\partial Y} J$,

$$\begin{aligned} \mathrm{d}\overline{H}(t) &= (\overline{\mu}^H \overline{H} - \overline{H} r)(t)\mathrm{d}t + \frac{1}{S^{(0)}(t)}(\frac{\partial H}{\partial Y} J)(t)\mathrm{d}W(t) \\ &= (\overline{\mu}^H \overline{H} - \overline{H} r)(t)\mathrm{d}t + \frac{1}{S^{(0)}(t)}(\widetilde{\pi}'\sigma)(t)\mathrm{d}W(t) + \frac{1}{S^{(0)}(t)}w(t)'\mathrm{d}W(t) \end{aligned}$$

Next, let $\lambda \in \mathcal{P}$. By the Girsanov's theorem (e.g., Karatzas and Shreve (1991) (thm. 5.1 p. 191)), the definition of $\mathcal{P}$ and lemma 3.4, and the fact that $w \in$

$\langle \sigma \rangle^{\perp}$,

$$
\begin{aligned}
d\overline{H}(t) &= (\overline{\mu}^H \overline{H} - \overline{H}r - \tfrac{1}{S^{(0)}}\widetilde{\pi}'\sigma\lambda - \tfrac{1}{S^{(0)}}w'\lambda)(t)dt + \tfrac{1}{S^{(0)}(t)}(\widetilde{\pi}'\sigma)(t)dW^*(t) \\
&\quad + \tfrac{1}{S^{(0)}(t)}w(t)'dW^*(t) \\
&= (\overline{\mu}^H \overline{H} - \overline{H}r - \tfrac{1}{S^{(0)}}\widetilde{\pi}'\sigma\widetilde{\lambda} - \tfrac{1}{S^{(0)}}w'\eta)(t)dt + \tfrac{1}{S^{(0)}(t)}(\widetilde{\pi}'\sigma)(t)dW^*(t) \\
&\quad + \tfrac{1}{S^{(0)}(t)}w(t)'dW^*(t)
\end{aligned}
$$

where $\eta \in \langle \sigma \rangle^{\perp}$ and W^* is a $(Q \in \mathcal{Q})$-$\mathcal{F}(t)$-Brownian motion. Hence, by assumption 3.7 and the preceding relation we get that:

$$
\begin{aligned}
(\overline{\mu}^H H)(t) &= H(t)r(t) + (\widetilde{\pi}'\sigma\widetilde{\lambda})(t) + (w'\eta)(t) \\
&= H(t)r(t) + \widetilde{\pi}(t)'(\mu(t) - \mathbf{1}r(t)) + (w'\eta)(t).
\end{aligned}
$$

Substituting this into eq. (3.14), making use of the definition of w, and the fact that $\eta \in \langle \sigma \rangle^{\perp}$ yield the result. $\|$

3.9 REMARKS. (1) $\sigma'\widetilde{\pi} = \sigma'(\sigma\sigma')^{-1}\sigma J'\frac{\partial H}{\partial Y}'$ is the orthogonal projection in $\mathbb{R}^m$ of $J'\frac{\partial H}{\partial Y}'$ onto the space generated by the rows of σ. It represents a sort of 'hedged volatility', or that part of the contingent claim price volatility which can be hedged by $\widetilde{\pi}$-trading in the existing primitive assets. w is instead an 'intrinsic risk' which is only inherent to an incomplete market setting. In fact, if $m = d$, w is the zero process, $\widetilde{\pi}$ coincides with the standard Black-Scholes type hedging and $\mathcal{H}_0^T = 0$. Yet, in the incomplete markets case, $\mathcal{H}_0^T = E(\int_0^T \|w(t)\|^2 dt) > 0$.

(2) As noted before, Hofmann et al. (1992) leave π unspecified; they only represent the contingent claim volatility in its orthogonal decomposition: $\widetilde{\gamma} = v + \sigma'\pi$ for some $v \in \langle \sigma \rangle^{\perp}$ (our notation), where $\widetilde{\gamma}$ is as in eq. (3.7).

(3) The cumulative hedging cost process satisfies: $C(t) \equiv H(t) - \sum_{i=0}^m \int_0^t (\widetilde{\theta}^{(i)} dS^{(i)})(u) = H(t) - H(t, \widetilde{\pi}) = H^c(t, \widetilde{\pi})$, $t \in [0, T]$.

3.3 Applications to stochastic volatility

A well-known specialization of the framework of the previous section is the one in which the state space is resumed by the dynamics of two state variables, namely the price of one primitive asset and its instantaneous volatility, which will be denoted as ν. In this section, then, the two state variables are (S, ν), and the primitive market model is incomplete because there is obviously only one primitive asset.

3.3.1 FEYNMAN-KAC REPRESENTATION OF THE SOLUTION(S)

The primitive is a stock price process solution of the following stochastic differential equation system

$$
\begin{aligned}
dS(t) &= S(t) \cdot (\bar{\mu}(S(t))dt + \bar{\sigma}(t)dW^{(1)}(t)) \\
d\nu(t) &= \bar{\varphi}(\bar{\sigma}(t))dt + \bar{\psi}(\bar{\sigma}(t))d(\rho W^{(1)}(t) + (1 - \rho^2)^{1/2}W^{(2)}(t))
\end{aligned}
\tag{3.22}
$$

where ν is a non-decreasing, continuously differentiable function of $\bar{\sigma}$ and $\bar{\mu}(.)$, $\bar{\varphi}(.)$ and $\bar{\psi}(.)$ are progressively $\mathcal{F}(t)$-measurable functions as in (3.1). Finally, we simplify and take ρ to be a constant with modulus strictly less than one.

The European contingent claim rational price process is of the form

$$
H = H(t, S(t), \nu(t)).
$$

Let $\mathcal{D}^*[.]$ be the Dynkin operator taken with respect to system (3.22). Under the same conditions of the previous subsection, H is the solution of the following stochastic differential equation

$$
\begin{aligned}
dH(t) &= \mathcal{D}^*[H]dt + (\frac{\partial H}{\partial S}\sigma S)(t)dW^{(1)}(t) \\
&+ (\frac{\partial H}{\partial \nu}\bar{\psi})(t)d(\rho W^{(1)}(t) + (1 - \rho^2)^{1/2}W^{(2)}(t))
\end{aligned}
$$

with terminal condition

$$
H(T, x, y) = \tilde{X} \quad \forall (x, y) \in \mathbb{R}^2_{++}.
\tag{3.23}
$$

We mantain assumption 3.7. Let $\widehat{W}^{(j)}(t) = W^{(j)}(t) + \int_0^t du \lambda^{(j)}(u)$, $j = 1, 2$, where $\lambda = \{\lambda(t) = (\lambda^{(1)}(t), \lambda^{(2)}(t))'\}_{t \in [0,T]}$ is a $\mathcal{F}(t)$-adapted process that satisfies

$$
\int_0^t du \cdot \|\lambda(u)\|^2 < \infty \quad P\text{-a.s.}
$$

By the Girsanov's theorem, $\widehat{W}$ is a standard Brownian motion under a new probability measure Q with Radon-Nikodym derivative with respect to P on $\mathcal{F}_T$ given by

$$
\frac{dQ}{dP} = \exp(-\int_0^T \lambda(u)'dW_u - \frac{1}{2}\int_0^T du \cdot \|\lambda(u)\|^2),
$$

and the previous integrability condition on λ accommodates the Novikov's condition which makes Q be well defined.

Under the new measure, system (3.22) is solution of

$$
\begin{aligned}
dS(t) &= S(t) \cdot (\bar{\mu} - \bar{\sigma}\lambda^{(1)})(t)dt + \bar{\sigma}(t)d\widehat{W}^{(1)}(t)) \\
d\nu &= (\bar{\varphi} - \bar{\psi}(\rho\lambda^{(1)} + (1 - \rho^2)^{1/2}\lambda^{(2)}))(t)dt \\
&+ \bar{\psi}(t)d(\rho\widehat{W}^{(1)}(t) + (1 - \rho^2)^{1/2}\widehat{W}^{(2)}(t))
\end{aligned}
\tag{3.24}
$$

and H is solution of

$$dH = (\mathcal{D}^*[H] - \tfrac{\partial H}{\partial S}\overline{\sigma}S\lambda^{(1)} - \tfrac{\partial H}{\partial v}\overline{\psi}(\rho\lambda^{(1)} + (1-\rho^2)^{1/2}\lambda^{(2)}))(t)dt$$
$$+ (\tfrac{\partial H}{\partial S}\overline{\sigma}S)(t)d\widehat{W}^{(1)}(t) + (\tfrac{\partial H}{\partial v}\overline{\psi})(t)d(\rho\widehat{W}^{(1)}(t) + (1-\rho^2)^{1/2}\widehat{W}^{(2)}(t)).$$

If $Q \in \mathcal{Q}$, it must be the case that

$$\begin{cases} r(t) &= \mu(t) - (\ \overline{\sigma}(t) \quad 0\ )(\ \lambda^{(1)}(t) \quad \lambda^{(2)}(t)\ )' \equiv \mu(t) - \sigma(t)\lambda(t) \\ \mathcal{D}[H] &= r(t)H(t) \end{cases}$$

$$(3.25)$$

where

$$\begin{aligned} \mathcal{D}[.] &\equiv \mathcal{D}^*[.] - \overline{\sigma}S\lambda^{(1)}\tfrac{\partial}{\partial S}. - \overline{\psi}(\rho\lambda^{(1)} + (1-\rho^2)^{1/2}\lambda^{(2)})\tfrac{\partial}{\partial v}. \\ &= \mathcal{D}^*[.] - (\mu - r)(S\tfrac{\partial}{\partial S}. + \tfrac{\psi}{\overline{\sigma}}\rho\tfrac{\partial}{\partial v}.) - \overline{\psi}(1-\rho^2)^{1/2}\lambda^{(2)}\tfrac{\partial}{\partial v}., \end{aligned}$$

and by the Feynman-Kac representation (e.g., Karatzas and Shreve (1991) (thm. 7.6 p. 366)) of the solution of the partial differential equation in (3.25)— with (3.23) as boundary condition—, one has:

$$H(t) = E^Q(\frac{S^{(0)}(t)}{S^{(0)}(T)} \cdot \widetilde{X} \ / \ \mathcal{F}(t)), \quad Q \in \mathcal{Q}.$$

Here $card(\mathcal{Q}) = \infty$ since the solution to the first equation in (3.25) is indeterminate: there exists an infinity of rational pricing functions that are consistent with absence of arbitrage opportunities.

To caracterize $\mathcal{Q}$, we proceed as in section 3.2: $\mathcal{P}$ can be written here as

$$\mathcal{P} = \left\{ \lambda \ / \ \lambda(t) = \widetilde{\lambda}(t) + \eta(t), \ \eta \in \langle\sigma\rangle^\perp \right\}, \tag{3.26}$$

where the risk-premia process inducing the minimal equivalent martingale measure is

$$\widetilde{\lambda}(t) = (\sigma'(\sigma\sigma')^{-1})(t) \cdot (\mu(t) - r(t)) = (\ \tfrac{\mu(t)-r(t)}{\overline{\sigma}(t)} \quad 0\ )',$$

which is bounded since v is bounded. As announced in the previous section, agents do not demand a risk premium to be compensated for the fluctuations of stochastic volatility under the minimal martingale measure.

To determine the volatility risk-premium within the framework of section 3.2.3, one simply adapts formula (3.13) to the model of this section and obtains:

$$\lambda^{(2)} = \overline{\psi}(1-\rho^2)^{1/2}\frac{\mathcal{J}_{Vv}}{\mathcal{J}_V}.$$

Such a result is known since at least Wiggins (1987). In the Heston (1993b) specification, for instance, $\overline{\psi}(\rho\lambda^{(1)} + (1-\rho^2)^{1/2}\lambda^{(2)}) \propto \overline{\sigma}^2$, where $\overline{\psi}$ was proportional to $\overline{\sigma}$, $\overline{\varphi}$ affine and $v = \overline{\sigma}^2$, which implies that the drift function of volatility is linear under the risk neutral measure, but the preceding formula also suggests to take a general approach.

In Fornari and Mele (1999b), we take a data-oriented approach in which we propose to estimate the risk premium by making use of cross-sectional information given by observed option prices. Precisely, we took $\nu(t) = \sigma(t)^\delta$, $\overline{\varphi}(t) = \overline{\omega} - \varphi\sigma(t)^\delta$, $\overline{\psi}(t) = \psi\sigma(t)^\delta$, where $a = (\delta, \varphi, \overline{\omega}, \psi, \rho)$ are real paramaters: notice that this is exactly the model in correspondence of which we produced approximation results in the previous chapter. After estimating a by only using time series returns, with the methods described in chapter 5, we calibrated the volatility risk premium which generates dynamics of the primitive asset price and volatility with the aim of matching as closely as possible observed cross-sections of option prices. While the identification of the risk premium can be done through a representative agent argument, as before, we assumed that it could be represented by means of a polynomial structure. This idea follows from $\lambda^{(2)}$ being measurable with respect to the filtration of $(W^{(1)}, W^{(2)})$ and, further, by combining a result of Harrison and Kreps (1979) with Romano and Touzi (1997), from the circumstance that the filtration of $(W^{(1)}, W^{(2)})$ and the filtration of (S, σ) must coincide: then $\lambda^{(2)}$ is a functional of past and current values of (S, σ). We restricted attention to a Markovian structure and took $\lambda^{(2)}(t) = \Lambda(S(t), \sigma(t))$, where

$$\begin{aligned}\Lambda(S(t), \sigma(t)) &= p_1 + p_2\sigma(t)^\delta + p_3\sigma(t)^{2\delta} + p_4\sigma(t)^{-\delta}\\ &\quad + p_5 S(t) + p_6 S(t)^2 + p_7 S(t)^{-1} + p_8 S(t)\sigma(t)^\delta\end{aligned}$$

and $\vartheta = (p_i)_{i=1}^8$ are real parameters to be estimated. We called Λ *volatility risk premium surface*.

To estimate ϑ, one can simulate system (3.24) up to maturities $T = [T_1,..., T_{N_1}]$, where T matches the maturities of observed cross-sections of traded options. In practice, one simulates with a being fixed at the estimates obtained via time series information. For each simulation i, the call prices are evaluated for the observed strike prices as $C_{j,T_\ell}(\vartheta) = \frac{1}{sim}e^{-r(T_\ell - t)}\sum_{i=1}^{sim}(S_{T_\ell, i}(\vartheta) - K_j)^+$, where $S_{T_\ell, i}(\vartheta)$ denotes the price at T_ℓ at the i-th simulation obtained with the parameter vector ϑ, K_j is the strike K_j-th strike $(j = 1, ..., N_2)$ and sim is the number of simulations. The measure of distance between observed and simulation-based prices can be constructed as $D(\vartheta) = \sum_{\ell=1}^{N_1}\sum_{i=1}^{N_2}(C_{i,T_\ell} - C_{i,T_\ell}(\vartheta))^2$, where C_{i,T_ℓ} denotes the observed option price. An estimator of ϑ is $\arg\min_\vartheta[D(\vartheta)]$.

A recent paper related to ours is Chernov and Ghysels (1999). The authors apply EMM techniques (see section 5.3 in chapter 5) and estimate the parameters of the Heston's (1993b) model which, as noted above, implies a linear drift function of the volatility process under the risk neutral measure. Figure 3.1 depicts the shape of the volatility risk premium that we estimated in Fornari and Mele (1999b). The estimates were obtained with data covering the period from December 18, 1995 to January 31, 1997 and referring to 7,621 prices of options on Italian bond futures with moneyness ranging between 0.97 and 1.03 and maturities ranging between 21 and 147 days. The volatility risk premium curve we fitted had the following form: $\Lambda(S, s) \equiv p_1 + p_2 s^\delta + p_3 s^{2\delta} + p_4 s^{-\delta}$.

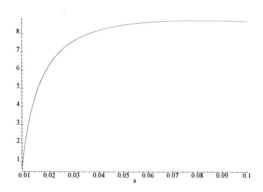

FIGURE 3.1. Volatility risk premium curve

3.3.2   INSPECTING THE MECHANISM: HEDGING COST PROCESSES AND DECOMPOSITION FORMULAE

In the stochastic volatility setting, $\frac{\partial H}{\partial Y} = (\; H_S \quad H_\nu \;)$,

$$J = \begin{pmatrix} \overline{\sigma} S & 0 \\ \overline{\psi}\rho & \overline{\psi}(1 - \rho^2)^{1/2} \end{pmatrix},$$

and $\widetilde{\pi}$ is the strategy that best approximates (in projection terms) the volatility vector $\frac{\partial H}{\partial Y} J = (\; H_S \overline{\sigma} S + H_\nu \overline{\psi}\rho \quad H_\nu \overline{\psi}(1 - \rho^2)^{1/2} \;)$, where $H_x \equiv \frac{\partial H}{\partial x}$. Recalling that $\sigma = (\; \overline{\sigma} \quad 0 \;)$, the solution (3.17) writes here

$$
\begin{aligned}
\widetilde{\pi}(t) &= (\frac{\partial H}{\partial Y} J)(t) \cdot (\sigma'(\sigma\sigma')^{-1})(t) \\
&= (\frac{\partial H}{\partial Y} J)(t)(\; \overline{\sigma}(t)^{-1} \quad 0 \;)' \\
&= (H_S S + H_\nu \overline{\psi}\rho\overline{\sigma}^{-1})(t).
\end{aligned}
$$

The hedging demand arises from two sources of change in the investment opportunity set. It is partly related to the standard Black-Scholes hedging rule (but with H being here different from the Black-Scholes function), and partly related to the fluctuations of the contingent claim price volatility that are most highly correlated with the fluctuations of the volatility of the volatility.

As concerns the decomposition of theorem 3.8, $H(t, \widetilde{\pi})$ satisfies

$$\mathrm{d}H(t, \widetilde{\pi}) = ((H_S S + H_\nu \overline{\psi}\rho\overline{\sigma}^{-1})(\mu - r) + rH)(t)\mathrm{d}t + (H_S S\overline{\sigma} + H_\nu \overline{\psi}\rho)(t)\mathrm{d}W^{(1)}(t).$$

The intrinsic risk is computed as

$$w(t) = (\frac{\partial H}{\partial Y} J(\mathbf{I}_{2\times 2} - \sigma'(\sigma\sigma')^{-1}\sigma))(t)' = (\; 0 \quad (H_\nu \overline{\psi}(1 - \rho^2)^{1/2})(t) \;)',$$

and, by virtue of remark 3.9(3), the cumulative hedging cost process under $\tilde{\pi}$ satisfies:

$$
\begin{aligned}
dC(t) &= (\ (H_S\bar{\sigma}S + H_\nu\bar{\psi}\rho)(t) \quad (H_\nu\bar{\psi}(1-\rho^2)^{1/2})(t)\ )\eta(t)dt \\
&\quad + (H_\nu\bar{\psi}(1-\rho^2)^{1/2})(t)dW^{(2)}(t), \ \eta \in \langle\sigma\rangle^\perp.
\end{aligned}
$$

Notice that

$$
\eta \in \langle\sigma\rangle^\perp \iff \eta_1\bar{\sigma} = 0 \iff \eta_1 = 0 \quad P \otimes dt\text{-a.s.},
$$

which shows that η must be of the form:

$$
\eta(t) = (\ 0 \quad \eta_2(t)\ )',
$$

for all $\eta_2 \in L^2_{0,T,1}(\Omega, \mathcal{F}, P)$

3.10 REMARK. By the definition of $\mathcal{P}$ (see (3.26)) and lemma 3.4, and the fact that $\tilde{\lambda}^{(2)} = 0$, one has that $\lambda^{(2)} = \eta_2$.

The dynamics of the $\tilde{\pi}$-hedging is thus:

$$
dC(t) = (H_\nu\bar{\psi}(1-\rho^2)^{1/2}\lambda^{(2)})(t)dt + (H_\nu\bar{\psi}(1-\rho^2)^{1/2})(t)dW^{(2)}(t).
$$

Finally, we note that

$$
\mathcal{H}^t_s(\tilde{\pi}) = E(\textstyle\int_s^t \|w(u)\|^2\, du\ /\ \mathcal{F}(s)) = E(\textstyle\int_s^t ((H_\nu\bar{\psi})^2(1-\rho^2))(u)du\ /\ \mathcal{F}(s)),
$$

and by defining

$$
\partial\mathcal{H}(s) \equiv \left.\frac{\partial}{\partial t}\mathcal{H}^t_s\right|_{t=s} = ((H_\nu\bar{\psi})^2(1-\rho^2))(s),
$$

then it holds that

$$
dC(t) = \lambda^{(2)}(t) \cdot (\partial\mathcal{H}(t))^{1/2} \cdot dt + (\partial\mathcal{H}(t))^{1/2}dW^{(2)}(t) \tag{3.27}
$$

This shows, in particular, that the conditional variance of the cumulative hedging cost process is in fact the $\tilde{\pi}$-loss due to market incompleteness:

$$
\text{var}(H^c(t, \tilde{\pi})\ /\ \mathcal{F}(0)) = \mathcal{H}^t_0.
$$

3.4 On mean self-financing strategies and the minimal martingale measure

Eq. (3.27) shows that the cumulative hedging cost is a martingale under P if and only if the true pricing measure is the minimal martingale measure.

This claim follows directly from lemma 3.4 and in fact extends to the general case treated in theorem 3.8. To heuristically see that such an extension holds indeed, inspect the way used to show thm. 3.8 and notice that η is inducing the true (unknown) pricing measure (along the lines of lemma 3.4). Such a key observation is missing in Hofmann et al. (1992), and now we wish to provide a further rigorous check of it. This check takes two steps. In the first step (lemma 3.12), it will be shown that the drift of the cumulative hedging cost process is identically zero under any candidate $Q \in \mathcal{Q}$. In the second step (lemma 3.14), it will be shown that the phenomenon described in lemma 3.12 is explained by the fact that η induces the (true) pricing measure in the drift defined under the primitive measure space. The desired extension will thus be the object of corollary 3.15. Finally we prove that the cumulative hedging cost arising from $\tilde{\pi}$ is a martingale if and only if $\tilde{Q}$ is the true martingale measure (theorem 3.16). Remark 3.9(3) and theorem 3.16 thus provide a possible sense in which the existence of a Föllmer-Schweizer -type decomposition:

$$\widetilde{X} = H(0) + \int_0^T \sum_{i=0}^m \widetilde{\theta}^{(i)}(t) dS^{(i)}(t) + L^H(T)$$

(where L^H is a local P-martingale orthogonal to $\int \sum \widetilde{\theta}^{(i)} dS^{(i)}$) is to be related with the minimal martingale measure.

We start with the following definition.

3.11 DEFINITION. Let Z be a probability measure on $(\Omega, \mathcal{F})$. $\tilde{\pi}$ is Z-mean-self-financing if the resulting cumulative hedging cost process $\{C(t)\}_{t \in [0,T]}$ is a martingale under Z.

We have:

3.12 LEMMA. *Let assumption 3.7 hold. Then, $\tilde{\pi}$ is Q-mean-self-financing under all measures $Q \in \mathcal{Q}$.*

PROOF. If W^* is a standard Brownian motion under $Q \in \mathcal{Q}$, and $\eta \in \langle \sigma \rangle^\perp$ (as in (3.5)), then, by the Girsanov's theorem, C is the solution of the following stochastic differential equation:

$$
\begin{aligned}
-dC(t) &= (\tilde{\pi}'(\mu - \mathbf{1}_m r) + rH - \overline{\mu}^H H + w'\lambda)(t)dt - w'dW^*(t) \\
&= (\tfrac{\partial H}{\partial Y} J\widetilde{\lambda} + rH - \overline{\mu}^H H - \tilde{\pi}'\sigma\lambda + \tfrac{\partial H}{\partial Y} J\lambda)(t)dt - w(t)'dW^*(t) \\
&= (\tfrac{\partial H}{\partial Y} J\widetilde{\lambda} + rH - \overline{\mu}^H H - \tilde{\pi}'\sigma\widetilde{\lambda} + \tfrac{\partial H}{\partial Y} J(\widetilde{\lambda} + \eta))(t)dt \\
&\qquad\qquad\qquad\qquad\qquad\qquad\qquad\qquad -w(t)'dW^*(t) \\
&= (2\tfrac{\partial H}{\partial Y} J\widetilde{\lambda} + rH - \overline{\mu}^H H - \tfrac{\partial H}{\partial Y} J\sigma'(\sigma\sigma')^{-1}\sigma\widetilde{\lambda} + \tfrac{\partial H}{\partial Y} J\eta)(t)dt \\
&\qquad\qquad\qquad\qquad\qquad\qquad\qquad\qquad -w(t)'dW^*(t) \\
&= (rH - \overline{\mu}^H H + \tfrac{\partial H}{\partial Y} J(\widetilde{\lambda} + \eta))(t)dt - w(t)'dW^*(t)
\end{aligned}
$$

under Q. In the preceding relations, the first line follows from (3.14), (3.20), (3.21) and remark 3.9(3); the second line follows from the definition of $\widetilde{\lambda}$, the solution for $\widetilde{\pi}$ and the definition of w given during the course of the proof of thm. 3.8; the third line follows from lemma 3.4; the fourth line follows from the solution for $\widetilde{\pi}$, and the fifth again from the definition of $\widetilde{\lambda}$.

The result now follows directly from assumption 3.7. ||

Hofmann et al. (1992) (p. 168) conjecture that the minimal martingale measure "will in general not be a martingale measure for the non-tradable assets", or $H^c(\widetilde{\pi})$ (our notation). The previous result shows that not only does the cumulative hedging cost process become a martingale under the minimal martingale measure, it even is a martingale under *all* candidate measures $Q \in \mathcal{Q}$. Notice that lemma 3.12 obtains with essentially the same assumptions as those in Hofmann et al. (1992).

We now turn to our program stated before definition 3.11.

Theorem 3.8 and the Girsanov's theorem, lemma 3.4, and finally the definition of w, respectively, inform us that the dynamics of the cumulative hedging cost process is also given by:[8]

$$
\begin{aligned}
dC(t) &= (\frac{\partial H}{\partial Y}J\eta - w'\lambda^{**})(t)dt + w(t)'dW^{**}(t), \\
&= (\frac{\partial H}{\partial Y}J(\eta - \eta^{**}))(t)dt + w(t)'dW^{**}(t), \quad \eta, \eta^{**} \in \langle \sigma \rangle^{\perp}, \quad (3.28)
\end{aligned}
$$

under an arbitrary measure $Q^{**} \in \mathcal{Q}$; here $W^{**} \equiv W + \int(\widetilde{\lambda} + \eta^{**})dt$ is a Brownian motion under Q^{**} and accordingly $\lambda^{**} \in \mathcal{P}$. By virtue of lemma 3.12, however, it must be the case that

$$
(\frac{\partial H}{\partial Y}J(\eta - \eta^{**}))(t) = 0, \quad \eta, \eta^{**} \in \langle \sigma \rangle^{\perp}, \qquad (3.29)
$$

if Q^{**} is to be the pricing measure. We claim that this is possible only when:

$$
\eta = \eta^{**}, \qquad (3.30)
$$

but before providing the formal proof, we wish to present heuristics based on informal economic arguments, and an example.

The arguments run as follows. Because $\frac{H}{S(0)}$ is a Q-martingale ($Q \in \mathcal{Q}$), H is the solution of:

$$
rH - \mu^H H + \frac{\partial H}{\partial Y}J(\widetilde{\lambda} + \eta_1) = 0 \qquad (3.31)
$$

---

[8]The second line of eq. (3.28) follows from the fact that $\widetilde{\lambda} = \sigma'(\sigma\sigma')^{-1}\sigma\widetilde{\lambda}$ and:

$$
\begin{aligned}
w'\lambda^{**} &= \frac{\partial H}{\partial Y}J(\mathbf{I}_{d\times d} - \sigma'(\sigma\sigma')^{-1}\sigma)(\widetilde{\lambda} + \eta^{**}) \\
&= \frac{\partial H}{\partial Y}J(\widetilde{\lambda} + \eta^{**} - \sigma'(\sigma\sigma')^{-1}\sigma\widetilde{\lambda} - \sigma'(\sigma\sigma')^{-1}\sigma\eta^{**}) \\
&= \frac{\partial H}{\partial Y}J(\widetilde{\lambda} + \eta^{**} - \sigma'(\sigma\sigma')^{-1}\sigma\widetilde{\lambda}) \\
&= \frac{\partial H}{\partial Y}J(\widetilde{\lambda} + \eta^{**} - \widetilde{\lambda}).
\end{aligned}
$$

for a given $\eta_1 \in \langle \sigma \rangle^{\perp}$. But it can also be the case that:

$$rH - \mu^H H + \frac{\partial H}{\partial Y} J(\tilde{\lambda} + \eta_2) = 0 \qquad (3.32)$$

for another $\eta_2 \in \langle \sigma \rangle^{\perp}$. Yet, (3.29) simply does *not* follow from (3.31)-(3.32). The reason is that H can not simultaneously satisfy (3.31) and (3.32): it either satisfies (3.31) or (3.32). Absence of arbitrage opportunities is not enough to give more information. This implies that relation (3.29) holds in (3.28) (by lemma 3.12) only when (3.30) holds.

3.13 EXAMPLE (Stochastic volatility). Pick, without loss of generality, $\eta^{**}(t) = \mathbf{0}_d$. Then relation (3.29) in (3.28) can be rewritten as:

$$(\frac{\partial H}{\partial Y} J\eta)(t) = 0, \text{ for all } \eta \in \langle \sigma \rangle^{\perp}. \qquad (3.33)$$

To show that (3.33) does not hold, we provide a counter-example. We make use of the stochastic volatility example. Using the notation of section 3.3 we have:

$$(\frac{\partial H}{\partial Y} J\eta)(t) = ((H_S \bar{\sigma} S + H_{\nu}\psi\rho)\eta_1 + (H_{\nu}\psi(1 - \rho^2)^{1/2})\eta_2)(t).$$

Suppose now that (3.33) holds in this case. Because $\lambda = \tilde{\lambda} + \eta \equiv (\frac{\mu - r}{\sigma} \quad 0)' + (0 \quad \eta_2)'$, this is:

$$(H_{\nu}\psi(1 - \rho^2)^{1/2}\eta_2)(t) = 0.$$

Select further $\rho = 0$, so as to simplify the above condition to:

$$(H_{\nu}\psi\eta_2)(t) = 0.$$

Under the assumptions underlying the diffusion in (3.1), the above equality holds if and only if:

$$(H_{\nu}\eta_2)(t) = 0,$$

which shows that $\eta_2 = 0$, at least when $H_{\nu} \neq 0$ for otherwise stochastic volatility would not affect the price of the European contingent claim; in fact, under all of our assumptions, and the condition that η_2 does not depend on s, Bajeux and Rochet (1996) showed that H_{ν} is always strictly positive. In all cases, $\frac{\partial H}{\partial Y} J\eta = 0$ is true if and only if $\eta_2 = 0$, thus contradicting (3.33).

This completes the stochastic volatility example.

We now generalize:

3.14 LEMMA. *Let assumption 3.7 hold. Then, relation (3.29) in (3.28) holds if and only if relation (3.30) holds.*

PROOF. Suppose, on the contrary, that

$$\frac{\partial H}{\partial Y} J\epsilon = 0 \quad \text{for all } \epsilon, \tag{3.34}$$

where $\epsilon \equiv \eta - \eta^{**}$, $\eta, \eta^{**} \in \langle\sigma\rangle^{\perp}$, with $\eta \neq \eta^{**}$. Because

$$\sigma\epsilon = \mathbf{0}_m, \tag{3.35}$$

relations (3.34)-(3.35) now show that every candidate vector in $\langle\sigma\rangle^{\perp}$ must be orthogonal to $\frac{\partial H}{\partial Y} J$. Thus, $\frac{\partial H}{\partial Y} J$ must belong to the range of σ'. This is:

$$\exists\, p \in L^2_{0,T,m}(\Omega, \mathcal{F}, P) : p'\sigma = \frac{\partial H}{\partial Y} J,$$

which is impossible for m strictly less than d. Thus (3.34)-(3.35) imply that the only candidate is $\epsilon = \mathbf{0}_d$.

The proof of the converse is trivial. ‖

Theorem 3.8, lemma 3.12 and lemma 3.14 now imply:

3.15 COROLLARY. *Let assumption 3.7 hold. Then, $\widetilde{Q}$ is the pricing measure if and only if $\eta = 0$ in the decomposition of theorem 3.8.*

We can now state:

3.16 THEOREM. *Let assumption 3.7 hold. Then, $\widetilde{\pi}$ is P-mean-self-financing if and only if $\widetilde{Q}$ is the true pricing measure.*

To grasp a better understanding of the preceding theorem, note that the cumulative hedging cost process is a martingale under all measures $Q \in \mathcal{Q}$. Since the cumulative hedging cost process solves the same stochastic differential equation under P as under $\widetilde{Q}$ (the proof is nearly identical to that of thm. 3.1 in Hofmann et al. (1992)), this would contradict (3.21) if $\eta \neq 0$. This confirms (heuristically) theorem 3.16.

PROOF OF THEOREM 3.16. By definition 3.11, we have to show that the cumulative hedging cost process is a P-martingale if and only if the pricing measure is $\widetilde{Q}$. The if part follows from theorem 3.8, corollary 3.15, and lemma 3.4. The converse is true thanks to an argument identical to that used after relations (3.34)-(3.35) given in the course of the proof of lemma 3.14. ‖

Appendix: relative entropy and the minimal martingale measure

The Kullback-Leibler distance, or relative entropy, of two probability measures on the (common) probability space $(\Omega, \mathcal{F})$ is defined as follows:

$$\text{En}(Q \mid P) = \begin{cases} \int (\log \frac{dQ}{dP}) dQ & \text{if } Q \text{ is absolutely continuous with respect to } P. \\ +\infty & \text{otherwise} \end{cases}$$

and

$$\text{En}(Q \mid P) = 0 \iff Q = P.$$

The following is the multivariate, 'Brownian' version of thm. 3.11 p. 402 in Föllmer and Schweizer (1991):

3A.1 THEOREM. *Among all martingale measures $Q \approx P$ with fixed expectation $E^Q(\int_0^T \left\| \tilde{\lambda}(t) \right\|^2 dt)$, the minimal martingale measure $\tilde{Q}$ is the one which minimizes the relative entropy $\text{En}(. \mid P)$.*

PROOF.

$\text{En}(Q \mid P)$

$$\begin{aligned}
&= \text{En}(Q \mid \tilde{Q}) + \int \log \tilde{\xi}(T) dQ \\
&= \text{En}(Q \mid \tilde{Q}) + \int (-\int_0^T \tilde{\lambda}(t)' dW(t) - \tfrac{1}{2} \int_0^T \left\| \tilde{\lambda}(t) \right\|^2 dt) dQ \\
&= \text{En}(Q \mid \tilde{Q}) + \int (-\int_0^T \tilde{\lambda}(t)' (dW^*(t) - \lambda(t) dt) - \tfrac{1}{2} \int_0^T \left\| \tilde{\lambda}(t) \right\|^2 dt) dQ \\
&= \text{En}(Q \mid \tilde{Q}) + \int (\int_0^T (\tilde{\lambda}'\lambda)(t) dt - \tfrac{1}{2} \int_0^T \left\| \tilde{\lambda}(t) \right\|^2 dt) dQ \\
&= \text{En}(Q \mid \tilde{Q}) + \int (\int_0^T (\left\| \tilde{\lambda} \right\|^2 + \tilde{\lambda}'\eta)(t) dt - \tfrac{1}{2} \int_0^T \left\| \tilde{\lambda}(t) \right\|^2 dt) dQ \\
&= \text{En}(Q \mid \tilde{Q}) + \tfrac{1}{2} \int (\int_0^T \left\| \tilde{\lambda}(t) \right\|^2 dt) dQ
\end{aligned}$$

$$(3A.1)$$

The second line is the definition of the Radon-Nikodym derivative of $\tilde{Q}$ with respect to P; the third and fourth lines follow by the Girsanov's theorem (in the third line, W^* is a standard $\mathcal{F}(t)$-Brownian motion under the measure Q, and $\lambda \in \mathcal{P}$) and the corresponding property that $E^Q(\int_0^T \tilde{\lambda}(t) dW^*(t)) = 0$; the last lines follow from the definition of $\mathcal{P}$.

From (3A.1), we eventually get:

$$\text{En}(Q \mid P) - \frac{1}{2} E^Q(\int_0^T \left\| \tilde{\lambda}(t) \right\|^2 dt) = \text{En}(Q \mid \tilde{Q}) \geq 0,$$

which is clearly minimized by $Q = \tilde{Q}$. ∥

MODELS OF THE TERM STRUCTURE WITH STOCHASTIC VOLATILITY

4.1 Introduction

The aim of this chapter is to introduce the reader to the basic continuous time models designed to determine the term structure of interest rates. We make use of the standard framework in which the whole term structure of interest rates can be modeled starting from the knowledge of the short term interest rate dynamics, and focus essentially on the case in which the instantaneous interest rate is the solution of a stochastic differential system with stochastic volatility, as for instance in system (1.1) of chapter 1.

As reminded in the introductory chapter, researchers, including Fong and Vasicek (1991), Longstaff and Schwartz (1992), Fornari and Mele (1994, 1995), Chen (1996) or Andersen and Lund (1997b) have proposed continuous time stochastic volatility models of the term structure that generalize previous models with fixed volatility, such as those of Vasicek (1977), Dothan (1978), or Cox et al. (1985a). Apart from the model of Longstaff and Schwartz, however, none of the above cited stochastic volatility models actually stems from an equilibrium theory explaining how risk-premia are generated by standard preference restrictions. Fornari and Mele (1999a) accomplished such a task, but instead of presenting the derivation of their model in detail, we prefer to pursue the following three objectives here.

First, we start by presenting the basic econometric techniques that are required to estimate the parameters of the single factor model of Cox et al. (1985a) and their (single factor) extensions. Such a choice mainly reflects the original plan and motivation of our first paper in this area (Fornari and Mele (1994)), in which we were essentially concerned with underlining some counterfactual features of these models, namely the fact that they obviously do not consider volatility as a stochastic factor. Naturally, the early nineties was an exciting period in which many researchers tried to incorporate stochastic volatility features into standard models of the short term interest rate by making use of the ARCH scheme: see, for instance, the paper of Brenner et al.

(1996) and the references therein; it is also instructive, at this point, to remind the reader that the first paper dealing with related issues was made by the Engle et al. (1987) in a celebrated work that gave birth to the so-called 'ARCH-M' model. The originality of our 1994 article lied in an attempt to use the early approximation results of Nelson (1990) in order to bring together the literature on ARCH models and the literature on arbitrage-free models with diffusion state variables, and this chapter intends to reproduce the intuitive reasoning that we intended to follow in order to accomplish such a task. In this sense, then, our original paper can be conceived as a logical antecedent of our current research agenda on the theory of the term structure with stochastic volatility.

The second objective of this chapter is to describe the analytical difficulties that result when one attempts at constructing models of the term structure by utilizing the continuous time volatility equations towards which ARCH models converge in distribution (see chapter 2). We show that the resulting models do not give rise to intensity rates that are affine functions of the state variables; in technical terms, such models do not belong to the class of the *exponential-affine* models. The literature on exponential-affine models has received a somewhat detailed treatment in mathematical finance (see, for instance, Brown and Schaefer (1995), the generalizing framework of Duffie and Kan (1996), and the references therein); nevertheless, we choose to include it here mainly for pedagogical reasons, for we wish to show how one can destroy or preserve affinity in the very special case of stochastic volatility. We believe that until the recent past, this was an important modeling issue that has influenced the way how applied researchers thought about their factor dynamics. Sometimes, the main concern was to obtain simple analytical expressions of the intensity rates in terms of the factors of the economy, but we believe that such a concern is not justified today: the modern computer capabilities allow one to rapidly obtain very accurate numerical solutions of analytically intractable models, and this should encourage the researcher to specifying realistic factor dynamics (despite the fact that they may give rise to analytically intractable models), instead of specifying unrealistic factor dynamics that allow to obtain analytically tractable models. In the next chapter, we will describe the numerical techniques that are needed to solve continuous time models of the term structure with stochastic volatility, by illustrating them in the specific case of the equilibrium model in Fornari and Mele (1999a), in which the volatility equation is the diffusion limit of the A-PARCH model (see chapter 2). The researcher who feels himself uncomfortable with such a particular choice—and that in fact wishes to consider a different model—must be ensured that a simple change in our computer code is sufficient to make that code solve any related well-behaved problem.

The third objective of this chapter is to present a class of equilibrium models of the term structure that includes the model in Fornari and Mele (1999a) as a particular case. This class of models is based on an encompassing version of the single-state variable model studied by Cox et al. (1985a); in fact, our primitive is the diffusion-state model of the preceding chapter (section 3.2), which is essentially the Cox et al. (1985b) setup modified to take account of stocks more in the vein of the discrete time Lucas (1978) model.[1] An important contribution to the equilibrium theory of the term structure with stochastic volatility was developed by Longstaff and Schwartz (1992). As noted in the introductory chapter (section 1.3.2), the class of models we generate is more in line with the formulations that are receiving attention in the applied econometric literature. In order to keep the mathematical presentation as simple as possible, the solution techniques that we use to solve for the model are based on the standard dynamic programming techniques that generated the optimality equations (3.11) of the previous chapter (section 3.2.3); more modern techniques (based on martingale methods) are in Fornari and Mele (1999a) where, however, we only study a specific case of the class of the models that is presented here.

The organization of this chapter exactly reflects the preceding three issues: the first two points are treated in sections 2 and 3, while the third one is covered in sections 4 and 5; the chapter then concludes with a very short section describing our current research agenda on the empirical modeling of nonlinearities of the short-term interest rate dynamics.

4.2 From the one factor model to the modeling of conditional heteroskedasticity

Among many single-factor models for the analysis of the term structure of interest rates along the lines outlined in the previous section, the model developed by Cox et al. (1985a,b) is the one that has received the greatest attention; see, for instance, Aït-Sahalia (1996a) (table 1) for a list of many alternative models. According to the hypotheses of the basic model developed in Cox et al. (1985a), preferences are logarithmic, and the state space is spanned by a unique factor, which is the solution of the following stochastic differential equation:

$$dy(t) = (\kappa y(t) + \zeta)dt + \sigma y(t)^{1/2}dW(t),$$

where κ, ζ, σ are constants and W is a standard Brownian motion. By making use of the equilibrium framework developed in Cox et al. (1985b), Cox et al. (1985a) show that by imposing certain restrictions, the instantaneous interest

---

[1]One of the reasons for such a modification is to understand the impact of standard factor restrictions à la Cox et al. (1985a) on the dynamics of the stock prices.

rate is then the solution of the following stochastic differential equation

$$dr(t) = (\iota - \theta r(t))dt + \sigma r(t)^{1/2}dW(t), \tag{4.1}$$

and that the unit risk premium demanded by agents to be compensated for the fluctuation of the stochastic factor is

$$\lambda(t) = \lambda \cdot r(t)^{1/2}, \tag{4.2}$$

where ι, θ, σ and λ are real constants.

Let $B_T(r(t), t)$ be the *rational* price as of time t of a zero-coupon bond maturing at time T. Given (4.1) and (4.2), a viable price process is the one for which $\{(\exp(-\int_0^t r(u)du)) \cdot B_T(r(t), t)\}_{t \in [0,T]}$ is a $(Q \in \mathcal{Q})$-martingale with Radon-Nikodym derivative of the form that is implicitly defined in lemma 3.4 of the previous chapter, with $d \equiv 1$ and $\lambda(.)$ defined by (4.2); see the preceding chapter for the introduction to the terminology and notation that we are using here. By the Girsanov's theorem, the Itô's lemma, and the previous martingale property of the discounted price process, then, the term structure of interest rates can be determined by solving the following partial differential equation:

$$\begin{cases} \frac{1}{2}\sigma^2 r B_{rr}(r, \tau) + (\iota - (\theta + \sigma\lambda)r)B_r(r, \tau) - B_\tau(r, \tau) - rB(r, \tau) = 0, \ t \in [0, T) \\ B(r, 0) = 1 \end{cases}$$
$$\tag{4.3}$$

where we have posed $B(r, \tau) \equiv B_T(r, t)$ and $\tau \equiv T - t$ (time to maturity). The solution of eq. (4.3) is of the form:

$$B(r(t), \tau; a_+) = H_1(\tau; a_+) \exp(-H_2(\tau; a_+) \cdot r(t)),$$

where H_1, H_2 are well-defined functions of τ and $a_+ \equiv (\iota, \theta, \sigma, \lambda)$. Equivalently, the term structure of the *intensity rates* $R(r(t), \tau) = -\frac{1}{\tau} \log B(r(t), \tau)$ can be determined by

$$R(r(t), \tau) = -\tau^{-1} \log(H_1(\tau)) + \tau^{-1} H_2(\tau) \cdot r(t). \tag{4.4}$$

Relation (4.4) shows that the intensity rate R is a linear function of the state of the economy resumed by r: it is due to such a property that this model is called *exponential-affine* model.

One estimation technique of the model's parameters a_+ can be based on non-linear least squares fitted to a cross section of prices of zero-coupon bonds. An alternative procedure can be based on two steps that make use of different information sets. In the first step, one estimates $a \equiv (\iota, \theta, \sigma)$ by fitting the stochastic differential equation (4.1) to time series data; in the second step, one searches the λ that makes theoretical prices close to the observed prices according to a well-defined criterion. It is the objective of this section to provide some information about the first step of this procedure.[2]

---

[2]See section 5.5 in the next chapter for some details concerning a possible estimation procedure of the risk-premia in a stochastic volatility setting.

The first problem that naturally emerges when one attempts to estimate a from time series data is obviously the choice of the data set to use. One can make use of proxies, such as the overnight rate or the three-months rate, but in some cases the use of such proxies can alter significantly the interpretation of the final results (see Chapman et al. (1999)).

The second problem is that even if we dispose of a reliable data set, data are only collected at discrete time points. As reminded in the introductory chapter, the likelihood function that is associated with the measure induced by a discretely sampled diffusion is not always known explicitly, although this is not the case here (see Cox et al. (1985a)). However, the exact discretization of eq. (4.1) is not known; while one can always discretize eq. (4.1) by means of the Euler's scheme, it is clear that an estimation of a based on such a scheme is subject to a discretization bias.

Broze et al. (1995a) propose an estimation strategy that is based on the indirect inference principle and that corrects for the discretization bias induced by the Euler's scheme. Let h denote sample frequency and consider a finite dimensional Markov process $\{_h X_{hk}\}_{k=0}^{\infty}$:

$$_h X_{h(k+1)} = \iota_h + (1 - \theta_h) \, _h X_{hk} + h^{-1/2}\sigma_h \, _h X_{hk}^{1/2} \, _h u_{h(k+1)},$$

where h indicates frequency scale, ι_h, θ_h and σ_h are real-valued non-stochastic parameters, and $_h u_{hk}$ is independently, identically, and normally distributed with mean zero and variance h. It is not hard to show that if the following moment conditions hold:

$$\begin{cases} \lim_{h \downarrow 0} h^{-1} \iota_h = \iota \\ \lim_{h \downarrow 0} h^{-1} \theta_h = \theta \\ \lim_{h \downarrow 0} h^{-1} \sigma_h^2 = \sigma^2 \end{cases} \tag{4.5}$$

the finite dimensional Markov process $\{_h X_{hk}\}_{k=0}^{\infty}$ converges in distribution to the solution of eq. (4.1) as $h \downarrow 0$. The estimation of a can then be based on simulations of eq. (4.1) by means of the high frequency simulator

$$_h r_{h(k+1)} - \, _h r_{hk} = (\iota - \theta \cdot \, _h r_{hk})h + \sigma \, _h r_{hk}^{1/2} \, _h u_{h(k+1)}. \tag{4.6}$$

Precisely, consider the ML estimator of $b_1 \equiv (\iota_1, \theta_1, \sigma_1)$,

$$\widehat{b}_1 = \arg\max_{b_1} \mathcal{L}_N(_1 r; b_1),$$

where $_1 r$ is the observation set (of dimension N) and $\mathcal{L}$ is the likelihood function that is generated by the following discrete time auxiliary model,

$$r_{n+1} = \iota_1 + (1 - \theta_1) \, r_n + \sigma_1 \, r_n^{1/2} \, u_{n+1}, \tag{4.7}$$

where u is a standard normal variate. Upon assigning values to a, one simulates eq. (4.6) for small values of h; after sampling the simulated interest rates data at a frequency identical to the sampling frequency of the available data, one then obtains simulated data—say $_{1,h}r^{(s)}(.)$—, and then computes:

$$\widehat{b}_{1,s}^{(h)}(a) = \arg\max_{b_{1,s}^{(h)}} \mathcal{L}_N\big(_{1,h}r^{(s)}(a); b_{1,s}^{(h)}\big), \quad s = 1, ..., S,$$

where S is the number of simulations and $\widehat{b}_{1,s}^{(h)}(x)$ is obtained by using $a = x$ in *all* the simulations. Finally, a is calibrated by making $\widehat{b}_{1,s}^{(h)}(.)$ the closest possible to $\widehat{b}_1$:

$$\widehat{a} = \arg\min_a \left\| \widehat{b}_1 - \frac{1}{S} \sum_{s=1}^S \widehat{b}_{1,s}^{(h)}(a) \right\|,$$

where $\|.\|$ is a given norm. The following chapter provides technical details concerning the asymptotics of $\widehat{a}$, by illustrating them when one is concerned with systems that have stochastic volatility.

As shown by Broze et al. (1995b), the validity of such a scheme rests on the weak convergence of the high frequency simulator towards the data generating mechanism. Furthermore, if the high frequency generator reduces to the auxiliary model when the simulation frequency tends to the frequency of the available data—as in (4.6) and (4.7)—, the procedure can then be thought as a natural device to correct the discretization bias of the discrete time auxiliary model. As noted in the introductory chapter (section 1.4), this is, in essence, the strategy that Gouriéroux et al. (1993) considered as "particularly promising" (p. S108): constructing criteria that are based on approximations of the likelihood function or time discretizations, thereby creating a natural interpretation of the parameters of the auxiliary model in terms of the parameters of the continuous time model. Here, the "natural interpretation" is given by the moment conditions (4.5), and the indirect inference procedure is then designed to correct the discretization bias of an estimator based on those conditions. As we shall see in the following chapter, one can apply the same type of reasoning when the system of interest is one with continuous time stochastic volatility and the auxiliary model is an ARCH model that converges in distribution to it (see chapter 2).

While conditionally 'heteroscedastic', the solution of eq. (4.1) is not a truly stochastic volatility model. To this end, one has to add any well-behaved stochastic volatility equation, but as we shall see in section 4.5, theory provides little guidance about the choice of such an equation. On the other hand, one objective of this monograph is to provide tools by which one can gauge the behavior of ARCH as diffusion approximations in empirical work. Following such a program, in the next section we start by considering the following simple volatility equation,

$$d\sigma(t)^2 = (\overline{\omega} - \varphi\sigma(t)^2)dt + \psi\sigma(t)^2 dW^\sigma(t), \tag{4.8}$$

which represents the diffusion limit to which a simple GARCH(1,1) process

$$
\begin{aligned}
{}_h r_{h(k+1)} &= \iota_h + (1 - \theta_h)\,_h r_{hk} + \,_h \sigma_{h(k+1)}\,\,_h r_{hk}^{1/2} \cdot \,_h u_{h(k+1)} \\
{}_h u_{hk} &\sim \text{ i.i.d.}(0, 1), \\
{}_h \sigma_{h(k+1)}^2 &= \omega_h + \alpha_h \,_h \varepsilon_{hk}^2 h^{-1} + \beta_h \,_h \sigma_{hk}^2, \quad \varepsilon \equiv u \cdot \sigma
\end{aligned}
\tag{4.9}
$$

converges in distribution (see chapter 2).

At this point, however, one has destroyed the one-factor set-up and has originated a two-factor model (interest rate and its conditional volatility) which jointly affect the price of bonds.

4.3 Searching for affinity

A natural extension of the single factor Cox et al. (1985a) model that takes account of stochastic volatility is a multifactor model, but the price to be paid for such a generalization would be measured in terms of analytical difficulties. Working with two highly related state variables (such as the interest rate and *its* volatility) introduces nonlinearities in the partial differential equation that has to be solved by the price of the bond. Apart from the exponential-affine class of models, one typically has to implement numerical approximations of the kind that is presented in the following chapter.

The aim of this section is to show that models including equations as (4.8) as volatility equation cannot give rise to this class of models. Example of affine models are instead Fong and Vasicek (1991) (see eq. (1.16) in chapter 1, section 1.3.2), and Longstaff and Schwartz (1992) (to be succinctly presented in the following section). The proof is rather simple, and can be produced via a constructive example (presented originally in Fornari and Mele (1994)) that rests on the volatility equation (4.8) of the previous section. Consider the following simple two-factor model:

$$
\begin{aligned}
dr(t) &= (\iota - \theta r(t))dt + v(t)^{1/2}dW^{(1)}(t) \\
dv(t) &= (\bar{\omega} - \varphi v(t))dt + \psi v(t)dW^{\sigma}(t)
\end{aligned}
$$

where we are simplifying the presentation by neglecting correlation issues. The first step now consists in specifying the risk-premia that would be demanded by agents to be compensated for the fluctuations of the stochastic factors r, v. Although such a specification can be made by making reference to a fully articulated equilibrium model, as in Fornari and Mele (1999a) and in its simplified presentation of section 4.5, we shall only show here the *existence* of such premia when arbitrage conditions are absent. Take then as primitive the model of the previous chapter (section 3.2), and suppose that the only available assets are $d+1$ pure discount bonds. We know that assumption 3.3 in chapter 3 rules out arbitrage opportunities. Now we show that absence of arbitrage opportunities also implies the content of that assumption.

Indeed, the dynamics of the value of a portfolio of the $d+1$ bonds and the accumulation factor is:

$$dV(t) = (\pi(t)'(\mu^\ell(t) - \mathbf{1}_{d+1}r(t)) + r(t)V(t))dt + \pi(t)'\sigma_\ell(t)dW(t),$$

where μ^ℓ and σ_ℓ are well-defined functions that can be found by the Itô's lemma (see eq. (4.10) below). Suppose now to find a portfolio π such that $\underline{\pi}'\sigma_\ell = 0$. This is an arbitrage opportunity if there exist events in which $\mu^\ell - \mathbf{1}_d r \neq 0$ (use $\underline{\pi}$ when $\mu^\ell - \mathbf{1}_d r > 0$, and use $-\underline{\pi}$ when $\mu^\ell - \mathbf{1}_d r < 0$: the drift of V will then be appreciating at a deterministic rate that is strictly greater than r). To rule out arbitrage opportunities, it must thus be the case that $\pi'(\mu^\ell - \mathbf{1}_d r) = 0$ whenever $\pi'\sigma_\ell = 0$. In other terms, arbitrage opportunities are ruled out when every vector in the null space of σ_ℓ is orthogonal to $\mu^B - \mathbf{1}_d r$, or when there exists a λ such that $\mu^\ell - \mathbf{1}_d r = \sigma_\ell \lambda$. The claim that absence of arbitrage opportunities implies that there exists a measure Q that belongs to $\mathcal{Q}$ now follows by Girsanov's theorem. Notice that λ does not depend on the institutional characteristics of the bonds, such as the date-to-expiration.

Let $B(t) \equiv B_T(r, v, t)$ be the *rational* price at time t of a pure discount bond with maturity τ. By Itô's lemma,

$$\frac{dB(t)}{B(t)} = \mu(t)dt + \Phi(t)dW^{(1)}(t) + \Psi dW^\sigma(t), \tag{4.10}$$

where

$$
\begin{aligned}
\mu B &= B_t + B_r(\iota - \theta r) + B_v(\bar{\omega} - \varphi v) + \tfrac{1}{2}B_{rr}v + \tfrac{1}{2}(\psi v)^2 B_{vv}\\
\Phi B &= B_r v^{1/2}\\
\Psi B &= B_v \psi v
\end{aligned}
$$

As shown above, $\{(\exp(-\int_0^t r(u)du)) \cdot B_T(r(t), t)\}_{t\in[0,T]}$ must be a martingale under any measure $Q \in \mathcal{Q}$ if and only if there are not arbitrage opportunities. Hence,

$$\mu = r + q\Phi + p\Psi, \tag{4.11}$$

where q and p are the market price of risk referred to interest rate and volatility changes, respectively. As noted above, these prices are obviously independent on the date-to-expiration of any bond. Unlike q, we are also going to assume that p is time-varying, however. Specifically, we model q and p by letting them vary proportionally to the square root and the level of v respectively, viz.,

$$
\begin{aligned}
q(t) &= \lambda v(t)^{1/2}, \ \lambda \in \mathbb{R}\\
p(t) &= \eta(t)v(t)
\end{aligned}
$$

Substituting this into relation (4.11), yields, for $t \in [0, T)$,

$$B_t + B_r(\iota - \theta r) + B_v(\bar{\omega} - \varphi v) + \frac{1}{2}B_{rr}v + \frac{1}{2}(\psi v)^2 B_{vv} - rB - \lambda v B_r - \eta\psi v^2 B_v = 0, \tag{4.12}$$

with the usual boundary condition.

Suppose, now, that the price of a pure-discount bond is given by the following expression:

$$B(\tau, r, v) = \exp(-rD(\tau) + vF(\tau) + G(\tau)) \tag{4.13}$$

with the boundary conditions $D(0) = F(0) = G(0) = 0$. The model we are examining would then belong to the exponential-affine class, since the term structure of the intensity rates,

$$R(\tau, r(t), v(t)) \equiv -\tau^{-1} \log B(\tau, r(t), v(t)),$$

would be affine in the two state variables of the economy (r, v). Now we wish to obtain parametric restrictions ensuring that the model is indeed affine. As it turns out, the parametric restrictions we obtain seriously undermine the interest of this model as an affine model.

To show this, we take the appropriate derivatives in (4.13) and substitute in (4.12); we get the following conditions:

$$
\begin{aligned}
0 &= \dot{D} + \theta D - 1 \\
0 &= -\dot{F} - \varphi F + \tfrac{1}{2}F^2 + \lambda D \\
0 &= \dot{G} - \bar{\omega}F + \iota D \\
0 &= \tfrac{1}{2}\psi^2 F^2 - \eta \psi F
\end{aligned}
$$

The last condition shows that the risk-premium due to the fluctuations of $W^{(\sigma)}$ depends on time to maturity: as explained above, however, this is impossible; it then follows that $\psi = 0$ is the only restriction ensuring that (4.13) is indeed the solution of (4.12), but in this case, volatility is deterministic!

That models including eq. (4.8) as volatility equation do not give rise to the exponential affine class of term structure models comes as no surprise. Duffie and Kan (1996), generalizing a previous result of Brown and Schaefer (1995), have shown that a condition for an affine model to be obtained is that the variance of the factors is linear in the factors. We now show why and in which case this is also true when one considers a stochastic volatility model of the following kind:

$$
\begin{aligned}
dr(t) &= \chi(r(t))dt + \sigma(t)dW^{(1)}(t) \\
d\sigma(t)^{\delta} &= (\bar{\omega} - \varphi\sigma(t)^{\delta})dt + (\psi_0 + \psi_1\sigma(t)^{\delta})^{1/2}dW^{\sigma}(t)
\end{aligned}
$$

where $\delta \in \mathbb{R}_{++}$. First,[3] it is not hard to show that by assuming the previous model, one ends with an affine model when $\delta = 2$ and $\chi(.)$ is affine. For the

---

[3]In what follows, we are going to neglect risk-premia issues. Alternatively, the reasoning that follows can be interpreted as applied to risk adjusted drift terms.

converse, suppose that we are given

$$
\begin{aligned}
dr(t) &= \chi(r(t))dt + \sigma(t)\beta(r(t))^{1/2}dW^{(1)}(t) \\
d\sigma(t)^\delta &= (\overline{\omega} - \varphi\sigma(t)^\delta)dt + \psi(\sigma(t)^\delta)^{1/2}dW^\sigma(t)
\end{aligned}
$$

In this case the evaluation partial differential equation becomes:

$$
0 = B_t + B_r\chi(r) + B_{\sigma^\delta}(\overline{\omega} - \varphi\sigma^\delta) + \frac{1}{2}(B_{rr}\sigma^2\beta(r) + B_{\sigma^\delta\sigma^\delta}\psi(\sigma^\delta)) - rB.
$$

In an affine model, $B(\tau, r, v) = \exp(-D(\tau)r + F(\tau)\sigma^\delta + G(\tau))$; substituting this into the preceding equation yields:

$$
0 = \dot{D}r - \dot{F}\sigma^\delta - \dot{G} + D\chi(r) + F(\overline{\omega} - \varphi\sigma^\delta) + \frac{1}{2}(D^2\sigma^2\beta(r) + F^2\psi(\sigma^\delta)) - rB.
$$

For such an equation to hold with non degenerate drift and diffusion functions, it suffices to take $\delta = 2$, $\beta(r) = 1$ and $\chi(.)$ and $\psi(.)$ affine functions.

The first proponents of exponential-affine models of the term structure with stochastic volatility are Fong and Vasicek (1991) (see eqs. (1.16) in chapter 1). More recently, Chen (1996) considers richer dynamics—notably, by assuming the presence of a sort of 'moving target long-term interest rate' that represents a third factor, and allowing for correlation issues—, and destroys affinity.[4]

A shortcoming of these papers is that they do not include an equilibrium theory justifying the models they propose. As shown above, arbitrage arguments are not enough to recover the risk premia demanded by agents to be compensated for the fluctuations of the uncertainty factors. Longstaff and Schwartz (1992) took care of this, and the purpose of the following section is to show how.

4.4   Early equilibrium-based models

In the model of Longstaff and Schwartz (1992), the primitive is the return on physical investments given by:

$$
dQ(t)/Q(t) = (\mu x(t) + \vartheta y(t))dt + \sigma y(t)^{1/2}dW^{(1)}(t)
$$

with μ, ϑ, σ real parameters and $W^{(1)}$ a Brownian motion, and (x, y) two states variables. The dynamics of the two state variables (which can be identified as proxies of 'productivity' and 'variability') are given by:

$$
\begin{aligned}
dx(t) &= (a - bx(t))dt + cx(t)^{1/2}dW^{(2)}(t) \\
dy(t) &= (d - ey(t))dt + fy(t)^{1/2}dW^{(3)}(t)
\end{aligned}
\tag{4.14}
$$

---

[4]A very similar three factor (non affine) model has subsequently been considered by Andersen and Lund (1999*b*).

with a, b, c, d, e, f real parameters and $(W^{(2)}, W^{(3)})$ two Brownian motions. Making use of the Cox et al. (1985b) scheme, and assuming logarithmic preferences, Longstaff and Schwartz are able to show that the short term rate is simply given by an 'expected return-minus-variance' formula:

$$r(t) = \mu x(t) + (\vartheta - \sigma^2) y(t).$$

Expanding the preceding relation yields:

$$dr(t) = \mu dx(t) + (\vartheta - \sigma^2) dy(t).$$

From (4.14), the instantaneous variance of r is thus:

$$v(t) \equiv (\mu c)^2 x(t) + [f(\vartheta - \sigma^2)]^2 y(t).$$

By inverting the mapping $(x, y) \mapsto (r, v)$ one gets: $(x, y) = (\ \frac{v - A_1 r}{B_1}, \quad \frac{A_2 r - v}{B_2}\ )$, where A_1, A_2, B_1, B_2 are constants that depend on the deep parameters. Last, by Itô's lemma and the solution of (x, y), one can derive the dynamics of (r, v) that are only expressed in terms of themselves. Such dynamics display the following features: (1) the volatility of volatility is linear in v; (2) the Brownian motions driving r are the same as the Brownian motions driving v. The first property is attractive on an analytical standpoint, since it makes the resulting model belong to the exponential affine class of models, indeed.[5] The second property makes the resulting model depart from standard formulations in which stochastic volatility is typically not adapted to the filtration generated by the instantaneous interest rate, as in the model we present in the next section.

4.5 A class of equilibrium models of the term structure with stochastic volatility

We provide here an equilibrium model of the term structure of interest rates with stochastic volatility. Our main objective is to deliver a theory of the risk-premia determinants within simple preference restrictions. We take as primitive the scheme of the previous chapter, section 3.2. The results we obtain here are essentially those which we would have obtained by working directly with the Cox et al. (1985b) model, but we pursue the analysis with the scheme of section 3.2 because we are also interested in pointing out the economic implications of the restrictions we impose to the stock price dynamics (see remarks 4.1). Since our specification of the state-space is different from the one of Longstaff

---

[5]However, the authors propose to estimate the model via an ARCH-M scheme (Engle et al. (1987)), which in turn does not converge in distribution to their theoretical model (see chapter 2).

and Schwartz (1992), however, our final model will differ from the Longstaff-Schwartz model.

We let a representative agent behave as to maximize the expected flows of her instantaneous, logarithmic utility under the constraint of a generalized version of eq. (3.3) that also includes trading with bonds, which are zero-net supply assets. As it will be clear, our model will be completed by these assets, and this will justify our use of the representative agent object. As mentioned in the introductory chapter (see section 1.3.2), we will make use of the standard dynamic programming techniques that generated eq. (3.11) in chapter 3, section 3.2. Please notice that such a choice is motivated by pedagogical reasons only: the full derivation of the model within CRRA preference restrictions and more theoretical sounded foundations is in Fornari and Mele (1999*a*), where the solution method we use is based on the modern martingale methods.

4.5.1   PRELIMINARY OPTIMALITY RESULTS

The model of the preceding chapter can be used to obtain a theory of the term structure of interest rates. We take $m = 1$, and interpret the non productive asset as a pure discount bond with price B. By using the first order conditions summarized by eqs. (3.11) as a starting point, we can proceed along lines very similar to the ones presented in Cox et al. (1985*a*). At the equilibrium, $\pi = V$ and $\pi_\ell = 0$ and, under logarithmic preferences, it is well known that $\frac{\mathcal{J}_V}{V \mathcal{J}_{VV}} = -1$ and $\mathcal{J}_{VY} = \mathbf{0}_2$ (no 'hedging demand'). Hence, the first equation in (3.11) implies the standard result that the equilibrium interest rate is given by an expected return-minus-variance formula:

$$r(t) = \mu(t) - (\sigma\sigma')(t). \tag{4.15}$$

4.5.2   THE CONSTRUCTION OF THE MODEL

We now present our two-factor model. We split the presentation into four stages. In the first one, we specify the state space; in the second one, we impose and/or derive factor restrictions; in the third one, we derive the risk premia of the resulting setup; in the fourth one, we derive the partial differential equation followed by the price of a default free-risk bond.

- *1st step: construction of the primitive diffusion state model.* The diffusion state process $y \equiv (y_1, y_2)$ is solution of

$$
\begin{aligned}
\mathrm{d}\left(\begin{array}{c} y_1(t) \\ \nu(t) \end{array} \right) = {}& \left(\begin{array}{c} a(y(t)) \\ \widetilde{\varphi}(y(t)) \end{array} \right) \mathrm{d}t \\
& + \left(\begin{array}{cc} b(y_1(t)) \cdot y_2(t) & 0 \\ (\widetilde{\psi} \cdot \rho)(y(t)) & (\widetilde{\psi} \cdot (1-\rho^2)^{1/2})(y(t)) \end{array} \right) \mathrm{d}W(t)
\end{aligned}
\tag{4.16}
$$

where $\nu = v(y_2)$, and v is an homeomorphism with an inverse denoted as β; we assume that the functions $a, \widetilde{\varphi}, \widetilde{\psi}, \rho, b, v$ satisfy the same properties of the corresponding functions appearing in system (3.1) of the previous chapter. For reasons developed below, we shall also require that the function b satisfies, for each $B > 0$, $b(B \cdot x) = \widetilde{b}(B) \cdot \widehat{b}(x)$, $\forall x > 0$, where $\widetilde{b}$ and $\widehat{b}$ are other continuous functions. The justification for selecting the primitive dynamics as in (4.16) is as follows. We wish to find out, as in Cox et al. (1985a), an equilibrium in which the interest rate is a linear function of the first state variable. This is so because that representation may yield a simple model in which the interest rate matches the kind of stochastic volatility which we wish to study; but a sufficient condition for this is just modeling the second state variable as we did (see the following step).

- *2nd step: determining the factor restrictions.* Consistently with the motivation of the first step, we encompass the Cox et al. (1985a) single factor model, and suppose that the following restrictions hold

$$\begin{cases} \mu(t) &= \widehat{\mu} \cdot y_1(t) \\ \sigma(t) &= \widehat{\sigma} \cdot y_1(t)^{1/2} \end{cases} \tag{4.17}$$

where $\widehat{\mu}$ and $\widehat{\sigma}$ are, respectively, a constant and a vector of constants in $\mathbb{R}^2$. Substituting this into relation (4.15), we get the following expression for the equilibrium interest rate:

$$r(t) = A \cdot y_1(t), \ A \equiv \widehat{\mu} - \widehat{\sigma}\widehat{\sigma}', \tag{4.18}$$

where we suppose that $A > 0$. By differentiating r,

$$\begin{aligned} \mathrm{d}r(t) &= Aa(y(t))\mathrm{d}t + Ab(y_1(t))y_2(t)\mathrm{d}W^{(1)}(t) \\[2mm] &= Aa(y(t))\mathrm{d}t + Ab(A^{-1}r(t))y_2(t)\mathrm{d}W^{(1)}(t) \\[2mm] &= Aa(y(t))\mathrm{d}t + \widehat{b}(r(t))A\widetilde{b}(A^{-1})y_2(t)\mathrm{d}W^{(1)}(t) \\[2mm] &= Aa(y(t))\mathrm{d}t + \widehat{b}(r(t))\vartheta(t)\mathrm{d}W^{(1)}(t) \end{aligned}$$

where

$$\vartheta(t) \equiv A\widetilde{b}(A^{-1})y_2(t).$$

By differentiating $\vartheta(t)$,

$$
\begin{aligned}
\mathrm{d}\vartheta(t) &= A\widetilde{b}(A^{-1})\mathrm{d}y_2(t) \\[2mm]
&= A\widetilde{b}(A^{-1})\mathrm{d}\beta(\nu(t)) \\[2mm]
&= A\widetilde{b}(A^{-1})\beta'(\nu(t))\mathrm{d}\nu(t) + \tfrac{1}{2}A\widetilde{b}(A^{-1})\beta''(\nu(t))\widetilde{\psi}(y(t))^2\mathrm{d}t \\[2mm]
&= u(r(t),\vartheta(t))\mathrm{d}t + w(r(t),\vartheta(t))\cdot(\widehat{\rho}(r(t),\vartheta(t))\mathrm{d}W^{(1)} \\
&\qquad\qquad +(1-\widehat{\rho}(r(t),\vartheta(t))^2)^{1/2}\mathrm{d}W^{(2)}(t))
\end{aligned}
$$

(4.19)

where

$$
\begin{aligned}
u(r,\vartheta) &\equiv A\widetilde{b}(\tfrac{1}{A})(\beta'(v(\tfrac{1}{A}\widetilde{b}(\tfrac{1}{A})^{-1}\vartheta)))\widetilde{\varphi}(\tfrac{1}{A}r,\tfrac{1}{A}\widetilde{b}(\tfrac{1}{A})^{-1}\vartheta) \\
&\quad +\tfrac{1}{2}\beta''(v(\tfrac{1}{A}\widetilde{b}(\tfrac{1}{A})^{-1}\vartheta))\widetilde{\psi}(\tfrac{1}{A}r,\tfrac{1}{A}\widetilde{b}(\tfrac{1}{A})^{-1}\vartheta)^2), \\[2mm]
w(r,\vartheta) &\equiv A\widetilde{b}(\tfrac{1}{A})\beta'(v(\tfrac{1}{A}\widetilde{b}(\tfrac{1}{A})^{-1}\vartheta))\widetilde{\psi}(\tfrac{1}{A}r,\tfrac{1}{A}\widetilde{b}(\tfrac{1}{A})^{-1}\vartheta) \\[2mm]
\widehat{\rho}(r,\vartheta) &\equiv \rho(\tfrac{1}{A}r,\tfrac{1}{A}\widetilde{b}(\tfrac{1}{A})^{-1}\vartheta)
\end{aligned}
$$

Finally, the interest rate equation can be expressed as:

$$
\mathrm{d}r(t) = \widehat{a}(r(t),\vartheta(t))\mathrm{d}t + \widehat{b}(r(t))\vartheta(t)\mathrm{d}W^{(1)}(t),
$$

(4.20)

where $\widehat{a}(r,\vartheta)\equiv Aa(\tfrac{1}{A}r,\tfrac{1}{A}\widetilde{b}(\tfrac{1}{A})^{-1}\vartheta)$.

- *3rd step: construction of the martingale measure implied by the model.* The second equation in (3.11), combined with the equilibrium conditions $\pi=V$ and $\pi_\ell=0$, yields under logarithmic utility,

$$
\mu^\ell(t)-r(t)=(\sigma_\ell\sigma')(t).
$$

This shows that $\{\frac{B(t)}{S^{(0)}(t)}\}_{t\in[0,T]}$ is a $(\widehat{Q}\in\mathcal{Q})$-martingale, where $\widehat{Q}$ has density process:

$$
\left.\frac{\mathrm{d}\widehat{Q}}{\mathrm{d}P}\right|_{\mathcal{F}(t)} = \exp(-\textstyle\int_0^t \widehat{\lambda}(u)'\mathrm{d}W(u)-\tfrac{1}{2}\int_0^t \left\|\widehat{\lambda}(u)\right\|^2 \mathrm{d}u),
$$

with

$$
\widehat{\lambda}(t)=\sigma(t)',
$$

which has the interpretation of the vector of unit risk premia demanded by agents to be compensated for the fluctuations of the 2-dimensional Brownian motion; using (4.17) and (4.18),

$$
\begin{aligned}
\widehat{\lambda}(t) &= \widehat{\sigma}'A^{-1}\cdot r(t)^{1/2} \\
&\equiv (\ \lambda_1\quad \lambda_2\ )'\cdot r(t)^{1/2},
\end{aligned}
$$

(4.21)

where λ_1 and λ_2 are two constants. Under all of our assumptions, $\widehat{\lambda}$ satisfies the Novikov condition.

- *4th step: derivation of the partial differential equation of the equilibrium bond price.* Follows from Itô's lemma and the above step:

$$
\begin{aligned}
\mathcal{L}[B](r(t), \vartheta(t), t) &= \Lambda(r(t), \vartheta(t), t) + r(t)B(r(t), \vartheta(t), t), \ t \in [0, T) \\
B(r, \vartheta, T) &= 1, \ \forall(r, \vartheta) \in \mathbb{R}^2_{++}
\end{aligned}
$$

$$(4.22)$$

where

$$
\begin{aligned}
\mathcal{L}[B](r, \vartheta, t) &\equiv B_t + B_r \cdot \widehat{a}(r, \vartheta) + B_\vartheta \cdot u(r, \vartheta) + \tfrac{1}{2}(B_{rr} \cdot \widehat{b}(r)^2 \vartheta^2 \\
&\quad + 2B_{r\vartheta} \cdot \widehat{b}(r)w(r, \vartheta)\vartheta\rho(r, \vartheta) + B_{\vartheta\vartheta} \cdot w(r, \vartheta)^2),
\end{aligned}
$$

$$
\begin{aligned}
\Lambda(r, \vartheta, t) &\equiv B_r \cdot \lambda_1 \widehat{b}(r)\vartheta r^{1/2} + B_\vartheta \cdot (\lambda_1 \rho(r, \vartheta) \\
&\quad + \lambda_2(1 - \rho(r, \vartheta)^2)^{1/2}) \cdot w(r, \vartheta)r^{1/2}
\end{aligned}
$$

The construction of the model is complete.

4.1 REMARKS. (1) In this model, the equilibrium interest rate is a linear function of the first state variable (see eq. (4.18)). By re-interpreting the model in terms of linear activities, this shows that our model has the same nature of the Cox et al. (1985a) model. This is not surprising since we explicitly made use of the same factor restrictions used by Cox et al. (1985a) (cf. (4.17)). The added value here is that our model extends the one of Cox et al. (1985a) by explicitly introducing stochastic volatility. In addition, the model nests stochastic volatility in exactly the way that has been suggested in the early contributions cited in the introductory chapter. To appreciate the first point, for instance, notice that this model predicts that there is a unique measure belonging to $\mathcal{Q}$ with unit risk premia given by (4.21). Such a result should be compared with the original Cox et al. (1985a) result in which information was driven by a single Brownian motion, to which a single risk premium corresponded that had exactly the same form as (4.21). Furthermore, in addition to the restrictions in (4.17), the simple analytical form of the risk premia in (4.21) is also attributable to the assumption that the process $\{(\mu - \overline{\mu})(t)\}_{t \in [0,T]}$ is a deterministic function of time (see Fornari and Mele (1999a)); one can relax such an assumption while keeping at the same time the factor restrictions in (4.17), and obtaining nonetheless more complicated risk-premia functions.

(2) In this model, the stock price and the short term interest rate can not display volatility dynamics sharing the same qualitative properties. If we accept the restrictions of this section, for instance, $\frac{dS(t)}{S(t)} = \widehat{\mu}y_1(t)dt + \widehat{\sigma}\sqrt{y_1(t)}dW(t)$, and if $y_1 = s$, then $\frac{dS(t)}{S(t)} = \widehat{\mu}S(t)dt + \widehat{\sigma}\sqrt{S(t)}dW(t)$, which contradicts that

S has stochastic volatility! While such negative results depend on the preference structure that has been assumed for the representative agent and the restrictions in (4.17), it seems nonetheless difficult to formulate a general model with: (1) stock prices that are rationally formed, as in (3.2); and (2) equilibrium dynamics of (r, ϑ) both exhibiting the kind of stochastic volatility of this section.

4.6   Concluding remarks: taking account of nonlinearities

The model presented in the preceding section does not impose any economic restrictions on the drift and diffusion functions of the various model's variables; similarly, the risk-premia demanded by agents to be compensated for the fluctuations of the uncertainty factors are invariant with respect to changes of such drift and diffusion functions.[6] While in the first application of this model to real data Fornari and Mele (1999a) assume linearity of the drift functions (see the next chapter for further details), one can also adopt a much more data-oriented approach. Within a single-factor model, for instance, Aït-Sahalia (1996b), Stanton (1997) and Conley et al. (1997) suggested to model the drift in a nonlinear way. They find that the 'strength' at which the interest rate is forced to come back to 'normal' levels is higher when the short term interest rate is 'high' rather than low, as suggested by a nonlinear drift function.[7] Of course, these are issues that deserve a deeper theoretical understanding on an economic standpoint, but one can also adopt a pragmatic approach that consists in specifying nonparametric drift or even nonlinear but ad hoc functions.

An example is the one considered by Aït-Sahalia (1996b) within a single factor model,

$$dr(t) = \widehat{a}(r(t))dt + \widehat{b}(r(t))dW(t),$$

in which both $\widehat{a}$ and $\widehat{b}$ where nonlinear functions of the state; as regards the drift function, for instance, Aït-Sahalia (1996b) considered the following form:

$$\widehat{a}(x) = a_0 + a_1 x + a_2 x^2 + a_3 x^{-1}, \tag{4.23}$$

where a_0, a_1, a_2, a_3 are parameters to be estimated.

---

[6]Fornari and Mele (1999a) use a more equilibrium-oriented version of the model presented in the preceding section, and argue that in addition to the factor restrictions (4.17), what can be responsible for such an invariance property of the risk premia could be the particular assumption that one makes about the stochastic process followed by the dividend associated with the primitive asset. Their explanation is consistent with previous results obtained by Pham and Touzi (1996) in a different context.

[7]See, however, the recent work of Chapman and Pearson (1999).

Ahn and Gao (1999) propose a more parsimonious structure

$$\mathrm{d}r(t) = r(t)(\iota - \theta r(t))\mathrm{d}t + \sigma r(t)^{3/2}\mathrm{d}W(t),$$

where ι, θ, σ are constants.

As is clear, one can apply the preceding ideas to a model with stochastic volatility—notably by specifying a drift function of the form (4.23)—, and even generalize and apply the same ideas to the volatility propagation mechanism. Empirical evidence suggests indeed that the description we gave with concern of the interest rate dynamics might also help understanding volatility dynamics; a natural question that can be addressed is then: does volatility tend to revert more rapidly towards 'normal values' when it has reached very high levels ? The model that we are currently considering in Fornari and Mele (1999c) tries to answer this question by applying the specification suggested by Ahn and Gao (1999) with concern of the instantaneous interest rate dynamics to the volatility generating mechanism:

$$\mathrm{d}\vartheta(t) = \vartheta(t)(\overline{\omega} - \varphi\vartheta(t))\mathrm{d}t + \psi\vartheta(t)^{3/2}\mathrm{d}W^{\vartheta}(t),$$

where $\overline{\omega}, \varphi, \psi$ are real parameters and W^{ϑ} is a Brownian motion. It is also clear, at this point, that one can further generalize the preceding formulation by inventing other appropriate forms for the drift and diffusion functions of the volatility and in fact, all such objectives make the object of our current research agenda.

Next chapter adopts the more modest objective to describe the estimation and solution strategies that one can apply to standard equations that result from the model formulated in the previous section. As it will be clear, however, many of the generalizations succinctly discussed here present technical difficulties that can be handled in a quite straight forward manner.

5

FORMULATING, SOLVING
AND ESTIMATING MODELS OF
THE TERM STRUCTURE USING
ARCH MODELS AS
DIFFUSION APPROXIMATIONS

5.1   Introduction

The purpose of this chapter is to show how to implement models belonging to the framework developed in section 4.5 of the previous chapter. As seen there, the main conceptual difficulty is that theory provides little guidance about the choice of the various drift and diffusion functions of the short term interest rate and its instantaneous volatility. In fact, the next section shows how to backward engeneer the drift and diffusion functions of the state variables that generate arbitrary models of the short term interest rate with stochastic volatility.

If theory provides little guidance, a data oriented approach could instead be pursued. While a general research strategy would then consist in comparing general specifications of the drift and diffusion functions with data, as for instance in Gallant and Tauchen (1998), here we wish to present a model that allows for the possibility of testing whether the approximation and filtering results for ARCH models are indeed valid (see section 5.2). As discussed in chapter 2 (section 2.4), a condition to accomplish such a task is to formulate the theoretical model so as to represent the diffusion limit of ARCH models. In recognition of the possibility that ARCH models may not converge to any diffusion limit (see section 2.3), we show how to construct a testing procedure of the validity of the moment conditions needed to guarantee the convergence to a well-defined diffusion limit. Such a testing procedure is described in section 5.3, where we also present the general philosophy of statistical inference procedures designed to estimate the parameters of stochastic differential equations that rest on simulation based methods.

In section 5.4, we show how to solve numerically for the equilibrium bond price. Although there exist many numerical procedures to integrate multi-dimensional partial differential equations (see, e.g., Gilli et al. (1999) for a comparative analysis of such methods applied to multivariate option pricing with deterministic volatility), we will make reference to the so-called Crank-Nicholson method, since it represents a stable algorithm which is at the same time relatively easy to implement.

Section 5.5 provides an illustrative but succinct example of the implementation of the material contained in the previous sections, and an appendix presents an alternative solution technique for the equilibrium bond price that is based on a method of iterated approximations.

5.2   Specification of the theoretical models

We specialize the model of section 4.5 of the preceding chapter by backward engineering the drift and diffusion functions in (4.16) that exactly match the drift and diffusion functions of two models that have been presented in chapter 1 as pedagogical devices. These are models (1.15) and model (1.16), respectively.

To obtain model (1.15), we first rewrite the volatility equation in terms of the standard deviation,

$$d\sigma(t) = \sigma(t)(\frac{\kappa}{2}(\alpha - \log\sigma(t)^2) + \frac{\psi^2}{8})dt + \sigma(t)\frac{\psi}{2}dW^{(2)}(t),$$

and try setting $\nu = \log y_2^2$ in (4.16); then, by comparing the preceding equation with eq. (4.19) and setting $\rho(y) \equiv 0$, we identify drift and diffusion functions in (4.16) as follows:[1] $\widetilde{\varphi}(y) = \kappa(\alpha - \log y_2^2) - \kappa\log(\widetilde{Ab}(\frac{1}{A}))^2$ and $\widetilde{\psi}(y) = \psi$. The first equation of system (1.15) follows trivially by an identification argument involving eq. (4.20).

To obtain model (1.16), we proceed as in the above example. We rewrite the volatility equation in terms of the standard deviation and, by trying with $\nu = y_2^2$ and setting $\rho(y) \equiv 0$, we identify $\widetilde{\varphi}(y) = \kappa(\frac{\alpha}{(\widetilde{Ab}(\frac{1}{A}))^2} - y_2^2)$ and $\widetilde{\psi}(y) = \frac{\psi}{\widetilde{Ab}(\frac{1}{A})}y_2$. Again, the first equation of the system follows trivially.

Motivated by the considerations spelled out in the introduction of this chapter, now we present a model that we use as the benchmark example to which we apply the techniques of this chapter. Such a model has been considered by Fornari and Mele (1999a), and assumes that $a(y) \equiv \kappa y_1 + \zeta$, $b(y_1) \equiv y_1^{1/2}$, $\widetilde{\varphi}(y) \equiv \widetilde{\omega} - \varphi y_2^\delta$, $\widetilde{\psi}(y) \equiv \psi y_2^\delta$, $v(y_2) \equiv y_2^\delta$, $\rho(y) \equiv \rho$, where κ, ζ, $\widetilde{\omega}$, φ, ψ, δ, ρ are real constants. This implies that the *equilibrium* instantaneous interest

---

[1] A and $\widetilde{b}(.)$ are a constant and a function that have been introduced in chapter 4, section 4.5.2.

rate process r satisfies:

$$
\begin{aligned}
dr(t) &= (\iota - \theta r(t))dt + \sigma r(t)^{1/2}dW^{(1)}(t) \\
d\sigma(t)^\delta &= (\overline{\omega} - \varphi\sigma(t)^\delta)dt + \psi\sigma(t)^\delta d(\rho W^{(1)}(t) + (1-\rho^2)^{1/2}W^{(2)}(t))
\end{aligned}
$$

$$(5.1)$$

where $\iota \equiv A\zeta$, $\theta \equiv -\kappa$, and $\overline{\omega} \equiv \widetilde{\omega}A^{\frac{\delta}{2}}$.

We know that the equilibrium bond price satisfies the partial differential equation (4.22) found in the previous chapter. With the parametrization in (5.1), the equilibrium price $B(r, \sigma^\delta, t)$ thus solves:

$$
\begin{aligned}
\mathcal{L}[B](x, \sigma^\delta, t) &= \Lambda(x, \sigma^\delta, t) + xB(x, \sigma^\delta, t), \ t \in [0, T) \\
B(x, \sigma^\delta, T) &= 1, \ \forall (x, \sigma) \in \mathbb{R}^2_{++}
\end{aligned}
$$

$$(5.2)$$

where

$$
\begin{aligned}
\mathcal{L}[B](x, \sigma^\delta, t) &\equiv B_t + B_x \cdot (\iota - \theta x) + B_{\sigma^\delta} \cdot (\overline{\omega} - \varphi\sigma^\delta) \\
&\quad + \tfrac{1}{2}(B_{xx} \cdot x\sigma^2 + 2B_{x\sigma^\delta} \cdot \psi\rho x^{1/2}\sigma^{\delta+1} + B_{\sigma^\delta\sigma^\delta} \cdot \psi^2\sigma^{2\delta}),
\end{aligned}
$$

$$
\Lambda(x, \sigma^\delta, t) \equiv B_r \cdot \lambda_1 x\sigma + B_{\sigma^\delta} \cdot (\lambda_1\rho + \lambda_2(1-\rho^2)^{1/2})\psi\sigma^\delta x^{1/2},
$$

and λ_1, λ_2 are two constants entering the unit risk premia functions that have been derived in the preceding chapter (see eqs. (4.21)).

The volatility process in (5.1) offers an interesting contrast with previous stochastic volatility models, since it allows for the possibility that the 'volatility concept' be not constrained to variance or standard deviation, say; rather, in (5.1), δ is a new parameter that can be estimated from data. In the empirical section of Fornari and Mele (1999a), for instance, we find that $\delta \cong 1$ for US data. As shown in chapter 2 (lemma 2.4), the volatility process σ^δ has a steady state distribution that is an inverted Gamma. Figure 5.1, taken from Fornari and Mele (1999a), depicts the stationary density of the standard deviation $f(s, d) \equiv P^d_{(s)}(s)$ found in chapter 2, appendix B (lemma 2B.2) in correspondence of the parameter estimates for the US interest rate obtained in Fornari and Mele (1999a) (see section 5.5). The density shrinks to the left as δ decreases, but such a phenomenon has to be understood as the product of a comparative statics exercise.

The volatility equation in (5.1) encompasses other formulations already encountered in the stochastic volatility literature (see, for instance, Ball and Roma (1994) and Taylor (1994) for a list of models that have been typically used in the stochastic volatility option pricing literature). As discussed at length in Fornari and Mele (1999a), however, such a distribution does not encompass the important case of the log-volatility equations used in the empirical work of Andersen and Lund (1997a, b) or Gallant and Tauchen (1998). In practice, however, the presence of δ should make model (5.1) be more flexible than models like (1.15) or (1.16); see Fornari and Mele (1999a) for further details.

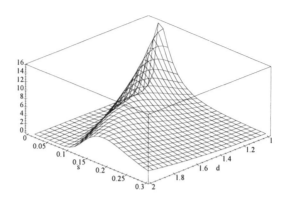

FIGURE 5.1. Stationary distribution $f(s,d)$ of the standard deviation s, for $d \in [1,2]$.

5.3   Econometric strategy

We implement the indirect inference principle to estimate the parameters of the stochastic differential system (5.1). As discussed in chapter 1, we are also interested in providing some basic tools by which one can gauge the uselfulness of ARCH models as diffusion approximations. Accordingly, we start by presenting a vary basic approach to obtain an initial estimate of $a \equiv (\iota, \theta, \overline{\omega}, \varphi, \psi, \rho, \delta)$. It consists in replacing the (intractable) likelihood function implied by the true measure induced by (5.1) with an approximation of it that is based on a well-chosen ARCH model converging in distribution to it (see chapter 2). Since the resulting likelihood function refers to a model converging in distribution to the solution of (5.1) that is *not* an Euler approximation of (5.1), however, we call the resulting criterion 'quasi'-approximated likelihood function. The advantage of the quasi-approximated ML estimator is that it demands no computational efforts, and its main drawback is that it is not necessarily consistent, since the ARCH models we use are typically not closed under temporal aggregation, which is theoretically the case only when the concept of an ARCH model is weakened, as discussed in chapter 1, section 1.4. Furthermore, the model we use may even fail to converge to any diffusion limit, as explained in chapter 2, section 2.3. In recognition of these facts, we show here how to construct a very precise testing procedure of the validity of the moment conditions needed to guarantee the convergence to well-defined diffusion limits; as it turns out, such a testing procedure also gives important information about the importance of disaggregation biases. Our strategy is based on the consistency test originally suggested by Gouriéroux et al. (1993) (section 4.2), and it can be viewed as the natural substitute of a global specification test in just-identified problems (see relation (5.8)).

Our starting point is based on the weak convergence results of the A-PARCH shown in chapter 2. We consider a model generated by a discrete time approximation of the short term interest rate equation with which we juxtapose the A-PARCH model:

$$
\begin{aligned}
\Delta r_{n+1} &= \Delta r_n + \iota_\Delta - \theta_\Delta \cdot \Delta r_n + \Delta \sigma_{n+1} \, \Delta r_n^{1/2} \cdot \Delta u_{n+1} \\
\Delta \epsilon_n &= \Delta u_n \cdot \Delta \sigma_n, \quad \tfrac{\Delta u_n}{\Delta^{1/2}} \sim \text{g.e.d.}_{(v)} \\
\Delta \sigma_{n+1}^\delta &= w_\Delta + \alpha_\Delta (|\Delta \epsilon_n| - \gamma \cdot \Delta \epsilon_n)^\delta + \beta_\Delta \cdot \Delta \sigma_n^\delta
\end{aligned}
\tag{5.3}
$$

where the indexing $n = 0, 1, 2, \dots$ refers to consecutive observations sampled at the same frequency Δ,[2] $\iota_\Delta, \theta_\Delta, w_\Delta$ are of the form $x_\Delta = x^{(\Delta)} \cdot \Delta$, with $\iota^{(\Delta)}, \theta^{(\Delta)}$ real parameters and $w^{(\Delta)} > 0, \alpha_\Delta, \beta_\Delta \geq 0, \delta > 0, \gamma \in (-1, 1)$. Such a representation is a natural generalization of the Brenner et al. (1996) model. It is easy to adapt the arguments utilized to show theorem 2.3 in chapter 2 to show the weak convergence of (5.3) to the solution of (5.1). Specifically, let

$$
\begin{aligned}
\varphi_h &\equiv 1 - n_{\delta, v}((1 - \gamma)^\delta + (1 + \gamma)^\delta)\alpha_h - \beta_h, \\
\psi_h &\equiv ((m_{\delta, v} - n_{\delta, v}^2)((1 - \gamma)^{2\delta} + (1 + \gamma)^{2\delta}) - 2n_{\delta, v}^2 (1 - \gamma)^\delta (1 + \gamma)^\delta)^{1/2} \cdot \alpha_h,
\end{aligned}
$$

and set ρ to formula (2.4) in chapter 2.

Let, further,

$$
{}_h\xi_{hk} \equiv \frac{\left| \frac{{}_h u_{hk}}{h^{1/2}} \right|^\delta (1 - \gamma s_k)^\delta - E(\left| \frac{{}_h u_{hk}}{h^{1/2}} \right|^\delta (1 - \gamma s_k)^\delta)}{((m_{\delta, v} - n_{\delta, v}^2)((1 - \gamma)^{2\delta} + (1 + \gamma)^{2\delta}) - 2n_{\delta, v}^2 (1 - \gamma)^\delta (1 + \gamma)^\delta)^{1/2}}.
$$

By utilizing the arguments in thm. 2.3, we have that if $\lim_{h \downarrow 0} h^{-1} \iota_h = \iota$, $\lim_{h \downarrow 0} h^{-1} \theta_h = \theta$ and:

$$
\begin{aligned}
\lim_{h \downarrow 0} h^{-1} w_h &= \bar{w} \in (0, \infty), \\
\lim_{h \downarrow 0} h^{-1} \varphi_h &= \varphi < \infty, \\
\lim_{h \downarrow 0} h^{-1/2} \psi_h &= \psi < \infty.
\end{aligned}
\tag{5.4}
$$

then the distribution of the sample paths generated by the following model,

$$
\begin{aligned}
{}_h r_{h(k+1)} - {}_h r_{hk} &= (\iota_h - \theta_h \cdot {}_h r_{hk}) + {}_h \sigma_{h(k+1)} \, {}_h r_{hk}^{1/2} \cdot {}_h u_{h(k+1)} \\
{}_h \sigma_{h(k+1)}^\delta - {}_h \sigma_{hk}^\delta &= (w_h - \varphi_h \cdot {}_h \sigma_{hk}^\delta) + \psi_h \cdot {}_h \sigma_{hk}^\delta \cdot {}_h \xi_{hk}
\end{aligned}
$$

gets closer and closer to the distribution generated by the sample paths generated by (5.1).

---

[2]Δ is the fraction of the sample frequency to the "numéraire" period: e.g., $\Delta = \frac{1}{24}$ if the sample frequency is hourly and the unity time is expressed in days, $\Delta = \frac{1}{52}$ if the sample frequency is weekly and the unity time is expressed in years, and so on.

As regards the intuition behind ρ in (2.4), this can be based on the appealing result that:

$$\psi^{-1}\frac{1}{h}E(\frac{{}_hr_{hk} - {}_hr_{h(k-1)}}{{}_hr^{1/2}_{h(k-1)} \cdot {}_h\sigma_{hk}} \cdot \frac{{}_h\sigma^\delta_{h(k+1)} - {}_h\sigma^\delta_{hk}}{{}_h\sigma^\delta_{hk}} \mid \mathcal{F}_{hk}) \underset{h\downarrow 0}{\rightarrow} \rho,$$

where $\mathcal{F}_{hk}$ denotes the sigma-algebra generated by ${}_hr_0, {}_hr_h, {}_hr_{2h}, \dots, {}_hr_{h(k-1)}$ and ${}_h\sigma^\delta_0, {}_h\sigma^\delta_h, {}_h\sigma^\delta_{2h}, \dots, {}_h\sigma^\delta_{hk}$.

The quasi-approximated ML (Q-AML) estimators of $\overline{\omega}, \varphi, \psi$ we propose are then

$$\begin{aligned}
\overline{\omega}_{\text{q-aml}} &\equiv \Delta^{-3/2}\widehat{w}_\Delta, \\
\varphi_{\text{q-aml}} &\equiv \Delta^{-1}\widehat{\varphi}_\Delta, \\
\psi_{\text{q-aml}} &\equiv \Delta^{-1/2}\widehat{\psi}_\Delta,
\end{aligned} \qquad (5.5)$$

where $\widehat{\varphi}_\Delta, \widehat{\psi}_\Delta$ are obtained by means of formulae (5.4) computed in correspondence of the QML estimator of model (5.3), $\widehat{w}_\Delta$ is the QML estimator of w_Δ of model (5.3). The Q-AML estimator of δ is the QML estimator of δ in model (5.3), and the Q-AML estimators of ι and θ are as those of $\overline{\omega}$ and φ above. Finally, the Q-AML estimator of ρ is obtained by plugging the QML estimators of $(\delta, \upsilon, \gamma)$ in formula (2.4), chapter 2.

The preceding estimators only rely on identifying moment conditions. One can now apply the indirect inference principle to test and correct for disaggregation biases. Formally, the Q-AML estimator of $b = (\Delta^{-1}\iota_\Delta, \Delta^{-1}\theta_\Delta, \Delta^{-3/2}w_\Delta, \Delta^{-1}\varphi_\Delta, \Delta^{-1/2}\psi_\Delta, \gamma, \delta, \upsilon)'$ in (5.3) is:

$$a_{\text{q-aml}} \equiv \widehat{b}_N = \arg\max_b \mathfrak{L}_N(\Delta r; b),$$

where $\mathfrak{L}_N(\Delta r; b)$ is the likelihood function implied by model (5.3), N is the sample size, and Δr is the observations set, which is supposed to be a discretely sampled diffusion from (5.1) when the true parameter vector is a_0. Note that $\dim(b) > \dim(a)$, but to simplify the exposition, we shall always consider the gaussian case in which $\upsilon \equiv 2$, and consistently with the assumptions and notation of chapter 2, we shall impose the time-scale invariance of δ and γ. Accordingly, now we re-interpret b as a vector in an open subset of $\mathbb{R}^5$ (with coordinates $\Delta^{-1}\iota_\Delta, \Delta^{-1}\theta_\Delta, \Delta^{-3/2}w_\Delta, \Delta^{-1}\varphi_\Delta, \Delta^{-1/2}\psi_\Delta$), $\mathfrak{L}_N(.)$ as a likelihood function that sets δ and γ to their Q-AML estimates and $\upsilon \equiv 2$, and a as a vector in an open subset of $\mathbb{R}^5$ (with coordinates $\iota, \theta, \overline{\omega}, \varphi, \psi$).

It is well known that under standard regularity conditions, such as $[N^{1/2}\frac{\partial \mathfrak{L}_N}{\partial b}(\Delta r; b)]_{b=b_0(a_0)} \xrightarrow{d} N(0, J(a_0))$, one has asymptotic normality of the pseudo-maximum likelihood estimator,

$$N^{1/2}(\widehat{b}_N - b_0(a_0)) \xrightarrow{d} N(0, \ddot{\mathfrak{L}}_\infty^{-1}(a_0; b_0(a_0)) \cdot J(a_0) \cdot \ddot{\mathfrak{L}}_\infty^{-1}(a_0; b_0(a_0))),$$

where $\mathfrak{L}_\infty(a_0; b) = \text{plim}_N \mathfrak{L}_N(\Delta r; b)$ say, uniformly in $b \in B \subset \mathbb{R}^5$, $\ddot{\mathfrak{L}}_\infty(a_0; b) = \text{plim}_N \frac{\partial^2 \mathfrak{L}_N}{\partial b \partial b'}(\Delta r; b)$, say, uniformly in $b \in B$, where $\frac{\partial^2 \mathfrak{L}_N}{\partial b \partial b'}(.)$ is invertible. In the preceding formulation, $b_0(.)$ is the so-called binding function:

$$b_0(a_0) = \arg\max_b \mathfrak{L}_\infty(a_0; b), \text{ the limit problem.}$$

However, the true law of $_\Delta r$, as implied by the continuous time data generating mechanism, say $\ell_0(_\Delta r)$, is most probably such that

$$\ell_0(_\Delta r) \notin \{\mathfrak{L}_N(_\Delta r; b), \ b \text{ varying}\},$$

and the discrete time model is expected to behave in a way that allows for a discretization bias

$$b(a_0) \neq a_0.$$

In Fornari and Mele (1999a, b), we test and correct the potential bias of the Q-AML estimator by the indirect inference principle; there we show that the identifying moment conditions (5.5) do a reasonable good work, for the correction introduced by the indirect inference procedure is not important in terms of a specification test based on the ex-post adequacy of an approximating model having the form (5.3) with parameter sequences as in (5.5) (see relation (5.8) below).

The indirect inference principle can be applied by using model (5.3) as one of the possible discrete time counterparts of the continuous time model with simulations drawn from

$$
\begin{aligned}
_h r_{h(k+1)} - {_h r_{hk}} &= (\iota - \theta \cdot {_h r_{hk}})h + {_h \sigma_{h(k+1)}} \cdot {_h r_{hk}^{1/2}} \cdot {_h u_{h(k+1)}} \\
_h \sigma_{h(k+1)}^\delta - {_h \sigma_{hk}^\delta} &= (\overline{\omega} - \varphi \cdot {_h \sigma_{hk}^\delta})h + \psi \cdot {_h \sigma_{hk}^\delta} \cdot {_h \xi_{hk}}
\end{aligned}
\quad (5.6)
$$

One can also double the dimension of the high frequency simulation generator by replacing $_h \xi_{hk}$ with $_h \widetilde{\xi}_{h(k+1)}$, where $E(_h \widetilde{\xi}_{hk}) = 0$, $\text{var}(_h \widetilde{\xi}_{hk}) = h$ and $\text{corr}(_h u_{hk} \cdot {_h \widetilde{\xi}_{hk}}) = \rho \cdot h$, all h.

The indirect inference estimation then runs as follows. After simulating (5.6) in correspondence of values of $a = (\iota, \theta, \overline{\omega}, \varphi, \psi)$, we obtain $_{h,h}\widetilde{r}^{(s)}(a) = \{_h\widetilde{r}_{hk}^{(s)}(a)\}_{k=0}^{N/h}$, $s = 1, ..., S$, where S is the number of simulations. For each simulation we retain the values of $\widetilde{r}^{(s)}$ which correspond to integer indexes of time and estimate the auxiliary model on each simulated series to get

$$\widehat{b}_{N,s}^{(h)}(a) = \arg\max_b \mathfrak{L}_N(_{1,h}\widetilde{r}^{(s)}(a); b), \quad s = 1, ..., S,$$

where $_{1,h}\widetilde{r}^{(s)}(.)$ denotes the set of interest rates that have integer indexes of time under simulation s and interval h. In our specific just-identified problem $(\dim(a) = \dim(b))$, the indirect estimator of a is then the solution (provided it exist) of the following five-dimensional system:

$$0 = \widehat{b}_N - \frac{1}{S}\sum_{s=1}^{S} \widehat{b}_{N,s}^{(h)}(a).$$

Call $_h\widehat{a}_N(a_0)$ the solution of the preceding system. To obtain heuristically its asymptotic distribution, expand the preceding system of equalities around a_0:

$$\widehat{b}_N - \frac{1}{S}\sum_{s=1}^{S}\widehat{b}_{N,s}^{(h)}(a_0) = (\frac{1}{S}\sum_{s=1}^{S}\frac{\partial\widehat{b}_{N,s}^{(h)}}{\partial a}(a_0))(_h\widehat{a}_N(a_0) - a_0)$$

For large N, the preceding is in fact an equality in distribution, and the covariance matrix of $(\frac{1}{S}\sum_{s=1}^{S}\frac{\partial\widehat{b}_{N,s}^{(h)}}{\partial a}(a_0))(_h\widehat{a}_N(a_0) - a_0)$ is the covariance matrix of $\widehat{b}_N - \frac{1}{S}\sum_{s=1}^{S}\widehat{b}_{N,s}^{(h)}(a_0)$, i.e. $(1 + \frac{1}{S})\text{cov}(\widehat{b}_{N,s}^{(h)}(a_0))$, and one has:

$$N^{1/2}(_h\widehat{a}_N(a_0) - a_0) \xrightarrow[N\uparrow\infty,\, h\downarrow 0]{d} N(0, (1 + \frac{1}{S})V_0^{-1}\Gamma_0 V_0'^{-1}), \qquad (5.7)$$

where Γ_0 is the covariance matrix of the simulated estimator and $V_0 \equiv \frac{\partial b}{\partial a}(a_0)$, i.e., the Jacobian of the binding function evaluated at a_0.[3] Broze et al. (1995b) proved the preceding result in great generality—i.e. in the case of a general diffusion in $\mathbb{R}^l$—, and to avoid bias due to the discretization step used during the simulations (hence the label 'quasi'-indirect inference), the authors also suggested to take $h = N^{-d}$ with $d > \frac{1}{2}$.

Finally, one can compute a global specification test that controls the adequacy of the approximated model. Such a consistency test aims at checking the validity of a sort of a fixed point of the binding function:

$$\text{H0} : a_0 = b(a_0).$$

Under H0, one has that:

$$N^{1/2}(\widehat{b}_N - \frac{1}{S}\sum_{s=1}^{S}\widehat{b}_{N,s}^{(h)}(\widehat{b}_N)) \xrightarrow{d} N(0, \mathfrak{B}), \qquad (5.8)$$

---

[3]In the over-identified case, the indirect estimator of a is given by

$$_h\widehat{a}_N(a_0) = \arg\min_a \left\| \widehat{b}_N - \frac{1}{S}\sum_{s=1}^{S}\widehat{b}_{N,s}^{(h)}(a) \right\|,$$

where $\|.\|$ is a given norm. When such a norm is generated by the identity matrix, for instance (i.e. the criterion is $\left\| \widehat{b}_N - \frac{1}{S}\sum_{s=1}^{S}\widehat{b}_{N,s}^{(h)}(a) \right\|^2$), asymptotics for $_h\widehat{a}_N(a_0)$ are as follows:

$$N^{1/2}(_h\widehat{a}_N(a_0) - a_0) \xrightarrow[N\uparrow\infty,\, h\downarrow 0]{d} N(0, \frac{S+1}{S}(V_0'V_0)^{-1}V_0'\Gamma_0 V_0(V_0'V_0)^{-1}).$$

When instead the norm is generated by an optimal choice of the weighting matrix, the variance above becomes equal to $\frac{S+1}{S}(V_0'\Gamma_0^{-1}V_0)^{-1}$.

A global specification test can be based on the quadratic form that generated the criterion. Under the null of correct specification of the theoretical model, N times the minimized criterion is asymptotically chi-squared with $\dim(b) - \dim(a)$ degrees of freedom.

where

$$\mathfrak{B} \equiv (\mathbf{I}_5 - \frac{\partial b}{\partial a}(a_0)) \,\ddot{\mathfrak{L}}_\infty^{-1} \, J \, \ddot{\mathfrak{L}}_\infty^{-1} \, (\mathbf{I}_5 - \frac{\partial b'}{\partial a}(a_0)) + \frac{1}{S} \, \ddot{\mathfrak{L}}_\infty^{-1} \, J \, \ddot{\mathfrak{L}}_\infty^{-1}$$

(see Gouriéroux et al. (1993)) (appendix 3). As discussed in chapter 1, such a test is particularly important here, since the continuous record asymptotics that we presented in chapter 2 do *not* deliver a theory of parameter estimation; rather, they were obtained by taking the parameters and their (converging) sequences as given.

Is an auxiliary ARCH-based criterion the only device to achieve consistent estimation of the parameters of interest ? Certainly not. The following diagram illustrates the situation. It conveys the main arguments that have to be used to show asymptotic normality of the parameters of interest of a diffusion system in a simulation-based context (see Broze et al. (1985b) and appendix C in Fornari and Mele (1999a) for further details).

$$
\begin{array}{ccc}
\mathfrak{L}_N(\Delta\tilde{r}(a_0); b) & \overset{h\downarrow 0}{\Longrightarrow} & \mathfrak{L}_N(\Delta r; b) \\[1em]
\downarrow^{N\uparrow\infty} & & \downarrow^{N\uparrow\infty} \\[1em]
\mathfrak{L}_\infty^{(h)}(a_0; b) & & \mathfrak{L}_\infty(a_0; b)
\end{array}
$$

convergence of the criterion

Suppose for instance that $\mathfrak{L}_N(.)$ corresponds to the exact likelihood that is associated with, say, an ARMA representation applied to the squared points of the discretely sampled simulated data. If the solution of the approximating scheme used for the simulations converges weakly to the solution of the data generating process, a_0 represent the true parameter vector, Δr and $\Delta\tilde{r}(a_0)$ represent real and simulated data sampled at frequency Δ, one has that $\mathfrak{L}_N(\Delta\tilde{r}(a_0); b) \Rightarrow \mathfrak{L}_N(\Delta r; b)$ under suitable conditions. This is obviously the case because the observation set Δr is assumed to have been generated by the data generating process. Consistency of the indirect estimator (i.e. for small N^{-1} and h) based on the auxiliary ARMA now follows from an argument, and conditions, similar to the one presented in appendix C in Fornari and Mele (1999a).

While there is not a theory concerning the optimal choice of the criterion in small sample sizes, one would like to require that the (already misspecified) auxiliary model fulfils some basic properties. Let M_Δ be a candidate auxiliary model. One property of M_Δ should be that it can be embedded into another model M_h, say, the solution of which converges in distribution towards the data generating process as $h \downarrow 0$. Such a choice is the most natural one, and indeed is the one that is both suggested and done in the literature; see, for instance, Broze et al. (1995a, b), and Gouriéroux and Monfort (1996) (p. 119-133). In view of the convergence results for ARCH models, choosing them as auxiliary devices is in line with such a principle. In addition, one can consider the case in which M_h is also used as the high frequency simulation generator. This, also, appears as a reasonable choice, and is suggested in the references above, too. This last case corresponds to the strategy discussed in chapter 1, section 1.4. Furthermore, it is more likely that properties that are sufficient for (5.7) to hold—such as the convergence of $\mathfrak{L}_N(\Delta\tilde{r}(a_0); b)$ to $\mathfrak{L}_\infty^{(h)}(a_0; b)$, uniformly in b; or the continuity of the partial application $a \mapsto \widehat{b}_{N,s}^{(h)}(a)$—are fulfilled in cases where $\mathfrak{L}_N(.)$ applies to discrete time counterparts of the data generating mechanism that are embedded in the high frequency simulation generator—as for (5.6)—, rather than in cases in which the criterion does not even fulfill such a requirement. However, we are unable to show that such circumstances hold in great generality.

Another approach has been put forward in the EMM theory of Gallant of Tauchen (1996). As discussed in the introductory chapter (section 1.4), the EMM estimator can achieve the same efficiency as the true (intractable) ML estimator when the auxiliary model generates a density that 'smoothly embeds' the true likelihood function of the discretely sampled diffusion. Following the results of Gallant and Long (1997), one can use a semi-nonparametric based likelihood function to provide the additional parameters that increment the efficiency of the EMM estimator. Thus, the EMM-based estimator typically relies on an auxiliary criterion that is based on an highly parametrized semi-nonparametric based likelihood function. In a first step, one obtains a qml estimate,

$$\widehat{b}_N = \arg\max_b \frac{1}{N} \sum_{t=1}^{N} \log \mathfrak{L}(r_t \,/\, \overline{r}_{t-1}; b),$$

where $\mathfrak{L}(.)$ is the likelihood of a single point, and $\overline{r}$ contains lagged values of r. The M^2 estimator with weighting matrix $\mathcal{I}_N$ is

$$\widehat{a}_N = \arg\min_a m_N(a, \widehat{b}_N)' \cdot \mathcal{I}_N^{-1} \cdot m_N(a, \widehat{b}_N), \qquad (5.9)$$

where

$$m_N(a, \widehat{b}_N) = \frac{1}{L} \sum_{j=1}^{L} \frac{\partial}{\partial b} \log \mathfrak{L}(\tilde{r}_j(a) \,/\, \tilde{\overline{r}}_{j-1}(a); b),$$

$\{\tilde{r}_j(x)\}_{j=1}^{L}$ is a discretely sampled simulated diffusion with parameter vector $a = x$, and L is the simulation length. If the score is a good data description, one can use $\mathcal{I}_N \doteq \frac{1}{N} \sum_{t=1}^{N} [\frac{\partial}{\partial b} \log \mathfrak{L}(r_t \,/\, \overline{r}_{t-1}; \widehat{b}_N)][\frac{\partial}{\partial b} \log \mathfrak{L}(r_t \,/\, \overline{r}_{t-1}; \widehat{b}_N)]'$ as a weighting matrix in (5.9). Asymptotics are derived similarly to the ones presented in footnote 3:

$$N^{1/2}(\widehat{a}_N - a_0) \xrightarrow{d} N(0, (A'\mathcal{I}_N^{-1}A)^{-1}),$$

where $A = \frac{\partial}{\partial a} m(a_0, b_0)$ and $m(.) = E(\frac{\partial}{\partial b} \log \mathfrak{L}(.))$; a global specification test that checks the correctness of the theoretical model is based on N times the minimized quadratic form $m_N(\widehat{a}_N, \widehat{b}_N)' \cdot \mathcal{I}_N^{-1} \cdot m_N(\widehat{a}_N, \widehat{b}_N)$, which is asymptotically chi-squared with $\dim(b) - \dim(a)$ degrees of freedom.

5.4 The pure numerical solution of the theoretical models

The present section describes a method that one may follow to integrate numerically partial differential equations that have the form of eq. (4.22) in the previous chapter. Such a method is based on the well-known Crank-Nicholson scheme (see, e.g., Ames (1977)). When compared with the usual Monte-Carlo methods, a numerical solution of a partial differential equation has the advantage to be much more flexible, especially when the researcher has to impose transversality conditions, or is interested in studying the dependence of the solution over a wide range of the initial states.

In section 5.4.1, we start and discuss the case in which the Cranck-Nicholson method is applied to a compact state-space; section 5.4.2 then shows how to manage the general noncompact state-space case, and focusses on the partial differential equation (5.2); finally, section 5.4.3 imposes limiting and transversality conditions to the approximating scheme that are used to eventually close the solution of the partial differential equation (5.2).

5.4.1 THE COMPACT STATE-SPACE CASE

Suppose we are given the following partial differential equation: for $(x, y, t) \in \mathcal{O}_1 \times \mathcal{O}_2 \times [0, T)$

$$0 = f_t + a(x, y)f_x + b(x, y)f_y + c(x, y)f_{xx} + d(x, y)f_{yy} + e(x, y)f_{xy} - R(x)f, \tag{5.10}$$

where $f \equiv f(x, y, t)$, a, b, c, d, e, R satisfy the usual regularity conditions contained for instance in the appendix of this chapter, and $\mathcal{O}_i$ are compacta of $\mathbb{R}_{++}$. The boundary condition we consider is $f(x, y, T) = 1 \ \forall (x, y) \in \mathcal{O}_1 \times \mathcal{O}_2$. We approximate the derivatives involved in the preceding equation by making use of both explicit and implicit approximations. We chop the state-space into a $N \times N$ grid, and time into J units:

$$\{(x_i, y_\ell)_{i,\ell=1}^N, (t_j)_{j=1}^J\} \subset \mathcal{O}_1 \times \mathcal{O}_2 \times [0, T];$$

here $x_i - x_{i-1} = \Delta x$, $y_\ell - x_{\ell-1} = \Delta y$, $t_j - t_{j-1} = \Delta t$, with $t_1 = 0$, $t_J = T$ and $N = \frac{x_N - x_1}{\Delta x} = \frac{y_N - y_1}{\Delta y}$, where $|x_N - x_1| < \infty$, and similarly for y. We define the approximation:

$$F_{i,\ell,j} \simeq f(x_i, y_\ell, t_j)$$

(and similarly for a, b, c, d, e, R), consider the primitive approximations:

$(f_x)_1$	$\simeq$	$\frac{F_{i+1,\ell,j} - F_{i-1,\ell,j}}{2\Delta x}$	(explicit at j)
$(f_x)_2$	$\simeq$	$\frac{F_{i+1,\ell,j+1} - F_{i-1,\ell,j+1}}{2\Delta x}$	(implicit at $j+1$)
$(f_y)_1$	$\simeq$	$\frac{F_{i,\ell+1,j} - F_{i,\ell-1,j}}{2\Delta y}$	(explicit at j)
$(f_y)_2$	$\simeq$	$\frac{F_{i,\ell+1,j+1} - F_{i,\ell-1,j+1}}{2\Delta y}$	(implicit at $j+1$)

$$(f_{xx})_1 \simeq \frac{F_{i+1,\ell,j}-2F_{i,\ell,j}+F_{i-1,\ell,j}}{(\Delta x)^2} \qquad \text{(explicit at } j)$$

$$(f_{xx})_2 \simeq \frac{F_{i+1,\ell,j+1}-2F_{i,\ell,j+1}+F_{i-1,\ell,j+1}}{(\Delta x)^2} \qquad \text{(implicit at } j+1)$$

$$(f_{yy})_1 \simeq \frac{F_{i,\ell+1,j}-2F_{i,\ell,j}+F_{i,\ell-1,j}}{(\Delta y)^2} \qquad \text{(explicit at } j)$$

$$(f_{yy})_2 \simeq \frac{F_{i,\ell+1,j+1}-2F_{i,\ell,j+1}+F_{i,\ell-1,j+1}}{(\Delta y)^2} \qquad \text{(implicit at } j+1)$$

$$(f_{xy})_1 \simeq \frac{F_{i+1,\ell+1,j}-F_{i+1,\ell-1,j}-F_{i-1,\ell+1,j}+F_{i-1,\ell-1,j}}{4\Delta x \cdot \Delta y} \qquad \text{(explicit at } j)$$

$$(f_{xy})_2 \simeq \frac{F_{i+1,\ell+1,j+1}-F_{i+1,\ell-1,j+1}-F_{i-1,\ell+1,j+1}+F_{i-1,\ell-1,j+1}}{4\Delta x \cdot \Delta y}$$

$$\text{(implicit at } j+1)$$

and construct the following estimates:

$$\widehat{f} \equiv F_{i,\ell,j}$$
$$\widehat{f_t} \equiv \frac{F_{i,\ell,j+1}-F_{i,\ell,j}}{\Delta t}$$
$$\widehat{f_x} \equiv \frac{1}{2}\sum_{i=1}^{2}(f_x)_i$$
$$\widehat{f_y} \equiv \frac{1}{2}\sum_{i=1}^{2}(f_y)_i$$
$$\widehat{f_{xx}} \equiv \frac{1}{2}\sum_{i=1}^{2}(f_{xx})_i$$
$$\widehat{f_{yy}} \equiv \frac{1}{2}\sum_{i=1}^{2}(f_{yy})_i$$
$$\widehat{f_{xy}} \equiv \frac{1}{2}\sum_{i=1}^{2}(f_{xy})_i$$

We plug the preceding estimates into eq. (5.10) and obtain:

$$\alpha_{i\ell}^{(1)} F_{i-1,\ell-1,j} + \alpha_{i\ell}^{(2)} F_{i,\ell-1,j} + \alpha_{i\ell}^{(3)} F_{i+1,\ell-1,j} + \alpha_{i\ell}^{(4)} F_{i-1,\ell,j} + \tilde{\alpha}_{i\ell}^{(5)} F_{i,\ell,j}$$
$$+\alpha_{i\ell}^{(6)} F_{i+1,\ell,j} + \alpha_{i\ell}^{(7)} F_{i-1,\ell+1,j} + \alpha_{i\ell}^{(8)} F_{i,\ell+1,j} + \alpha_{i\ell}^{(9)} F_{i+1,\ell+1,j}$$

$$=$$

$$-[\alpha_{i\ell}^{(1)} F_{i-1,\ell-1,j+1} + \alpha_{i\ell}^{(2)} F_{i,\ell-1,j+1} + \alpha_{i\ell}^{(3)} F_{i+1,\ell-1,j+1} + \alpha_{i\ell}^{(4)} F_{i-1,\ell,j+1}$$
$$+\alpha_{i\ell}^{(5)} F_{i,\ell,j+1} + \alpha_{i\ell}^{(6)} F_{i+1,\ell,j+1} + \alpha_{i\ell}^{(7)} F_{i-1,\ell+1,j+1} + \alpha_{i\ell}^{(8)} F_{i,\ell+1,j+1}$$
$$+\alpha_{i\ell}^{(9)} F_{i+1,\ell+1,j+1}]$$

$$(5.11)$$

where

$$\alpha_{i\ell}^{(1)} \equiv \frac{e_{i\ell}}{8\Delta x \cdot \Delta y}$$

$$\alpha_{i\ell}^{(2)} \equiv -\frac{b_{i\ell}}{4\Delta y} + \frac{d_{i\ell}}{2(\Delta y)^2}$$

$$\alpha_{i\ell}^{(3)} \equiv -\frac{e_{i\ell}}{8\Delta x \cdot \Delta y}$$

$$\alpha_{i\ell}^{(4)} \equiv -\frac{a_{i\ell}}{4\Delta x} + \frac{c_{i\ell}}{2(\Delta x)^2}$$

$$\tilde{\alpha}_{i\ell}^{(5)} \equiv -\frac{1}{\Delta t} - \frac{c_{i\ell}}{(\Delta x)^2} - \frac{d_{i\ell}}{(\Delta y)^2} - R_i$$

$$\alpha_{i\ell}^{(5)} \equiv \frac{1}{\Delta t} - \frac{c_{i\ell}}{(\Delta x)^2} - \frac{d_{i\ell}}{(\Delta y)^2}$$

$$\alpha_{i\ell}^{(6)} \equiv \frac{a_{i\ell}}{4\Delta x} + \frac{c_{i\ell}}{2(\Delta x)^2}$$

$$\alpha_{i\ell}^{(7)} \equiv -\frac{e_{i\ell}}{8\Delta x \cdot \Delta y}$$

$$\alpha_{i\ell}^{(8)} \equiv \frac{b_{i\ell}}{4\Delta y} + \frac{d_{i\ell}}{2(\Delta y)^2}$$

$$\alpha_{i\ell}^{(9)} \equiv \frac{e_{i\ell}}{8\Delta x \cdot \Delta y}$$

Next, we let

$$F_j = (F_{\cdot,1,j}, F_{\cdot,2,j}, ..., F_{\cdot,N-1,j}, F_{\cdot,N,j})'$$

$$F_{\cdot,\ell,j} = (F_{1,\ell,j}, F_{2,\ell,j}, ..., F_{N-1,\ell,j}, F_{N,\ell,j}), \ \ell = 1, ..., N.$$

Starting from the boundary condition[4]

$$F_J = \mathbf{1}_{N^2 \times 1}$$

(with $\mathbf{1}_{N^2 \times 1}$ being a vector of N^2 ones), eq. (5.11) can be solved by backward iterating the following equation

$$F_j = L \cdot F_{j+1}, \ j = J - 1, ..., 1,$$

where

$$L = -\widetilde{A}^{-1} \cdot A,$$

and $\widetilde{A}, A$ are block tridiagonal matrices:

$$\widetilde{A} = \begin{pmatrix} \widetilde{A}_{11} & A_{12} & 0 & 0 & ... & ... & ... & ... & 0 & 0 \\ A_{21} & \widetilde{A}_{22} & A_{23} & 0 & ... & ... & ... & ... & 0 & 0 \\ 0 & A_{32} & \widetilde{A}_{33} & A_{34} & ... & ... & ... & ... & 0 & 0 \\ ... & ... & ... & ... & \ddots & \ddots & ... & ... & ... & ... \\ 0 & 0 & 0 & 0 & ... & \widetilde{A}_{\ell\ell} & ... & ... & ... & 0 \\ ... & ... & ... & ... & \ddots & \ddots & ... & ... & ... & ... \\ 0 & 0 & 0 & 0 & ... & ... & ... & A_{N-1,N-2} & \widetilde{A}_{N-1,N-1} & A_{N-1,N} \\ 0 & 0 & 0 & 0 & ... & ... & ... & 0 & A_{N,N-1} & \widetilde{A}_{NN} \end{pmatrix},$$

$$A = \begin{pmatrix} A_{11} & A_{12} & 0 & 0 & ... & ... & ... & ... & 0 & 0 \\ A_{21} & A_{22} & A_{23} & 0 & ... & ... & ... & ... & 0 & 0 \\ 0 & A_{32} & A_{33} & A_{34} & ... & ... & ... & ... & 0 & 0 \\ ... & ... & ... & ... & \ddots & \ddots & ... & ... & ... & ... \\ 0 & 0 & 0 & 0 & ... & A_{\ell\ell} & ... & ... & ... & 0 \\ ... & ... & ... & ... & \ddots & \ddots & ... & ... & ... & ... \\ 0 & 0 & 0 & 0 & ... & ... & ... & A_{N-1,N-2} & A_{N-1,N-1} & A_{N-1,N} \\ 0 & 0 & 0 & 0 & ... & ... & ... & 0 & A_{N,N-1} & A_{NN} \end{pmatrix},$$

where $\mathbf{0}$ are $N \times N$ matrices of zeros and (with blanks denoting zeros)

---

[4]In section 5.4.3, we modify the boundary condition in order to take account of transversality conditions.

$$A_{\ell,\ell-1} = \begin{pmatrix} \alpha_{1\ell}^{(2)} & \alpha_{1\ell}^{(3)} & & & & & \\ \alpha_{2\ell}^{(1)} & \alpha_{2\ell}^{(2)} & \alpha_{2\ell}^{(3)} & & & & \\ & \alpha_{3\ell}^{(1)} & \alpha_{3\ell}^{(2)} & \alpha_{3\ell}^{(3)} & & & \\ & & & \ddots & & & \\ & & & & \alpha_{N-1,\ell}^{(1)} & \alpha_{N-1,\ell}^{(2)} & \alpha_{N-1,\ell}^{(3)} \\ & & & & & \alpha_{N\ell}^{(1)} & \alpha_{N\ell}^{(2)} \end{pmatrix},$$

$$\widetilde{A}_{\ell\ell} = \begin{pmatrix} \widetilde{\alpha}_{1\ell}^{(5)} & \alpha_{1\ell}^{(6)} & & & & & \\ \alpha_{2\ell}^{(4)} & \widetilde{\alpha}_{2\ell}^{(5)} & \alpha_{2\ell}^{(6)} & & & & \\ & \alpha_{3\ell}^{(4)} & \widetilde{\alpha}_{3\ell}^{(5)} & \alpha_{3\ell}^{(6)} & & & \\ & & & \ddots & & & \\ & & & & \alpha_{N-1,\ell}^{(4)} & \widetilde{\alpha}_{N-1,\ell}^{(5)} & \alpha_{N-1,\ell}^{(6)} \\ & & & & & \alpha_{N\ell}^{(4)} & \widetilde{\alpha}_{N\ell}^{(5)} \end{pmatrix},$$

and

$$A_{\ell,\ell+1} = \begin{pmatrix} \alpha_{1\ell}^{(8)} & \alpha_{1\ell}^{(9)} & & & & & \\ \alpha_{2\ell}^{(7)} & \alpha_{2\ell}^{(8)} & \alpha_{2\ell}^{(9)} & & & & \\ & \alpha_{3\ell}^{(7)} & \alpha_{3\ell}^{(8)} & \alpha_{3\ell}^{(9)} & & & \\ & & & \ddots & & & \\ & & & & \alpha_{N-1,\ell}^{(7)} & \alpha_{N-1,\ell}^{(8)} & \alpha_{N-1,\ell}^{(9)} \\ & & & & & \alpha_{N\ell}^{(7)} & \alpha_{N\ell}^{(9)} \end{pmatrix}.$$

Finally, $\widetilde{A}_{\ell\ell}$ differs from $A_{\ell\ell}$ in that the diagonal of $\widetilde{A}_{\ell\ell}$ is composed by $\widetilde{\alpha}_{i,\ell}^{(5)}$ whereas the diagonal of $A_{\ell\ell}$ is composed by $\alpha_{i,\ell}^{(5)}$.

The final step now consists in deriving limiting as well as transversality conditions that eventually place restrictions on the matrices $\widetilde{A}$ and A. As is clear, such a final step can only be implemented once the specific problem to solve becomes known. In the next subsection, for instance, we show how to switch the partial differential equation (5.2) to a compact state space formulation.

5.4.2 THE GENERAL CASE

When the state-space is not as in eq. (5.10)—as it usually happens in finance—, the implementation of the algorithm can only be done after a previous transformation of the original state-space. In the partial differential equation (5.2), for instance, we may introduce two new functions of (r, σ^δ) that take values on the compact $\mathcal{O}_1 \times \mathcal{O}_2$. A convenient choice is to set $\mathcal{O}_1 \times \mathcal{O}_2 = [0,1]^2$. Then we define $v \equiv \sigma^\delta$ and

$$
\begin{aligned}
x(r) &= \tfrac{\gamma r}{1+\gamma r}, \quad \gamma > 0 \\
y(v) &= \tfrac{\beta v}{1+\beta v}, \quad \beta > 0
\end{aligned}
\qquad (5.12)
$$

and write

$$
f(x,y,t) \equiv f(x(r),y(v),t) = B(r,v,t).
$$

In terms of (f,x,y) eq. (5.2) can be expressed in exactly the same format as eq. (5.10), with

$$
a(x,y) \equiv (\iota - \theta R(x) - R(x)V(y)^{\frac{1}{\delta}}\lambda_1)\tfrac{\gamma}{(1+\gamma R(x))^2} - R(x)V(y)^{\frac{2}{\delta}}\tfrac{\gamma^2}{(1+\gamma R(x))^3}
$$
$$
b(x,y) \equiv (\overline{w} - \varphi V(y) - \psi V(y)R(x)^{1/2}(\rho\lambda_1 + (1-\rho^2)^{1/2}\lambda_2))\tfrac{\beta}{(1+\beta V(y))^2}
$$
$$
\quad - \psi^2 V(y)^2 \tfrac{\beta^2}{(1+\beta V(y))^3}
$$
$$
c(x,y) \equiv \tfrac{1}{2}R(x)V(y)^{\frac{2}{\delta}}\tfrac{\gamma^2}{(1+\gamma R(x))^4}
$$
$$
d(x,y) \equiv \tfrac{1}{2}\psi^2 V(y)^2 \tfrac{\beta^2}{(1+\beta V(y))^4}
$$
$$
e(x,y) \equiv \psi\rho R(x)^{1/2}V(y)^{\frac{\delta+1}{\delta}}\tfrac{\gamma\beta}{(1+\gamma R(x))^2(1+\beta V(y))^2}
$$

where $(R,V)(.,.)$ is the inversion of (5.12):

$$
\begin{aligned}
R(x) &= \tfrac{x}{\gamma(1-x)} \\
V(y) &= \tfrac{y}{\beta(1-y)}
\end{aligned}
$$

Naturally, the previous formulae are valid for the partial differential equation (5.2) only. When one wishes to implement a different model, such formulae have to be modified to take into account the alternative drift and/or diffusion functions, but these are the *only* changes needed to implement the algorithm described in the previous subsection. However, one has to be very careful to check that the limiting and transversality conditions that we impose in the following subsection also hold for the new model.

Finally, it is worth noticing that the role of the new parameters β and γ in (5.12) in achieving precision is rather crucial. In practice, both should have to be chosen so that the state-space region that is the most visited region (theoretically) is overrepresented in the numerical procedure. To determine theoretically which is 'the most visited region', sometimes it would be sufficient to take a look at the simplest probabilistic properties of the diffusion generating mechanism in correspondence of the parameter values that will subsequently be used in the numerical procedure. In the case of model (5.2) with parameters fixed at the values reported in the following section, for instance, we use $\gamma = 70$ and $\beta = 100$ when $N = 30$.

5.4.3   Limiting and Transversality Conditions

Finally we impose two kinds of conditions. The first kind of conditions concerns the limiting behavior of the partial differential equation (5.10) when $R(x) =$

$0, R(x) = \infty, V(y) = 0, V(y) = \infty$. The second kind of conditions follows from a transversality argument, and stipulates that $\lim_{r \to \infty} B(r, v, t) = 0 \ \forall (v, t) \in \mathbb{R}_+ \times [0, T]$ and $\lim_{v \to \infty} B(r, v, t) = 0 \ \forall (r, t) \in \mathbb{R}_+ \times [0, T]$.

We call the first kind of conditions 'limiting conditions' and the second kind of conditions 'transversality conditions'.

To find the restrictions on the coefficients of $\widetilde{A}$ and A that correspond to $x = 0$ and $y = 0$, notice that, for each $t \in [0, T)$,

$$
\begin{aligned}
0 &= f_t(0, y, t) + a(0, y) f_x(0, y, t) + b(0, y) f_y(0, y, t) + d(0, y) f_{yy}(0, y, t) \\
0 &= f_t(x, 0, t) + a(x, 0) f_x(x, 0, t) + b(x, 0) f_y(x, 0, t) - R(x) f(x, 0, t)
\end{aligned}
$$

By plugging the following asymmetric approximations in the preceding equations,

$$
\begin{aligned}
\widehat{f_t}(0, y, t) &\equiv \frac{F_{1,\ell,j+1} - F_{1,\ell,j}}{\Delta t} \\
\widehat{f_t}(x, 0, t) &\equiv \frac{F_{i,1,j+1} - F_{i,1,j}}{\Delta t} \\
\widehat{f_x}(0, y, t) &\equiv \frac{F_{2,\ell,j} - F_{1,\ell,j}}{\Delta x} \\
\widehat{f_x}(x, 0, t) &\equiv \frac{F_{i+1,1,j} - F_{i,1,j}}{\Delta x} \\
\widehat{f_y}(0, y, t) &\equiv \frac{F_{1,\ell+1,j} - F_{1,\ell,j}}{\Delta y} \\
\widehat{f_y}(x, 0, t) &\equiv \frac{F_{i,2,j} - F_{i,1,j}}{\Delta y} \\
\widehat{f_{yy}}(0, y, t) &\equiv \frac{F_{1,\ell+1,j} - 2F_{1,\ell,j} + F_{1,\ell-1,j}}{(\Delta y)^2}
\end{aligned}
$$

we get the following difference equations:

$$
\begin{aligned}
\gamma_{1\ell}^{(1)} F_{1,\ell-1,j} + \gamma_{1\ell}^{(2)} F_{1,\ell,j} + \gamma_{1\ell}^{(3)} F_{2,\ell,j} + \gamma_{1\ell}^{(4)} F_{1,\ell+1,j} &= -\frac{1}{\Delta t} F_{1,\ell,j+1} \\
\eta_{i1}^{(1)} F_{i,1,j} + \eta_{i1}^{(2)} F_{i,2,j} + \eta_{i1}^{(3)} F_{i+1,1,j} &= -\frac{1}{\Delta t} F_{i,1,j+1}
\end{aligned}
$$

where

$$
\begin{aligned}
\gamma_{1\ell}^{(1)} &\equiv \frac{d_{1\ell}}{(\Delta y)^2} \\
\gamma_{1\ell}^{(2)} &\equiv -\frac{1}{\Delta t} - \frac{a_{1\ell}}{\Delta x} - \frac{b_{1\ell}}{\Delta y} - \frac{2d_{1\ell}}{(\Delta y)^2} \\
\gamma_{1\ell}^{(3)} &\equiv \frac{a_{1\ell}}{\Delta x} \\
\gamma_{1\ell}^{(4)} &\equiv \frac{b_{1\ell}}{\Delta y} + \frac{d_{1\ell}}{(\Delta y)^2} \\
\eta_{i1}^{(1)} &\equiv -\frac{1}{\Delta t} - \frac{a_{i1}}{\Delta x} - \frac{b_{i1}}{\Delta y} - R_i \\
\eta_{i1}^{(2)} &\equiv \frac{b_{i1}}{\Delta y} \\
\eta_{i1}^{(3)} &\equiv \frac{a_{i1}}{\Delta x}
\end{aligned}
$$

The matrices $\widetilde{A}$ and A must thus be constrained so that the elements $\alpha_{1\ell}^{(2)}$, $\alpha_{1\ell}^{(3)}, \widetilde{\alpha}_{1\ell}^{(5)}, \alpha_{1\ell}^{(5)}, \alpha_{1\ell}^{(6)}, \alpha_{1\ell}^{(8)}, \alpha_{1\ell}^{(9)}, \alpha_{i1}^{(4)}, \widetilde{\alpha}_{i1}^{(5)}, \alpha_{i1}^{(5)}, \alpha_{i1}^{(6)}, \alpha_{i1}^{(7)}, \alpha_{i1}^{(8)}$ and $\alpha_{i1}^{(9)}$ enter as $\alpha_{1\ell}^{(2)} = \gamma_{1\ell}^{(1)}, \alpha_{1\ell}^{(3)} = 0, \widetilde{\alpha}_{1\ell}^{(5)} = \gamma_{1\ell}^{(2)}, \alpha_{1\ell}^{(6)} = \gamma_{1\ell}^{(3)}, \alpha_{1\ell}^{(8)} = \gamma_{1\ell}^{(4)}, \alpha_{1\ell}^{(9)} = 0, \alpha_{i1}^{(4)} = 0,$ $\widetilde{\alpha}_{i1}^{(5)} = \eta_{i1}^{(1)}, \alpha_{i1}^{(6)} = \eta_{i1}^{(3)}, \alpha_{i1}^{(7)} = 0, \alpha_{i1}^{(8)} = \eta_{i1}^{(2)}, \alpha_{i1}^{(9)} = 0$ in matrix $\widetilde{A}$, and as

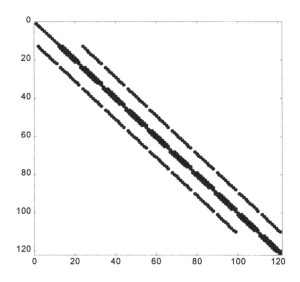

FIGURE 5.2. Pattern of nonzero elements in the $N^2 \times N^2$ dimensional matrix A

$\alpha_{1\ell}^{(2)} = 0$, $\alpha_{1\ell}^{(3)} = 0$, $\alpha_{1\ell}^{(5)} = \frac{1}{\Delta t}$, $\alpha_{1\ell}^{(6)} = 0$, $\alpha_{1\ell}^{(8)} = 0$, $\alpha_{1\ell}^{(9)} = 0$, $\alpha_{i1}^{(4)} = 0$, $\alpha_{i1}^{(5)} = \frac{1}{\Delta t}$, $\alpha_{i1}^{(6)} = 0$, $\alpha_{i1}^{(7)} = 0$, $\alpha_{i1}^{(8)} = 0$, $\alpha_{i1}^{(9)} = 0$ in matrix A. Finally, we derive and impose similar restrictions in the cases $x = 1$ and $y = 1$. Such restrictions were also the result of the transversality condition concerning the behavior of the price at $x = 1$: $F_{N,\ell,j} = 0$ ($\ell = 1, ..., N$, $j = 1, ..., J$) which implies starting with $F_J = \tilde{1}_{N^2 \times 1}$, where $\tilde{1}_{N^2 \times 1}$ is as $1_{N^2 \times 1}$ with the exception that zeroes replace ones at positions $N, 2N, ..., N^2$. As concerns $y = 1$, we took $F_{iNJ} = 0$ $\forall i$.

To summarize, figure 5.2 shows the final pattern of nonzero elements of A; in this figure $N = 11$, which implies that A has size 121×121. Such a size has been chosen for visualization purposes only; in the application in Fornari and Mele (1999a) that we succinctly describe in the following section, one has to take $N \geq 30$ to obtain reliable approximation results.

5.5   An illustrative example

We provide a very succinct overview of some results that Fornari and Mele (1999a) obtained in correspondence of model (5.1)-(5.2). Our first step in that paper consisted in fitting the stochastic differential system (5.1) to a time series that we used as a proxy of the instantaneous interest rate. We made use of weekly data referring to 3-month Treasury Bill rates to approximate the instantaneous interest rate.[5] We restricted attention to the sample spanning the period from May, 30 1973 to February, 22 1995, which has 1135 observations. Such a sampling period coincides with the period in which our target term structure (to which we fitted model (5.2)) is constructed. Following the procedure outlined in section 5.3, we first fitted model (5.3) (with normal errors) to data, finding that the estimates of δ and γ were statistically indistinguishable from 1 and 0.[6] Then we obtained estimates of the parameter vector $a = (\iota, \theta, \bar{\omega}, \varphi, \psi)$ by using both the q-aml rule (5.5) based on the moment conditions (5.4) and the indirect inference (II) rule. In implementing the II approach, we doubled the dimension of the high frequency simulation numbers in (5.6), and simulated the resulting setup by using 25 subintervals per week, which corresponds to fixing $h^{-1} \equiv 1300$. We used $S = 50$ simulations. Some of our estimation results were as follows.

TABLE 5.1

parameter	ι	θ	$\bar{\omega}$	φ	ψ
q-aml	0.0081	0.1067	0.0418	0.3736	0.6540
II	0.0082	0.1108	0.0301	0.3806	0.8092

The II estimates we obtained were all significant at standard levels, and the consistency test described in section 5.3 (see formula (5.8)) indicated the high quality of the approximation of the moment conditions needed to guarantee the convergence of model (5.3) towards the continuous time model (5.1).

To appreciate the filtering performances of the approximating discrete time model (5.3), we simulated 5000 times the stochastic differential system (5.1) with parameters fixed at the II estimates of table 5.1, sampled the resulting trajectories of the interest rate at the weekly frequency, and fitted model (5.3) to such simulated sampled data. Figure 5.3, taken from Fornari and Mele (1999a), depicts the distribution of the average volatility filtering error in all the simulations defined by the sequence $\{\mathcal{E}_i\}_{i=1}^{5000}$, where $\mathcal{E}_i \equiv \frac{1}{1135}\sum_{n=1}^{1135}(\sigma_{i,n} - \hat{\sigma}_{i,n})$, $\sigma_{i,n}$ is the volatility simulated at the ith round sampled at n, and $\hat{\sigma}_{i,n}$ is the corresponding (rescaled) ARCH estimate from model (5.3). The average filtering error was $9.610 \cdot 10^{-5}$ with a standard deviation of $3.275 \cdot 10^{-3}$, while the RMSE was 0.0209. These figures have to be compared with the average (rescaled) volatility as filtered by model (5.3) fitted to the previously described US data,

---

[5] Part of such a data set is available at http://www.frbchi.org/econinfo/finance/int-rates/welcome.html.

[6] The fact the we did not uncover evidence of volatility asymmetries is in contrast with some pieces of our previous empirical work on other data sets concerning interest rates (Fornari and Mele (1995)).

which was approximately 0.05.

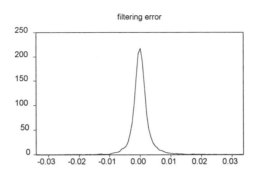

FIGURE 5.3. Distribution of the average volatility filtering error

In the final step, we estimated the coefficient (λ_1, λ_2) in (5.2) entering into the risk premia functions (4.21) by minimizing the squared differences between a given target term structure and that predicted by our theoretical model with parameters $a = (\iota, \theta, \bar{\omega}, \varphi, \psi)$ fixed at the II estimates of table 5.1, initial interest rate equal to our sample sample average level $(7.1 \cdot 10^{-2})$ and volatility also equal to the average (rescaled) standard deviation as filtered by the model (5.3) fitted to US data (0.05). In numerically solving the partial differential equation (5.2), we imposed the transversality conditions: $\lim_{r \to \infty} B(r, v, t) = 0$ $\forall (v, t) \in \mathbb{R}_+ \times [0, T]$, and $\lim_{v \to \infty} B(r, v, t) = 0 \ \forall (r, t) \in \mathbb{R}_+ \times [0, T]$. As noted in subsection 5.4.3, computations were performed in correspondence of a grid that sets $N = 30$ (see section 5.4 for the notation); furthermore, we set $J = T \times N$, where T (expressed in years) is equal to 30; we took $\Delta t = \frac{T}{J}$. Our target term structure was the Cox et al. (1985a) model estimated by Aït-Sahalia (1996a) in correspondence of the same sampling period that we use to estimate a. Our bootstrap estimates of λ_1 and λ_2 were -0.581 and 0.677, respectively. Such estimates were significant at any standard level and implied a mean absolute error (in terms of intensity rates) equal to $5.3027 \cdot 10^{-4}$. In figure 9 we reproduce our fitted term structure, which is the second curve starting from top: it is increasing, being very steep until 5 years, and then relatively flat for higher maturities, which corresponds to well-known stylized facts of the US term structure in our sample period.

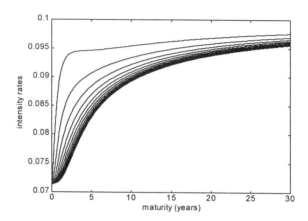

FIGURE 5.4. From bottom to top, the curves correspond to values of $\sigma(t)$ equal to 0.0100, 0.0114, 0.0131, 0.0150, 0.0173, 0.0200, 0.0233, 0.0275, 0.0329, 0.0400, 0.0500, 0.0650. The average level of the (rescaled) $\hat{\sigma}$ for US data was 0.0490, and the curve corresponding to $\sigma(t) = 0.0500$ was fitted to the target term structure.

In an empirical study, Litterman and Scheinkman (1991) identify three factor loadings that can correspond to changes in level, steepness and curvature of the term structure. Figure 9 then also shows how the term structure changes when volatility changes:[7] as is clear, the curve sharpens as volatility increases, and in way that suggests that volatility can be considered as a source of both curvature and steepness of the term structure. Results not reported here also unambiguously show that changes in the instantaneous rate generate shifts in the term structure that suggest to consider r as a level factor. Andersen and Lund (1997b) showed that in a model in which the interest rate drift function is driven by another Brownian motion, parallel shifts in the term structure have to be generated by simultaneous changes in the short term interest rate and the 'long run tendency' of that rate; see also Chen (1996) for earlier related work.

---

[7]Previous work on similar comparative statics exercises in models with stochastic volatility were done by Chen (1996) and Andersen and Lund (1997b). Their results were obtained in correspondence of models with arbitrary risk premia functions and arbitrary numerical values given to the parameters entering in such functions.

Appendix: a solution method based on the approach of iterated approximations

In this appendix we present an alternative solution technique of the partial differential equation (5.2) that is inspired by the work of Chen (1996), and that is based on a method of iterated approximations. Such a method relies on a functional iteration of a certain benchmark affine pricing rule under the action of the associated Arrow-Debreu state price density, and requires the computation of multi-dimensional integrals.

After setting some of the assumptions underlying our results in an operator-theoretic format in section 5A.1, section 5A.2 provides more standard conditions ensuring existence of solutions to partial differential equations. Results are in section 5A.3.

5A.1 ASSUMPTIONS

Let $\mathbb{S}(Z)$ denote the Banach space of complex valued bounded continuous functions on a compact set $Z \subset \mathbb{R}^l$, endowed with the norm

$$\|m\| = \sup_Z |m| \, .$$

In this appendix, we are concerned with the solution of equations of the following form:

$$m(x) = n(x) + \int_Z K(x, \xi) m(\xi) \mathrm{d}\xi, \tag{5A.1}$$

also known as Fredholm equations (e.g., Ruston (1986)); here $n \in \mathbb{S}(Z)$ and the kernel K is continuous on Z^2.

We aim at giving a condition ensuring existence and uniqueness of a solution $m \in \mathbb{S}(Z)$ to (5A.1).

Let $\mathcal{K}$ be the integral operator associated with K that makes a one-to-one correspondence between any function $v \in \mathbb{S}(Z)$ and the function

$$y = \mathcal{K}[v] \in \mathbb{S}(Z)$$

defined by

$$y(x) = \int_Z K(x, \xi) v(\xi) \mathrm{d}\xi.$$

Note that the norm of $\mathcal{K}$ is

$$\|\mathcal{K}\| = \sup_{x \in Z} \int_Z |K(x, \xi)| \, \mathrm{d}\xi,$$

that we suppose bounded by one:

$$\|\mathcal{K}\| < 1. \tag{5A.2}$$

In terms of $\mathcal{K}$, eq. (5A.1) is:

$$(I - \mathcal{K})[m] = n,$$

where $I[.]$ is the identity map.

Under condition (5A.2) the sequence

$$m_i = n + \mathcal{K}[m_{i-1}]$$

with $m_0 = 0$ (say), converges in $\mathbb{S}(Z)$ to the solution of (5A.1):

$$m = n + \sum_{i=1}^{\infty} \mathcal{K}^i[n],$$

where $\mathcal{K}^i[.]$ is the integral operator associated with the ith iterate of the kernel K^i defined as $K^1 = K$ and as:

$$K^{j+1}(x,\xi) = \int_{Z^j} K(x,\xi_1) K(\xi_1,\xi_2) \cdots K(\xi_j,\xi) \mathrm{d}\xi_1 \cdots \mathrm{d}\xi_j$$

for $j \geq 1$.

5A.2 GENERALITIES

Pricing with Brownian information often translates into problems involving finding the scalar function $u \in C^{2,1}(\mathbb{R}^N \times [0,T))$ which solves the following partial differential equation:

$$\begin{cases} \mathcal{L}[u](x,t) = -q(x,t), \ (x,t) \in \mathbb{R}^N \times [0,T) \\ u(x,T) = g(x), \ x \in \mathbb{R}^N \end{cases} \tag{5A.3}$$

where

$$\mathcal{L}[u](x,t) = \mathcal{D}[u](x,t) - r(x,t)u(x,t),$$

and:

$$\mathcal{D}[u](x,t) = u_t(x,t) + u_x(x,t)b(x,t) + \tfrac{1}{2}\mathrm{tr}[a(x,t)a'(x,t)u_{xx}(x,t)],$$

where, for an integer M, $a(x,t) : \mathbb{R}^N \times [0,T] \mapsto \mathbb{R}^{N \times M}$ (the space of the $N \times M$ real matrices), $b(x,t) : \mathbb{R}^N \times [0,T] \mapsto \mathbb{R}^N$, $(r,q)(x,t) : \mathbb{R}^N \times [0,T] \mapsto (\mathbb{R}_{++},\mathbb{R})$, and subscripts denote partial derivatives. Usually, in this context, $u(.)$ represents the price of a European claim, b and a are drift and diffusion coefficients of a N-dimensional diffusion driven by M Brownian motions on the probability space $(\Omega, \mathcal{F}, Q)$, with $Q \in \mathcal{Q}$, where $\mathcal{Q}$ is as in chapters 3 and 4. The usual interpretation of $q(.)$ is that it represents the flow of dividends associated with the European claim. It is the objective of this subsection, however, to give (5A.3) and $q(.)$ a broader mathematical interpretation that is useful for obtaining an approximating solution of the partial differential equation (5.2). In what follows, we suppose standard mild regularity conditions to hold (essentially, uniform ellipticity on a; boundness on a, b; Hölder continuity on a, b, r, q; polynomial growth on g, q—see, e.g., Karatzas and Shreve (1991) (p. 366-369)—) that are met in our problem.

The starting point is the existence of a nonnegative function $G(x, t; \xi, \tau)$, the so-called *Green's Function*, defined for $0 \le t < \tau \le T, x \in \mathbb{R}^n$, such that the function:

$$\hat{u}(x, t) = \int_{\mathbb{R}^N} G(x, t; \xi, \tau) g(\xi) d\xi, \ 0 \le t < \tau, \ x \in \mathbb{R}^N, \qquad (5A.4)$$

is bounded, belongs to $\mathcal{C}^{2,1}$ and satisfies:

$$\begin{cases} \mathcal{L}[\hat{u}](x, t) = 0, & (x, t) \in \mathbb{R}^N \times [0, \tau) \\ \lim_{t \uparrow \tau} \hat{u}(x, t) = g(x), & x \in \mathbb{R}^N \end{cases} \qquad (5A.5)$$

Further, by defining:

$$f(x, t) = G(x, t; \xi, \tau)$$

for fixed $(\xi, \tau) \in \mathbb{R}^N \times (0, T]$, one has that f satisfies (5A.5) in the *backward* variables (x, t), but with

$$\lim_{t \uparrow \tau} f(x, t) = \hat{\delta}(x - \xi),$$

where $\hat{\delta}(.)$ is the Dirac function (see, also, Arnold (1992) (thm. 2.6.6, p. 43)).

If $\mathcal{L}[\hat{u}] = 0$ is describing the no-arbitrage restriction of a securities market model, the economic interpretation of the Green's Function is that of the Arrow-Debreu state-price density of that model: it is the value as of time t in state x of a unit of numéraire at $\tau > t$ in state ξ. The preceding result then means that, if r does not depend on x, then the state price follows the same partial differential equation followed by the contingent claim, which is very intuitive. Here is a proof of this. Define $\hat{u}$ by (5A.4). Under the conditions given in chapter 3, section 3.2, $\hat{u}$ is arbitrage free if and only if there is a measure Q (with density π^Q, say) equivalent to P on $(\Omega, \mathcal{F})$ under which:

$$\hat{u}(x, t) = \int_{\mathbb{R}^N} \exp(-\int_t^\tau r(s) ds) \pi^Q(x, t; \xi, \tau) g(\xi) d\xi, \ 0 \le t \le \tau, \ x \in \mathbb{R}^N. \qquad (5A.6)$$

By construction, π^Q is the solution of the following backward Kolmogorov equation:

$$0 = \pi_t^Q(x, t; \xi, \tau) + \pi_x^Q(x, t; \xi, \tau) b(x, t) + \tfrac{1}{2} \text{tr}[a(x, t)a'(x, t)\pi_{xx}^Q(x, t; \xi, \tau)]. \qquad (5A.7)$$

Comparing (5A.4) with (5A.6), we see that it must be the case that:

$$G(x, t; \xi, \tau) = \exp(-\int_t^\tau r(s) ds) \pi^Q(x, t; \xi, \tau). \qquad (5A.8)$$

Differentiating both sides of (5A.8) with respect to t, and using (5A.7), we obtain that $\mathcal{L}[f] = 0$. This completes the proof.

Consider, next, eq. (5A.3) in its full generality. It is easily seen that if a function $G(x,t;\xi,\tau)$ satisfies, for fixed $(\xi,\tau) \in \mathbb{R}^N \times [0,T)$,

$$\begin{cases} \mathcal{L}[G](x,t;\xi,\tau) = 0, \ (x,t) \in \mathbb{R}^N \times [0,\tau) \\ G(x,\tau;\xi,\tau) = \widehat{\delta}(x-\xi), \ x \in \mathbb{R}^N \end{cases}$$

in the backward variables (x,t), then the solution of (5A.3) can be written in the following form:

$$\begin{aligned} u(x,t) &= \int_{\mathbb{R}^N} \int_t^T G(x,t;\xi_0,\tau_0)q(\xi_0,\tau_0)d\tau_0 d\xi_0 + \int_{\mathbb{R}^N} G(x,t;\xi,\tau)g(\xi)d\xi \\ &= \int_{\mathbb{R}^N} \int_t^T G(x,t;\xi_0,\tau_0)q(\xi_0,\tau_0)d\tau_0 d\xi_0 + \widehat{u}(x,t). \end{aligned}$$

Next, let $T[u](.)$ be an operator with the special property that:

$$T[u](x,t) = q(x,t). \tag{5A.9}$$

If our partial differential equation can be re-written in the same form as (5A.3), with $q(.)$ as above, the computation of u becomes then tractable once we are given a *known* $\widehat{u}$. In this case, in fact,

$$\begin{aligned} u(x,t) &= \widehat{u}(x,t) + \int_{\mathbb{R}^N} \int_t^T G(x,t;\xi_0,\tau_0)q(\xi_0,\tau_0)d\tau_0 d\xi_0 \\ &= \widehat{u}(x,t) + \int_{\mathbb{R}^N} \int_t^T G(x,t;\xi_0,\tau_0)T[u](\xi_0,\tau_0)d\tau_0 d\xi_0. \end{aligned}$$

Continuing:

$$u(x,t) = \widehat{u}(x,t) + \int_{\mathbb{R}^N} \int_t^T G(x,t;\xi_0,\tau_0)T[\widehat{u}](\xi_0,\tau_0)d\tau_0 d\xi_0 + \mathcal{R}_1(x,t),$$

where:

$$\mathcal{R}_1(x,t)$$
$$= \int_{\mathbb{R}^N} \int_t^T G(x,t;\xi_0,\tau_0)T\left[\int_{\mathbb{R}^N} \int_{\tau_0}^T G(\xi_0,\tau_0;\xi_1,\tau_1)T[u](\xi_1,\tau_1)d\tau_1 d\xi_1\right]d\tau_0 d\xi_0.$$

The procedure can go on by applying the preceding functional iteration: iterating n times means that one has to consider an increasing sequence $\{\tau_i\}_{i=0}^n$ of integrals to intervene in the brackets of the above formula. In a second order correction, for instance,

$$u(x,t) = \widehat{u}(x,t) + \widehat{u}_1(x,t) + \widehat{u}_2(x,t) + \mathcal{R}_2(x,t)$$

where

$$\widehat{u}_1(x,t) = \int_{\mathbb{R}^N} \int_t^T G(x,t;\xi_0,\tau_0)T[\widehat{u}](\xi_0,\tau_0)d\tau_0 d\xi_0,$$

$$\widehat{u}_2(x,t)$$
$$= \int_{\mathbb{R}^N} \int_t^T G(x,t;\xi_0,\tau_0)T\left[\int_{\mathbb{R}^N} \int_{\tau_0}^T G(\xi_0,\tau_0;\xi_1,\tau_1)T[\widehat{u}](\xi_1,\tau_1)d\tau_1 d\xi_1\right]d\tau_0 d\xi_0$$

and

$$\mathcal{R}_2(x,t) = \int_{\mathbb{R}^N} \int_t^T G(x,t;\xi_0,\tau_0) T \left[\int_{\mathbb{R}^N} \int_{\tau_0}^T G(\xi_0,\tau_0;\xi_1,\tau_1) \right.$$
$$\left. T \left[\int_{\mathbb{R}^N} \int_{\tau_1}^T G(\xi_1,\tau_1;\xi_2,\tau_2) T[\widehat{u}](\xi_2,\tau_2) d\tau_2 d\xi_2 \right] d\tau_1 d\xi_1 \right] d\tau_0 d\xi_0.$$

In formula (5A.11) to be stated in theorem 5A.1 below, for instance, we shall only consider a first order approximation:

$$u(x,t) \simeq \widehat{u}(x,t) + \widehat{u}_1(x,t).$$

The method thus consists in re-writing the original partial differential equation in a form that allows us to use $\widehat{u}$ to get progressively more accurate approximations of the pricing function u. Convergence is ensured by condition (5A.2) in the problem of section 5A.1 applied to the Laplace transform of $u(x,t)$ with respect to time t:

$$\widetilde{u}(x;a) = \int_0^\infty e^{-at} u(x,t) dt. \tag{5A.10}$$

In practice, the choice of $\widehat{u}$ (which is in fact implied by the choice of *which* $T[.]$ operator to use) should be a fair compromise between analytical convenience and informational richness of $\widehat{u}$. This is the principle followed in elaborating theorem 5A.1 below.

5A.3 AN ITERATED APPROXIMATION RESULT

The objective here is to apply the framework of the preceding subsections to the partial differential equation (5.2). For reasons of analytical convenience, we shall be working with the pricing function $B_T(r,\sigma^2,t)$ (instead of $B_T(r,\sigma^6,t)$) that satisfies eq. (5.2). The following is an approximating result:

5A.1 THEOREM: *Under the conditions given in sections 5A.1 and 5A.2, the sequence of functions obtained by iterated approximations,*

$$\widetilde{B}_T^{(n)}(r,\sigma^2) = \widetilde{B}_T(r,\sigma^2) + \mathcal{K}[\widetilde{B}_T^{(n-1)}](r,\sigma^2)$$

converges to $\widetilde{B}_T(r,\sigma^2)$, *i.e.:*

$$\widetilde{B}_T(r,\sigma^2) = \widetilde{B}_T(r,\sigma^2) + \lim_{N\to\infty} \sum_{n=1}^N \mathcal{K}^n[\widetilde{B}_T](r,\sigma^2),$$

where $\mathcal{K}[.]$ *and* $\mathcal{K}^n[.]$ *are the integral operators defined in section 5A.1,* $\widetilde{B}_T(r,\sigma^2)$ *and* $\widetilde{B}_T(r,\sigma^2)$ *are Laplace transforms of* $B_T(r,\sigma^2,t)$ *and*

$$B_T(r,\sigma^2,t) = \exp(-D(\tau^t)r + F(\tau^t)\sigma^2 + U(\tau^t))$$

with respect to t, *with* $D(.), F(.), U(.)$ *defined in the appendix and:*

$$\tau^t = T - t.$$

Up to a first order approximation,

$$
\begin{aligned}
B_T(r,\sigma^2,t) &\simeq \mathcal{B}_T(r,\sigma^2,t) \\
&\quad \int_{\mathbb{R}^2_{++}} \int_t^T G(r,\sigma^2,t;r_+,\sigma_+^2,s)\mathcal{T}[\mathcal{B}_T](r_+,\sigma_+^2,s)dsdr_+d\sigma_+^2,
\end{aligned}
$$

(5A.11)

where

$$
\begin{aligned}
&G(r,\sigma^2,t;r_+,\sigma_+^2,s) \\
&= \tfrac{1}{(2\pi)^2} \int\int e^{-ir_+\eta_1 - i\sigma_+^2\eta_2 - \widetilde{D}(\eta_1;\tau_s)r + \widetilde{F}(\eta_1,\eta_2;\tau_s)\sigma^2 + \widetilde{U}(\eta_1,\eta_2;\tau_s)} d\eta_1 d\eta_2,
\end{aligned}
$$

and the $\mathcal{T}[\mathcal{B}_T](.)$ *operator is given explicitly by*

$$
\begin{aligned}
\mathcal{T}[\mathcal{B}_T](r,\sigma^2,t) =\ & (\phi\sigma^2(\lambda_2 - \lambda_3 r^{1/2}) + w(\sigma^{2-\delta} - 1))F(\tau^t)\mathcal{B}_T(r,\sigma^2,t) \\
&+ \tfrac{1}{2}(\sigma^2(r-1)D^2(\tau^t) + \phi^2(\sigma^4 - 1)F^2(\tau^t))\mathcal{B}_T(r,\sigma^2,t) \\
&- (\lambda_1(\sigma - r)\sigma + \rho\phi\sigma^3 r^{1/2}F(\tau^t))D(\tau^t)\mathcal{B}_T(r,\sigma^2,t)
\end{aligned}
$$

with

$$
\begin{aligned}
\tau_s &= s - t, \\
w &= \tfrac{2\bar{\omega}}{\delta}, \\
\phi &= \tfrac{2\psi}{\delta}, \\
\lambda_3 &= \lambda_1\rho + \lambda_2(1 - \rho^2)^{1/2},
\end{aligned}
$$

$i \equiv (-1)^{1/2}$, *and* $\widetilde{D}(\eta_1;.), \widetilde{F}(\eta_1,\eta_2;.), \widetilde{U}(\eta_1,\eta_2;.)$ *are defined in the proof. The first order correction is given in the proof.*

As shown during the course of the proof below, G has the interpretation of the Arrow-Debreu state price associated with $\mathcal{B}_T$. It can be interpreted as the Green's function associated with a fundamental solution of the partial differential equation (5A.13) below. The model to which $\mathcal{B}_T$ corresponds is an affine model, and refers to an economy in which the instantaneous interest rate and its instantaneous volatility are jointly normal and independent. The idea of the preceding theorem is thus to start with a poor model, $\mathcal{B}_T$, which can nevertheless be exploited to get progressively more accurate approximations by its iteration under the action of $\mathcal{T}$ and G. For brevity, this iteration has been stopped at one in eq. (5A.11).

PROOF OF THEOREM 5A.1. As noted before the statement of the theorem, we work with the pricing function $B_T(r,\sigma^2,t)$ instead of $B_T(r,\sigma^\delta,t)$ for analytical purposes. Specifically, we make a change of variables $\sigma^\delta \mapsto \sigma^2$ and obtain eq. (5A.13) below. It is also possible to derive (5A.13) by noticing that, by Itô's lemma, the variance process satisfies:

$$
d\sigma(t)^2 = (w\sigma(t)^{2-\delta} - \vartheta\sigma(t)^2)dt + \phi\sigma(t)^2 dW^\sigma(t),
$$

where w and ϕ have been defined in the theorem and:

$$\vartheta \equiv \frac{2\varphi\delta - (2-\delta)\psi^2}{\delta^2}.$$

Because we are considering a *rational* price function, by Itô's lemma, the Girsanov's theorem and the Q-martingale property of $\{\frac{B_T(r,\sigma^2,t)}{S^{(0)}(t)}\}_{t\in[0,T]}$, we get:

$$
\begin{aligned}
0 = \;& B_t - rB + B_r(\iota - \theta r) + B_{\sigma^2}(w\sigma^{2-\delta} - \vartheta\sigma^2) + \tfrac{1}{2}B_{rr}r\sigma^2 + \tfrac{1}{2}B_{\sigma^2\sigma^2}\phi^2\sigma^4 \\
& + B_{r\sigma^2}r^{1/2}\sigma^3\phi\rho - (r^{1/2}\sigma B_r + \phi\sigma^2\rho B_{\sigma^2})\lambda^{(1)} - \phi\sigma^2(1-\rho^2)^{1/2}B_{\sigma^2}\lambda^{(2)},
\end{aligned}
$$
$$(5A.12)$$

where $\lambda^{(i)}$, interpreted as unit risk premia for the risks associated to the fluctuations of two standard $P\text{-}\mathcal{F}(t)$-Brownian motions $W^{(i)}$, $i = 1, 2$, are defined from

$$
\begin{cases}
\widetilde{W}^{(1)}(t) = W^{(1)}(t) - \int_0^t \lambda^{(1)}(u)du \\
\widetilde{W}^{(2)}(t) = W^{(2)}(t) - \int_0^t \lambda^{(2)}(u)du
\end{cases}
$$

where $\widetilde{W}^{(i)}$, $i = 1, 2$, are standard $Q\text{-}\mathcal{F}(t)$-Brownian motions, and $\lambda^{(i)}$ are taken to satisfy the Novikov condition. Plugging λ from (4.21) into (5A.12) we get the following partial differential equation:

$$
\begin{cases}
(\mathcal{L} + T)[B_T](x,t) = 0, \; (x,t) \in \mathbb{R}^2_{++} \times [0,T) \\
B_T(x,T) = 1, \; x \in \mathbb{R}^2_{++}
\end{cases}
$$
$$(5A.13)$$

where

$$
\begin{aligned}
\mathcal{L}[B_T](r,\sigma^2,t) = \;& -B_\tau - rB + (\iota - \theta r)B_r + (w - \vartheta\sigma^2)B_{\sigma^2} \\
& + \tfrac{1}{2}(\sigma^2 B_{rr} + \phi^2 B_{\sigma^2\sigma^2}) - \lambda_1\sigma^2 B_r - \lambda_2\phi\sigma^2 B_{\sigma^2},
\end{aligned}
$$

$\tau = T - t$, and

$$
\begin{aligned}
T[B_T](r,\sigma^2,t) = \;& [\phi\sigma^2(\lambda_2 - \lambda_3 r^{1/2}) + w(\sigma^{2-\delta} - 1)]B_{\sigma^2} + \tfrac{1}{2}\sigma^2(r-1)B_{rr} \\
& + \tfrac{1}{2}\phi^2(\sigma^4 - 1)B_{\sigma^2\sigma^2} + \lambda_1(\sigma - r)\sigma B_r + \rho\phi\sigma^3 r^{1/2}B_{r\sigma^2},
\end{aligned}
$$

where λ_3 has been defined in the theorem.

Eq. (5A.13) can be recognized as a special case of the scheme treated in sections 5A.2 and 5A.3. As suggested there, it is convenient to start with a simpler problem of the following kind. Solve for the following price:

$$
\begin{cases}
\mathcal{L}[\mathcal{B}_T](x,t) = 0, \; (x,t) \in \mathbb{R}^2_{++} \times [0,T) \\
\mathcal{B}_T(x,T) = 1, \; x \in \mathbb{R}^2_{++}
\end{cases}
$$
$$(5A.14)$$

and then compute the Green's function $G(x,t;\xi,T)$ associated with $\mathcal{B}_T$

$$\mathcal{B}_T(x,t) = \int_{\mathbb{R}^2_{++}} G(x,t;\xi,T)d\xi.$$

This will eventually enable one to apply the functional iteration discussed in section 5A.2, obtaining for instance the first order approximation given in (5A.11):

$$\mathcal{B}_T(x,t) \simeq \mathcal{B}_T(x,t) + \int_{\mathbb{R}^2_{++}} \int_t^T G(x,t;\xi_0,\tau_0)T[\mathcal{B}_T](\xi_0,\tau_0)\mathrm{d}\tau_0\mathrm{d}\xi_0,$$

where the first order correction is given by

$$\begin{aligned}&\mathcal{R}_1(x,t)\\ &= \int_{\mathbb{R}^2_{++}} \int_t^T G(x,t;\xi_0,\tau_0)T[\int_{\mathbb{R}^2_{++}} \int_{\tau_0}^T G(\xi_0,\tau_0;\xi_1,\tau_1)T[\mathcal{B}_T](\xi_1,\tau_1)\mathrm{d}\tau_1\mathrm{d}\xi_1]\mathrm{d}\tau_0\mathrm{d}\xi_0,\end{aligned}$$

or more generally, obtaining progressively more accurate approximations, as in the first part of the theorem, with $\mathcal{K}$ as defined in section 5A.1 and $\widetilde{B}_T$ and $\widetilde{\mathcal{B}}_T$ as in (5A.10).

The solution of (5A.14) can be interpreted as a no-arbitrage price of a bond in the case in which the primitives satisfy the following 'special interest rate dynamics':

$$\begin{cases} \mathrm{d}r(t) = (\iota - \theta r(t))\mathrm{d}t + \sigma(t)\mathrm{d}W^A(t) \\ \mathrm{d}\sigma(t)^2 = (w - \vartheta\sigma(t)^2)\mathrm{d}t + \phi\mathrm{d}W^B(t) \end{cases}$$

where W^i, $i = A, B$, are two standard $P\text{-}\mathcal{F}(t)$-Brownian motions, and the risk premia are $\lambda_1\sigma$ and $\lambda_2\sigma^2$. The solution of (5A.14) is that reported in the theorem, with $D(.), F(.)$ and $U(.)$ defined as:

$$D(\tau) = \frac{1-e^{-\theta\tau}}{\theta}$$
$$F(\tau) = \Upsilon_5 + \Upsilon_6 e^{-\Upsilon_1\tau} + \Upsilon_7 e^{-2\theta\tau} + \Upsilon_8 e^{-\theta\tau}$$
$$\begin{aligned}U(\tau) = &\Upsilon_9 + \Upsilon_{10}\tau + \Upsilon_{11}e^{-2\theta\tau} + \Upsilon_{12}e^{-2\Upsilon_1\tau} + \Upsilon_{13}e^{-4\theta\tau} + \Upsilon_{14}e^{-\Upsilon_1\tau} + \Upsilon_{15}e^{-\theta\tau}\\ &+ \Upsilon_{16}e^{-(2\theta+\Upsilon_1)\tau} + \Upsilon_{17}e^{-(\theta+\Upsilon_1)\tau} + \Upsilon_{18}e^{-3\theta\tau}\end{aligned}$$
$$\Upsilon_1 = \vartheta + \phi\lambda_2$$
$$\Upsilon_2 = \theta^2\Upsilon_1$$
$$\Upsilon_3 = 1 + 2\theta\lambda_1$$
$$\Upsilon_4 = 1 + \theta\lambda_1$$
$$\Upsilon_5 = \frac{\Upsilon_3}{2\Upsilon_2}$$
$$\Upsilon_6 = \frac{\Upsilon_4}{\Upsilon_2-\theta^3} - \frac{1}{2\Upsilon_2-4\theta^3} - \Upsilon_5$$
$$\Upsilon_7 = \frac{1}{2\Upsilon_2-4\theta^3}$$
$$\Upsilon_8 = -\frac{\Upsilon_4}{\Upsilon_2-\theta^3}$$
$$\Upsilon_9 = \frac{\iota}{\theta^2} + w\left(\frac{\Upsilon_6}{\Upsilon_1} + \frac{\Upsilon_7}{2\theta} + \frac{\Upsilon_8}{\theta}\right) + \frac{1}{2}\phi^2\Xi$$
$$\Xi = \frac{\Upsilon_6^2}{2\Upsilon_1} + \frac{\Upsilon_7^2}{4\theta} + \frac{\Upsilon_8^2}{2\theta} + \frac{2\Upsilon_5\Upsilon_6}{\Upsilon_1} + \frac{\Upsilon_5\Upsilon_7}{\theta} + \frac{2\Upsilon_5\Upsilon_8}{\theta} + \frac{2\Upsilon_6\Upsilon_7}{2\theta+\Upsilon_1} + \frac{2\Upsilon_6\Upsilon_8}{\theta+\Upsilon_1} + \frac{2\Upsilon_7\Upsilon_8}{3\theta}$$
$$\Upsilon_{10} = \frac{1}{2}\phi^2\Upsilon_5^2 + w\Upsilon_5 - \frac{\iota}{\theta}$$
$$\Upsilon_{11} = -\frac{\phi^2\Upsilon_8^2}{4\theta} - \frac{\phi^2\Upsilon_5\Upsilon_7}{2\theta} - \frac{w\Upsilon_7}{2\theta}$$
$$\Upsilon_{12} = -\frac{\phi^2\Upsilon_6^2}{4\Upsilon_1}$$
$$\Upsilon_{13} = -\frac{\phi^2\Upsilon_7^2}{8\theta}$$

$$\Upsilon_{14} = -\frac{\phi^2 \Upsilon_5 \Upsilon_6}{\Upsilon_1} - \frac{w \Upsilon_6}{\Upsilon_1}$$

$$\Upsilon_{15} = -\frac{\phi^2 \Upsilon_5 \Upsilon_8}{\theta} - \frac{\iota}{\theta^2} - \frac{w \Upsilon_8}{\theta}$$

$$\Upsilon_{16} = -\frac{\phi^2 \Upsilon_6 \Upsilon_7}{2\theta + \Upsilon_1}$$

$$\Upsilon_{17} = -\frac{\phi^2 \Upsilon_6 \Upsilon_8}{\theta + \Upsilon_1}$$

$$\Upsilon_{18} = -\frac{\phi^2 \Upsilon_7 \Upsilon_8}{3\theta}$$

Next, we turn to the computation of the Green's function associated with $\mathcal{B}_T$: we do that by first computing its Fourier transform:

$$\widehat{G}(\eta_1, \eta_2; x_1, x_2, \tau) = \int \int e^{i\xi_1 \eta_1 + i\xi_2 \eta_2} G(x_1, x_2, t; \xi_1, \xi_2, T) d\xi_1 d\xi_2.$$

Because $G(x_1, x_2; x_1, x_2, \tau)$ satisfies the same partial differential equation satisfied by $\mathcal{B}(x_1, x_2, \tau)$, its Fourier transform will follow the same partial differential equation as well. To find its boundary behavior, we exploit the boundary behavior of $G(x_1, x_2, t; \xi_1, \xi_2, T)$, and find:

$$
\begin{aligned}
\widehat{G}(\eta_1, \eta_2; x_1, x_2, 0) &= \int \int e^{i\xi_1 \eta_1 + i\xi_2 \eta_2} G(x_1, x_2, T; \xi_1, \xi_2, T) d\xi_1 d\xi_2 \\
&= \int \int \widehat{\delta}(x_1 - \xi_1) \widehat{\delta}(x_2 - \xi_2) e^{i\xi_1 \eta_1 + i\xi_2 \eta_2} d\xi_1 d\xi_2 \\
&\equiv \int \int \widehat{\delta}(x - \xi) \zeta(\xi) d\xi \\
&= \zeta(x) \equiv e^{ix_1 \eta_1 + ix_2 \eta_2}.
\end{aligned}
\tag{5A.15}
$$

Hence, we have to solve eq. (5A.14) (with $\widehat{G}$ replacing $\mathcal{B}_T$), but with (5A.15) serving as boundary condition. The solution is:

$$\widehat{G}(\eta_1, \eta_2; r, \sigma^2, \tau) = \exp(-\widetilde{D}(\eta_1; \tau) r + \widetilde{F}(\eta_1, \eta_2; \tau) \sigma^2 + \widetilde{U}(\eta_1, \eta_2; \tau)),$$

where:

$$\widetilde{D}(\eta_1; \tau) = \frac{1 - e^{-\theta \tau}}{\theta} - i\eta_1 e^{-\theta \tau}$$

$$\widetilde{F}(\eta_1, \eta_2; \tau) = \Upsilon_5 + \widetilde{\Upsilon}_6 e^{-\Upsilon_1 \tau} + \widetilde{\Upsilon}_7 e^{-2\theta \tau} + \widetilde{\Upsilon}_8 e^{-\theta \tau}$$

$$\widetilde{U}(\eta_1, \eta_2; \tau) = \widetilde{\Upsilon}_9 + \Upsilon_{10} \tau + \widetilde{\Upsilon}_{11} e^{-2\theta \tau} + \widetilde{\Upsilon}_{12} e^{-2\Upsilon_1 \tau} + \widetilde{\Upsilon}_{13} e^{-4\theta \tau} + \widetilde{\Upsilon}_{14} e^{-\Upsilon_1 \tau}$$
$$+ \widetilde{\Upsilon}_{15} e^{-\theta \tau} + \widetilde{\Upsilon}_{16} e^{-(2\theta + \Upsilon_1)\tau} + \widetilde{\Upsilon}_{17} e^{-(\theta + \Upsilon_1)\tau} + \widetilde{\Upsilon}_{18} e^{-3\theta \tau}$$

$$\widetilde{\Upsilon}_6 = \Upsilon_6 + i\eta_2 + \chi_1(i\eta_1) + \chi_2(i\eta_1)$$

$$\widetilde{\Upsilon}_7 = \Upsilon_7 - \chi_2(i\eta_1)$$

$$\widetilde{\Upsilon}_8 = \Upsilon_8 - \chi_1(i\eta_1)$$

$$\chi_1(i\eta_1) = \frac{\theta(\theta \lambda_1 - 1)}{\Upsilon_2 - \theta^3} i\eta_1$$

$$\chi_2(i\eta_1) = -\frac{\theta(\theta \eta_1^2 + 2i\eta_1)}{2(\Upsilon_2 - 2\theta^3)}$$

$$\widetilde{\Upsilon}_9 = \frac{\iota}{\theta^2} + w\left(\frac{\widetilde{\Upsilon}_6}{\Upsilon_1} + \frac{\widetilde{\Upsilon}_7}{2\theta} + \frac{\widetilde{\Upsilon}_8}{\theta}\right) + \frac{1}{2}\phi^2 \widetilde{\Xi} + \frac{\iota}{\theta} \cdot i\eta_1$$

$$\widetilde{\Xi} = \frac{\widetilde{\Upsilon}_6^2}{2\Upsilon_1} + \frac{\widetilde{\Upsilon}_7^2}{4\theta} + \frac{\widetilde{\Upsilon}_8^2}{2\theta} + \frac{2\Upsilon_5 \widetilde{\Upsilon}_6}{\Upsilon_1} + \frac{\Upsilon_5 \widetilde{\Upsilon}_7}{\theta} + \frac{2\Upsilon_5 \widetilde{\Upsilon}_8}{\theta} + \frac{2\widetilde{\Upsilon}_6 \widetilde{\Upsilon}_7}{2\theta + \Upsilon_1} + \frac{2\widetilde{\Upsilon}_6 \widetilde{\Upsilon}_8}{\theta + \Upsilon_1} + \frac{2\widetilde{\Upsilon}_7 \widetilde{\Upsilon}_8}{3\theta}$$

$$\widetilde{\Upsilon}_{11} = -\frac{\phi^2 \widetilde{\Upsilon}_8^2}{4\theta} - \frac{\phi^2 \Upsilon_5 \widetilde{\Upsilon}_7}{2\theta} - \frac{w \widetilde{\Upsilon}_7}{2\theta}$$

$$\tilde{\Upsilon}_{12} = -\frac{\phi^2 \tilde{\Upsilon}_6^2}{4\Upsilon_1}$$

$$\tilde{\Upsilon}_{13} = -\frac{\phi^2 \tilde{\Upsilon}_7^2}{8\theta}$$

$$\tilde{\Upsilon}_{14} = -\frac{\phi^2 \Upsilon_5 \tilde{\Upsilon}_6}{\Upsilon_1} - \frac{w\tilde{\Upsilon}_6}{\Upsilon_1}$$

$$\tilde{\Upsilon}_{15} = -\frac{\phi^2 \Upsilon_5 \tilde{\Upsilon}_8}{\theta} - \frac{\iota}{\theta^2} - \frac{w\tilde{\Upsilon}_8}{\theta} - \frac{\iota}{\theta} \cdot i\eta_1$$

$$\tilde{\Upsilon}_{16} = -\frac{\phi^2 \tilde{\Upsilon}_6 \tilde{\Upsilon}_7}{2\theta + \Upsilon_1}$$

$$\tilde{\Upsilon}_{17} = -\frac{\phi^2 \tilde{\Upsilon}_6 \tilde{\Upsilon}_8}{\theta + \Upsilon_1}$$

$$\tilde{\Upsilon}_{18} = -\frac{\phi^2 \tilde{\Upsilon}_7 \tilde{\Upsilon}_8}{3\theta}$$

The Green's function can now be recovered by inverting its Fourier transform:

$$G(r(t), \sigma(t)^2, t; r(T), \sigma(T)^2, T)$$

$$= \frac{1}{(2\pi)^2} \int \int e^{-i \cdot r(T) \cdot \eta_1 - i \cdot \sigma(T)^2 \cdot \eta_2} \cdot \widehat{G}(\eta_1, \eta_2; r(t), \sigma(t), \tau) d\eta_1 d\eta_2,$$

which is the formula given in the theorem. ‖

REFERENCES

Aït-Sahalia, Y. (1996a): "Nonparametric Pricing of Interest Rate Derivative Securities," *Econometrica*, 64, 527–560.

Aït-Sahalia, Y. (1996b): "Testing Continuous-Time Models of the Spot Interest Rate," *Review of Financial Studies*, 9, 385–426.

Aït-Sahalia, Y. (1998): "Maximum Likelihood Estimation of Discretely Sampled Diffusions: a Closed-Form Approach," unpublished manuscript.

Ahn, D-H. and B. Gao (1999): "A Parametric Nonlinear Model of Term Structure Dynamics," *Review of Financial Studies*, 12, 721-762.

Ames, W.F. (1977): *Numerical Methods for Partial Differential Equations*. New York: Academic Press.

Amin, K.I. and V.K. Ng (1993): "Option Valuation with Systematic Stochastic Volatility," *Journal of Finance*, 48, 881-910.

Andersen, T.G. and J. Lund (1997a): "Estimating Continuous-Time Stochastic Volatility Models of the Short-Term Interest Rate," *Journal of Econometrics*, 77, 343–377.

Andersen, T.G. and J. Lund (1997b): "Stochastic Volatility and Mean Drift in the Short Rate Diffusion: Sources of Steepness, Level, and Curvature in the Yield Curve," unpublished manuscript.

Arnold, L. (1992): *Stochastic Differential Equations. Theory and Applications*. Malabar, Florida: Krieger Publishing Company.

Bajeux, I. and J.C. Rochet (1996): "Dynamic Spanning: Are Options an Appropriate Instrument ?," *Mathematical Finance*, 6, 1-16.

Ball, C.A. and A. Roma (1994): "Stochastic Volatility Option Pricing," *Journal of Financial and Quantitative Analysis*, 29, 589-607.

Bensaid, B., J.-P. Lesne, H. Pagès and J.A. Scheinkman (1992): "Derivative Asset Pricing with Transaction Costs," *Mathematical Finance*, 2, 63-86.

Bera, A. and M. Higgins (1993): "ARCH Models: Properties, Estimation and Testing," *Journal of Economic Surveys*, 7, 305-366.

Billingsley, P. (1968): *Convergence of Probability Measures*. New York: Wiley.

Black, F. (1976): "Studies of Stock Price Volatility Changes," *Proceedings of the 1976 Meeting of the American Statistical Association*, 177-181.

Black, F. and M. Scholes (1973): "The Pricing of Options and Corporate Liabilities," *Journal of Political Economy*, 81, 637-659.

Bollerslev, T. (1986): "Generalized Autoregressive Conditional Heteroskedasticity," *Journal of Econometrics*, 31, 307-327.

Bollerslev, T. (1987): "A Conditional Heteroskedastic Time Series Model for Speculative Prices and Rates of Return," *Review of Economics and Statistics*, 69, 542-547.

Bollerslev, T. and P.E. Rossi (1996): "Introduction," in Rossi, P.E. (ed.), *Modeling Stock Market Volatility—Bridging the Gap to Continuous Time*. San Diego: Academic Press, xi-xviii.

Bollerslev, T., R. Chou and K. Kroner (1992): "ARCH Modeling in Finance: A Review of the Theory and Empirical Evidence," *Journal of Econometrics*, 52, 5-59.

Bollerslev, T., Engle, R. and D. Nelson (1994): "ARCH Models," in: McFadden, D. and R. Engle (eds.), *Handbook of Econometrics*, Volume 4, Amsterdam: North-Holland, 2959-3038.

Bouleau, N. and D. Lamberton (1989): "Residual Risks and Hedging Strategies in Markovian Markets," *Stochastic Processes and Their Applications*, 33, 131-150.

Brenner, R.J., R.H. Harjes and K.F. Kroner (1996): "Another Look at Alternative Models of the Short-Term Interest Rate," *Journal of Financial and Quantitative Analysis*, 31, 85-107.

Brown, R. and S. Shaefer (1995): "Interest Rate Volatility and the Shape of the Term Structure," in Howison, S., F. Kelly and P. Wilmott (eds.), *Mathematical Models in Finance*, London: Chapman & Hall, 113-125.

Broze, L., O. Scaillet and J. Zakoïan (1995a): "Testing for Continuous-Time Models of the Short Term Interest Rate," *Journal of Empirical Finance*, 2, 199-223.

Broze, L., O. Scaillet and J. Zakoïan (1995*b*): "Quasi-Indirect Inference for Diffusion Processes," CORE DP 9505.

Campbell, J. and L. Hentschel (1992): "No News is Good News. An Asymmetric Model of Changing Volatility in Stock Returns," *Journal of Financial Economics*, 31, 281-318.

Campbell, J. Y., A.W. Lo, and A.C. MacKinlay (1997): *The Econometrics of Financial Markets*. Princeton, NJ: Princeton University Press.

Chan, K.C., G.A. Karolyi, F.A. Longstaff and A.B. Sanders (1992): "An Empirical Comparison of Alternative Models of Short-Term Interest Rate," *Journal of Finance*, 47, 1209-1228.

Chapman, D.A and N.D. Pearson (1999): "Is the Short Rate Drift Actually Nonlinear ?," *Journal of Finance*, forthcoming.

Chapman, D.A., J.B. Long and N.D. Pearson (1999): "Using Proxies for the Short Rate: When Are Three Months Like an Instant ?," *Review of Financial Studies,* 12, 763-806.

Chen, L. (1996): *Interest Rate Dynamics, Derivative Pricing, and Risk Management*. Berlin: Springer, Lecture Notes in Economics and Mathematical Systems #435.

Chernov, M. and E. Ghysels (1999): " A Study towards a Unified Approach to the Joint Estimation of Objective and Risk Neutral Measures for the Purpose of Options Valuations," *Journal of Financial Economics*, forthcoming.

Chesney, M. and L. Scott (1989): "Pricing European Currency Options: a Comparison of the Modified Black-Scholes Model and a Random Variance Model," *Journal of Financial and Quantitative Analysis*, 24, 267-284.

Christie, A. (1982): "The Stochastic Behavior of Common Stock Variance: Value, Leverage and Interest Rate Effects," *Journal of Financial Economics*, 10, 407-432.

Clark, P.K. (1973): "A Subordinated Stochastic Process Model with Fixed Variance for Speculative Prices," *Econometrica*, 41, 135-156.

Comte, F. and E. Renault (1996): "Long Memory Continuous Time Models," *Journal of Econometrics*, 73, 101-149.

Comte, F. and E. Renault (1998): "Long Memory in Continuous-Time Stochastic Volatility Models," *Mathematical Finance*, 8, 291-323.

Conley, T.G., L.P. Hansen, E.G.J. Luttmer, and J.A. Scheinkman (1997): "Short-Term Interest Rates as Subordinated Diffusions," *Review of Financial Studies*, 10, 525-577.

Corradi, V. (1997): "Degenerate Continuous Time Limits of GARCH and GARCH-type Processes," unpublished manuscript.

Cox, J.C., J.E. Ingersoll and S.A. Ross (1985a): "A Theory of the Term Structure of Interest Rates," *Econometrica*, 53, 385-407.

Cox, J.C., J.E. Ingersoll and S.A. Ross (1985b): "An Intertemporal General Equilibrium Model of Asset Prices," *Econometrica*, 53, 363-384.

Cvitanic, J., H. Pham and N. Touzi (1997): "Super-Replication in Stochastic Volatility Models under Portfolio Constraints," unpublished manuscript.

Das, S.R. and R.K. Sundaran (1999): "Of Smiles and Smirks: a Term Structure Perspective," *Journal of Financial and Quantitative Analysis*, 34, 211-239.

Davis, M.H.A. (1997): "Option Pricing in Incomplete Markets," in: Dempster, M.A.H. and S.R. Pliska (eds.): *Mathematics of Derivative Securities.* Cambridge: Cambridge University Press, 216-226.

Ding, Z., R. F. Engle and C.W.J. Granger (1993): "A Long Memory Property of Stock Returns and a New Model," *Journal of Empirical Finance*, 1, 83-106.

Dothan, L.U. (1978): "On the Term Structure of Interest Rates," *Journal of Financial Economics*, 6, 59-69.

Drost, F.C. and T.E. Nijman (1993): "Temporal Aggregation of GARCH Processes," *Econometrica*, 61, 909-927.

Drost, F.C. and B.J.M. Werker (1996): "Closing the GARCH gap: Continuous-Time GARCH Modeling," *Journal of Econometrics*, 74, 31-57.

Duan, J.C. (1995): "The GARCH Option Pricing Model," *Mathematical Finance*, 5, 13-32.

Duan, J.C. (1997): "Augmented GARCH(p,q) process and its diffusion limit," *Journal of Econometrics*, 79, 97-127.

Duffie, D. (1996): *Dynamic Asset Pricing Theory*, 2nd ed. Princeton, NJ: Princeton University Press.

Duffie, D. and C. Huang (1985): "Implementing Arrow-Debreu Equilibria by Continuous Trading of few Long-Lived Securities," *Econometrica*, 53, 1337-1356.

Duffie, D. and R. Kan (1996): "A Yield-Factor Model of Interest Rates," *Mathematical Finance*, 6, 379-406.

Duffie, D. and K.J. Singleton (1993): "Simulated Moments Estimation of Markov Models of Asset Prices," *Econometrica*, 61, 929-952.

Engle, R.F. (1982): "Autoregressive Conditional Heteroskedasticity with Estimates of the Variance of United Kingdom Inflation," *Econometrica*, 50, 987-1008.

Engle, R.F. and T. Bollerslev (1986): "Modeling the Persistence of Conditional Variances," *Econometric Reviews*, 5, 1-50.

Engle, R.F. and C. Mustafa (1992): "Implied ARCH Models from Option Prices," *Journal of Econometrics*, 52, 289-311.

Engle, R.F. and V. Ng (1993): "Measuring and Testing the Impact of News on Volatility," *Journal of Finance*, 48, 1749-1778.

Engle, R.F. and G.G.J. Lee (1996): "Estimating Diffusion Models of Stochastic Volatility," in Rossi, P.E. (ed.): *Modeling Stock Market Volatility—Bridging the Gap to Continuous Time*. San Diego: Academic Press, 333-355.

Engle, R.F., D.M. Lilien and R.P. Robins (1987): "Estimating Time Varying Risk Premia in the Term Structure: the ARCH-M Model," *Econometrica*, 55, 391-407.

Föllmer, H. (1995): "Stock Price Fluctuations as a Diffusion in a Random Environment," in Howison, S., F. Kelly and P. Wilmott (eds.), *Mathematical Models in Finance*, London: Chapman & Hall, 21-33.

Föllmer, H. and D. Sondermann (1986): "Hedging of Non-Redudant Contingent Claims," in: A. Mas-Colell and W. Hildebrand (eds.), *Contributions to Mathematical Economics*. Amsterdam: North-Holland, 205-223.

Föllmer, H. and M. Schweizer (1991): "Hedging of Contingent Claims under Incomplete Information," in: Davis, M. and R. Elliott (eds.), *Applied Stochastic Analysis.* New York: Gordon & Breach, 389-414.

Föllmer, H. and M. Schweizer (1993): "A Microeconomic Approach to Diffusion Models for Stock Prices," *Mathematical Finance*, 3, 1-23.

Fama, E. (1965): "The Behaviour of Stock Market Prices," *Journal of Business*, 38, 34-105.

Fong, H.G. and O.A. Vasicek (1991): "Fixed Income Volatility Management," *The Journal of Portfolio Optimization*, Summer issue, 41-46.

Fornari, A. and A. Mele (1994): "A Two Factor Arbitrage Model with Optimal Filtering Behaviour," *Statistica*, 54, 293-312

Fornari, A. and A. Mele (1995): "Continuous Time Conditionally Heteroskedastic Models: Theory with Applications to the Term Structure of Interest Rates," *Economic Notes*, 25, 341-366.

Fornari, A. and A. Mele (1996): "Modeling the Changing Asymmetry of Conditional Variances," *Economics Letters*, 50, 197-203.

Fornari, A. and A. Mele (1997a): "Weak Convergence and Distributional Assumptions for a General Class of Non Linear ARCH Models," *Econometric Reviews*, 16, 205-227.

Fornari, A. and A. Mele (1997b): "Sign and Volatility Switching ARCH Models," *Journal of Applied Econometrics*, 12, 49-65.

Fornari, A. and A. Mele (1999a): "An Equilibrium Model of the Term Structure with Stochastic Volatility," unpublished manuscript.

Fornari, A. and A. Mele (1999b): "Recovering the Probability Density Function of Asset Prices using GARCH Models as Diffusion Approximations," unpublished manuscript.

Fornari, F. and A. Mele (1999c): "Modeling Nonlinear Volatility Dynamics of the Short Term Interest Rate," work in progress.

Gallant, A.R. and G. Tauchen (1996): "Which Moments to Match?," *Econometric Theory*, 12, 657-681.

Gallant, A.R. and J.R. Long (1997): "Estimating Stochastic Differential Equations Efficiently by Minimum Chi-Squared," *Biometrika*, 84, 125-141.

Gallant, A.R. and G. Tauchen (1997): "Estimation of Continuous Time Models for Stock Returns and Interest Rates," unpublished manuscript.

Gallant, A.R. and G. Tauchen (1998): "Reprojecting Partially Observed Systems with Applications to Interest Rate Diffusions," *Journal of American Statistical Association*, 93, 10-24.

Gallant, A.R., D. Hsieh and G. Tauchen (1997): "Estimation of Stochastic Volatility Models with Diagnostics," *Journal of Econometrics*, 81, 159-192.

Ghysels, E., A. Harvey and E. Renault (1996): "Stochastic Volatility," in: Maddala, G.S. and C.R. Rao (eds.), *Handbook of Statistics*, Vol.14: Statistical Methods in Finance. Amsterdam: North-Holland, 119-191.

Gilli, M., K. Hencken, Ph Huber, E. Këllezi, M. Kroedel and G. Pauletto (1999): "Numerical Methods in Multivariate Option Pricing," unpublished manuscript.

Glosten, L., R. Jagannathan and D. Runkle (1993): "On the Relation Between the Expected Value and the Volatility on the Nominal Excess Returns on Stocks," *Journal of Finance*, 48, 1779-801.

Gonzalez-Rivera, G. (1998): "Smooth Transition GARCH Models," unpublished.

Gouriéroux, C. and A. Monfort (1996): *Simulation-Based Econometric Methods*. Oxford: Oxford University Press.

Gouriéroux, C., A. Monfort and E. Renault (1993): "Indirect Inference," *Journal of Applied Econometrics*, 8, S85-S118.

Granger, C.W.J. and Z. Ding (1993): "Some Properties of Absolute Return, an Alternative Measure of Risk," unpublished manuscript, University of California at San Diego, Department of Economics.

Granger, C.W.J. and Z. Ding (1994): "Stylized Facts on the Temporal and Distributional Properties of Daily Data from Speculative Markets," unpublished manuscript, University of California at San Diego, Department of Economics.

Granger, C.W.J. and T. Teräsvirta (1993): *Modeling Nonlinear Economic Relationships*. Oxford University Press, Oxford.

Härdle, W. and O. Linton (1994): "Applied Nonparametric Methods," in: McFadden, D. and R. Engle (eds.), *Handbook of Econometrics*, Volume 4, Amsterdam: North-Holland, 2295-2339.

Hagerud, G.E. (1997): "A New Nonlinear GARCH Model," EFI, Stockholm School of Economics.

Hansen, L.P. (1982): "Large Sample Properties of Generalized Method of Moments Estimators," *Econometrica*, 50, 1029-1054.

Hansen, L.P. and J.A. Scheinkman (1995): "Back to the Future: Generating Moment Implications for Continuous Time Markov Processes," *Econometrica*, 63, 767-804.

Hansen, L.P. and J.J. Heckman (1996): "The Empirical Foundations of Calibration," *Journal of Economic Perspectives*, 10, 87-104.

Harrison, J.M. and D. Kreps (1979): "Martingales and Arbitrage in Multiperiod Securities Markets," *Journal of Economic Theory*, 20, 381-408.

Harrison, J.M. and S. Pliska (1983): "A Stochastic Calculus Model of Continuous Trading: Complete Markets," *Stochastic Processes and Their Applications*, 15, 313-316.

Harvey, A. (1989): *Forecasting, Structural Time Series and the Kalman Filter*, Cambridge: Cambridge University Press.

Harvey, A. and N. Shephard (1993a): "The Econometrics of Stochastic Volatility," London School of Economics, Financial Markets Group, Discussion Paper 166.

Harvey, A. and N. Shephard (1993b): "Estimation and Testing of Stochastic Variance Models," STICERD Econometrics Discussion Paper, London School of Economics.

Harvey, A., E. Ruiz and N. Shephard (1994): "Multivariate Stochastic Variance Models," *Review of Economic Studies*, 61, 247-264.

He, H. and N.D. Pearson (1991): "Consumptions and Portfolio Policies with Incomplete Markets and Short-Sale Constraints: the Infinite Dimensional Case,"

Journal of Economic Theory, 54, 259-304.

Heath, D., R. Jarrow and A. Morton (1992): "Bond Pricing and the Term Structure of Interest Rates: a New Methodology for Contingent Claim Valuation," *Econometrica*, 60, 77-105.

Heston, S.L. (1993*a*): "Invisible Parameters in Option Prices," *Journal of Finance*, 48, 933-947.

Heston, S.L. (1993*b*): "A Closed Form Solution for Options with Stochastic Volatility with Application to Bond and Currency Options," *Review of Financial Studies*, 6, 327-344.

Hobson, D.G and L.C.G. Rogers (1998): "Complete Models with Stochastic Volatility," *Mathematical Finance*, 8, 27-48.

Hofmann, N., E. Platen and M. Schweizer (1992): "Option Pricing Under Incompleteness and Stochastic Volatility," *Mathematical Finance*, 3, 153-187.

Hsieh, D. (1988): "Modeling Heteroskedasticity in Daily Foreign Exchange Rates," *Journal of Business and Economic Statistics*, 7, 307-317.

Huang, C. (1987): "An Intertemporal General Equilibrium Asset Pricing Model: the Case of Diffusion Information," *Econometrica*, 55, 117-142.

Hull, J. and A. White (1987): "The Pricing of Options with Stochastic Volatilities," *Journal of Finance*, 42, 281-300.

Ingram, B.F. and B.S. Lee (1991): "Estimation by Simulation of Time Series Models," *Journal of Econometrics*, 47, 197-207.

Jacquier, E., N.G. Polson and P.E. Rossi (1994): "Bayesian Analysis of Stochastic Volatility Models (with discussion)," *Journal of Business and Economic Statistics*, 12, 371-417.

Jacquier, E., N.G. Polson and P.E. Rossi (1999): "Stochastic Volatility: Univariate and Multivariate Extensions," unpublished manuscript.

Johnson, N.L. and S. Kotz (1970): *Distributions in Statistics. Continuous Univariate Distributions.* Boston: Houghton Mifflin.

Johnson, H. and D. Shanno (1987): "Option Pricing when the Variance is Changing," *Journal of Financial and Quantitative Analysis*, 22, 143-151.

Kallsen, J. and M.S. Taqqu (1998): "Option Pricing in ARCH-Type Models," *Mathematical Finance*, 8, 13-26.

Karatzas, I. (1997): *Lectures on the Mathematics of Finance*. American Mathematical Society, CRM Monograph Series (vol.8). Providence, Rhode Island.

Karatzas, I. and S. Shreve (1991): *Brownian Motion and Stochastic Calculus*. Berlin, Springer Verlag.

Karatzas, I., J.P. Lehoczky, S.E. Shreve and G.L. Xu (1991): "Martingale and Duality Methods for Utility Maximization in an Incomplete Market," *SIAM Journal of Control and Optimization*, 29, 702-730.

Kushner, H. (1984): *Approximations and Weak Convergence Methods for Random Processes, with Applications to Stochastic Systems Theory*. Cambridge, MA: The MIT Press.

Kydland, F.E. and E.C. Prescott (1982): "Time to Build and Aggregate Fluctuations," *Econometrica*, 50, 1345-1370.

Kydland, F.E. and E.C. Prescott (1996): "The Computational Experiment: an Econometric Tool," *Journal of Economic Perspectives*, 10, 69-85.

Lamoureux, C. and W. Lastrapes (1993): "Forecasting Stock Return Variances: Towards and Understanding of Stochastic Implied Volatilities," *Review of Financial Studies*, 6, 293-326.

Litterman, R. and J.A. Scheinkman (1991): "Common Factors Affecting Bond Returns," *Journal of Fixed Income*, 1, 54-61.

Lo, A.W. (1988): "Maximum Likelihood Estimation of Generalized Itô Processes with Discretely Sampled Data," *Econometric Theory*, 4, 231-247.

Longstaff, F. and E.S. Schwartz (1992): "Interest-Rate Volatility and the Term Structure: A Two Factor General Equilibrium Model," *Journal of Finance*, 47, 1259-1282.

Lucas,R.E. (1978): "Asset Prices in an Exchange Economy," *Econometrica* 46, 1429-1445.

Luce, R. (1980): "Several Possible Measures of Risk," *Theory and Decision*, 12, 217-228.

Mandelbrot, B. (1963): "The Variation of Certain Speculative Prices," *Journal of Business*, 36, 394-419.

Mankiw, N.G. (1987): "The Equity Premium and the Concentration of Aggregate Shocks," *Journal of Financial Economics*, 17, 211-219.

Marcet, A. (1994): "Simulation Analysis of Dynamic Stochastic Models: Applications to Theory and Estimation," in: Sims, C.A. (1994), 81-118.

McFadden, D. (1989): "A Method of Simulated Moments for Estimation of Discrete Response Models without Numerical Integration," *Econometrica*, 57, 995-1026.

Mele, A. (1998): *Dynamiques non linéaires, volatilité et équilibre*. Paris: Editions Economica.

Melino, A. (1994): "Estimation of Continuous Time Models in Finance," in: Sims, C.A. (1994), 313-351.

Melino, A. and S. Turnbull (1990): "Pricing Foreign Currency Options with Stochastic Volatility," *Journal of Econometrics*, 45, 239-266.

Merton, R. (1973): "Theory of Rational Option Pricing," *Bell Journal of Economics and Management Science*, 4, 637-654.

Modigliani, F. and M. Miller (1958): "The Cost of Capital, Corporation Finance and the Theory of Investment," *American Economic Review*, 48, 261-297.

Nelson, D.B. (1988): Thesis MIT.

Nelson, D.B. (1990): "ARCH Models as Diffusion Approximations," *Journal of Econometrics*, 45, 7-38.

Nelson, D.B. (1991): "Conditional Heteroskedasticity in Asset Returns: A New Approach," *Econometrica*, 59, 347-370.

Nelson, D.B. (1992): "Filtering and Forecasting with Misspecified ARCH Models I: Getting the Right Variance with the Wrong Model," *Journal of Econometrics*, 52, 61-90.

Nelson, D.B., and D.P. Foster (1994): "Asymptotic Filtering Theory for Univariate ARCH Models," *Econometrica*, 62, 1-41.

Pagan, A. and G. Schwert (1990): "Alternative Models for Conditional Stock Volatility," *Journal of Econometrics*, 45, 267-290.

Pakes, A. and D. Pollard (1989): "Simulation and the Asymptotics of Optimization Estimators," *Econometrica*, 57, 1027-1957.

Palm, F.C. (1996): "GARCH Models of Volatility," in: Maddala, G.S. and C.R. Rao (eds.), *Handbook of Statistics*, Vol.14: Statistical Methods in Finance. Amsterdam: North-Holland, 209-240.

Pham, H. and N. Touzi (1996): "Equilibrium State Prices in a Stochastic Volatility Model," *Mathematical Finance*, 6, 215-236.

Rabemananjara, R. and J. Zakoïan (1993): "Threshold ARCH Models and Asymmetries in Volatility," *Journal of Applied Econometrics*, 8, 31-49.

Renault, E. (1997): "Econometric Models of Option Pricing Errors," in Kreps, D., Wallis, K. (eds.): *Advances in Economics and Econometrics*, vol. 3, Cambridge: Cambridge University Press, 223-278.

Renault, E. and N. Touzi (1996): "Option Hedging and Implied Volatilities in a Stochastic Volatility Model," *Mathematical Finance*, 6, 279-302.

Romano, M. and N. Touzi (1997): "Contingent Claims and Market Completeness in a Stochastic Volatility Model," *Mathematical Finance*, 7, 399-412.

Rossi, P.E. (1996): *Modeling Stock Market Volatility—Bridging the Gap to Continuous Time*. San Diego: Academic Press.

Ruston, A. (1986): *Fredholm Theory in Banach Spaces*, Cambridge: Cambridge University Press.

Schwartz, B.A., D.B. Nelson and D.P. Foster (1993): "Variance Filtering with ARCH Models: a Monte-Carlo Investigation," Tel Aviv University, Tel Aviv, unpublished manuscript.

Schweizer, M. (1992): "Mean-Variance Hedging for General Claims," *Annals of Applied Probability*, 2, 171-179.

Schweizer, M. (1994): "Approximating Random Variables by Stochastic Integrals," *Annals of Probability*, 22, 1536-1575.

Schweizer, M. (1996): "Approximation Pricing and the Variance-Optimal Martingale Measure," *Annals of Probability*, 24, 206-236.

Schwert, W. (1989*a*): "Business Cycles, Financial Crises, and Stock Volatility," *Carnegie-Rochester Conference Series on Public Policy*, 39, 83-126.

Schwert, W. (1989*b*): "Why Does Stock Market Volatility Change Over Time ?," *Journal of Finance*, 44, 1115-1154.

Scott, L. (1987): "Option Pricing when the Variance Changes Randomly: Theory, Estimation, and an Application," *Journal of Financial and Quantitative Analysis*, 22, 419-438.

Sentana, E. (1991): "Quadratic ARCH Models: a Potential Re-Interpretation of ARCH Models," unpublished, LSE.

Shephard, N. (1996): "Statistical Aspects of ARCH and Stochastic Volatility," in: Cox, D.R., D.V. Hinkley and O.E. Barndorff-Nielsen (eds.): *Time Series Models in Econometrics, Finance and other Fields*. London: Chapman & Hall, 1-67.

Shreve, S. (1991): "A Control Theorist's View of Asset Pricing," in: Davis,M. and R. Elliot (eds.), *Applied Stochastic Analysis*. New York: Gordon & Breach, 415-445.

Sims, C.A. (1984): "Martingale-Like Behavior of Prices and Interest Rates," Mimeo, University of Minnesota.

Sims, C.A. (ed.) (1994): *Advances in Econometrics, Sixth World Congress*, Vol. II, Econometric Society Monographs. Cambridge: Cambridge University Press.

Sims, C.A. (1996): "Macroeconomics and Methodology," *Journal of Economic Perspectives*, 10, 105-120.

Smith, A.A. (1990): "Three Essays on the Solution and Estimation of Dynamic Macroeconometric Models," Thesis Duke University.

Smith, A.A. (1993): "Estimating Nonlinear Time Series Models Using Simulated Vector Autoregressions," *Journal of Applied Econometrics*, 8, S63-S84.

Stanton, R. (1997): "A Nonparametric Model of Term Structure Dynamics and the Market Price of Interest Rate Risk," *Journal of Finance*, 52, 1973-2002.

Stroock, D. and S. Varadhan (1979): *Multidimensional Diffusion Processes.* Berlin: Springer Verlag.

Tauchen, G. and M. Pitts (1983): "The Price Variability-Volume Relationship on Speculative Markets," *Econometrica*, 51, 485-505.

Taylor, S. (1986): *Modeling Financial Time Series.* Chichester, UK: Wiley.

Taylor, S. (1994): "Modeling Stochastic Volatility: a Review and Comparative Study," *Mathematical Finance*, 4, 183-204.

Vasicek, O. (1977): "An Equilibrium Characterization of the Term Structure," *Journal of Financial Economics*, 5, 177-188.

Wiggins, J. (1987): "Option Values and Stochastic Volatility. Theory and Empirical Estimates," *Journal of Financial Economics*, 19, 351-372.

Wong, E. (1964): "The Construction of a Class of Stationary Markov Processes," in: R.Bellman, ed., *Sixteen Symposia in Applied Mathematics. Stochastic Processes in Mathematical Physics and Engineering.* American Mathematical Society, 264-276.

Zakoïan, J.M. (1994): "Threshold Heteroskedastic Models," *Journal of Economic Dynamics and Control*, 18, 931-955.

Index

Dynamic Modeling and Econometrics in Economics and Finance

1. P.Rothman:
   *Nonlinear Time Series Analysis of Economic
   And Financial Data.* 1999   ISBN 0-7923-8379-6
2. D.Patterson, R.Ashley:
   *A Nonlinear Time Series Workshop: A Toolkit
   For Detecting and Identifying Nonlinear
   Serial Dependence.* 1999   ISBN 0-7923-8674-4
3. F.Fornari, A.Mele
   *Stochastic Volatility in Financial Markets:
   Crossing the Bridge to Continuous Time.* 2000 ISBN 0-7923-7842-3